To: Jackie & Glenn
Thanks for your
continued support —

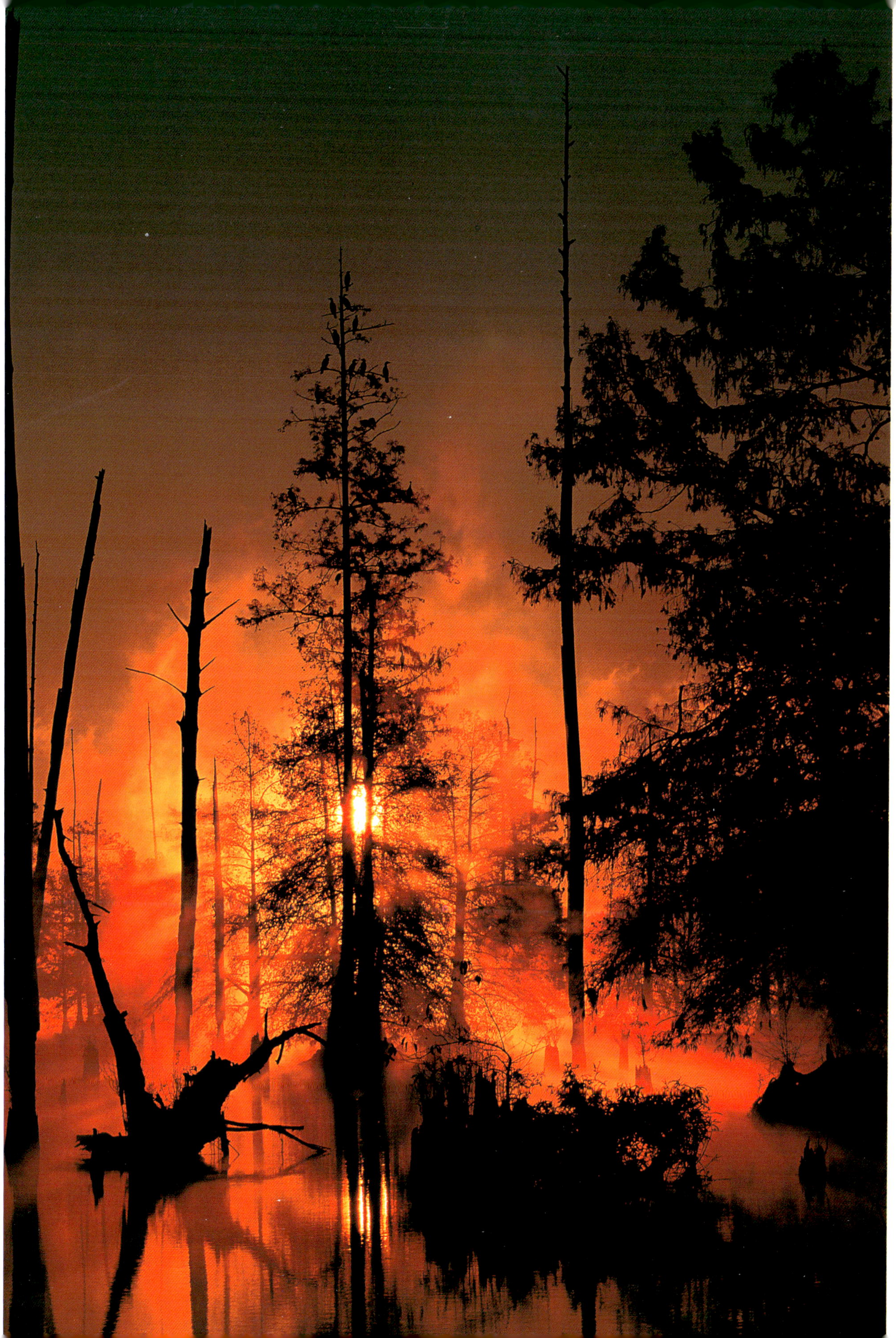

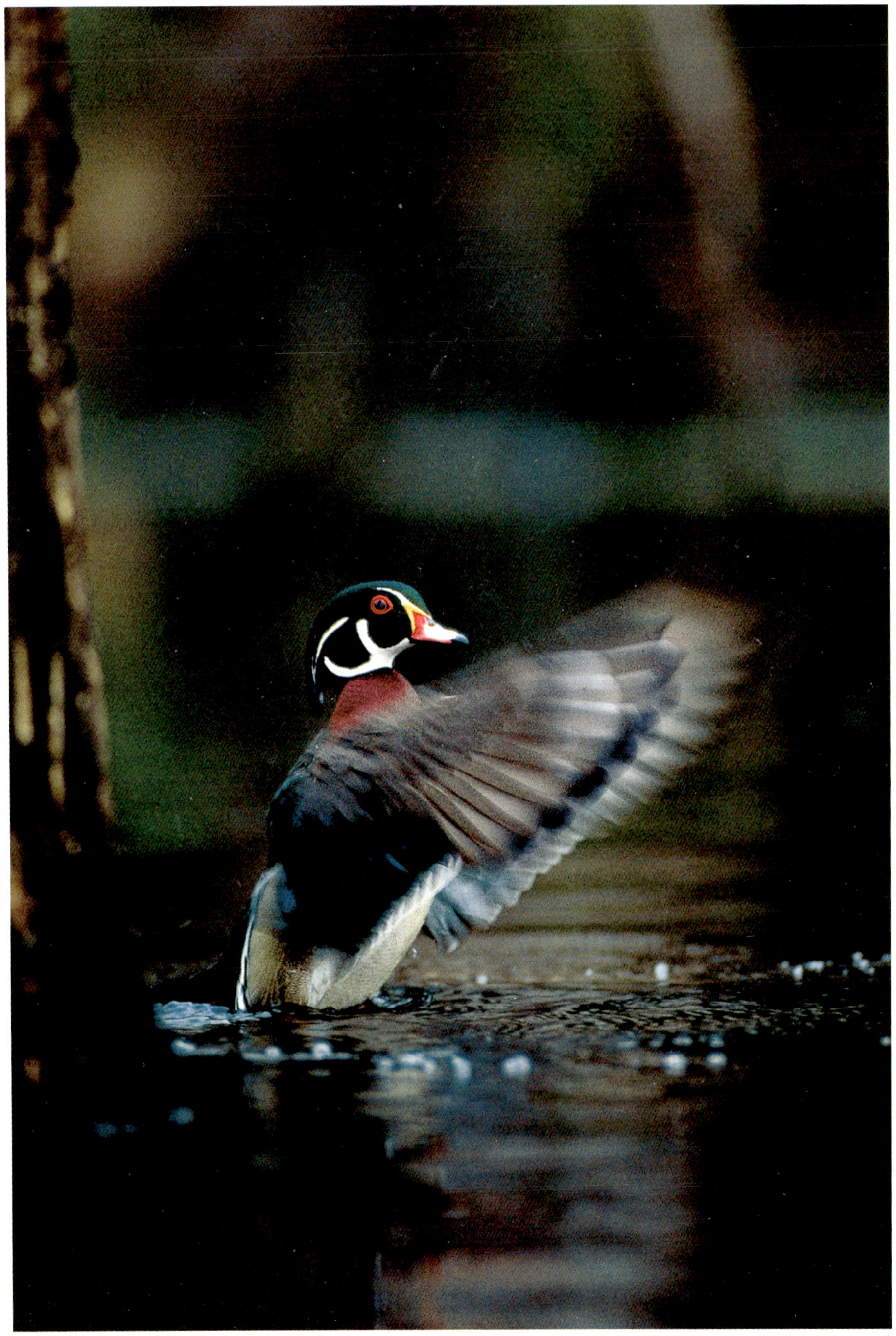

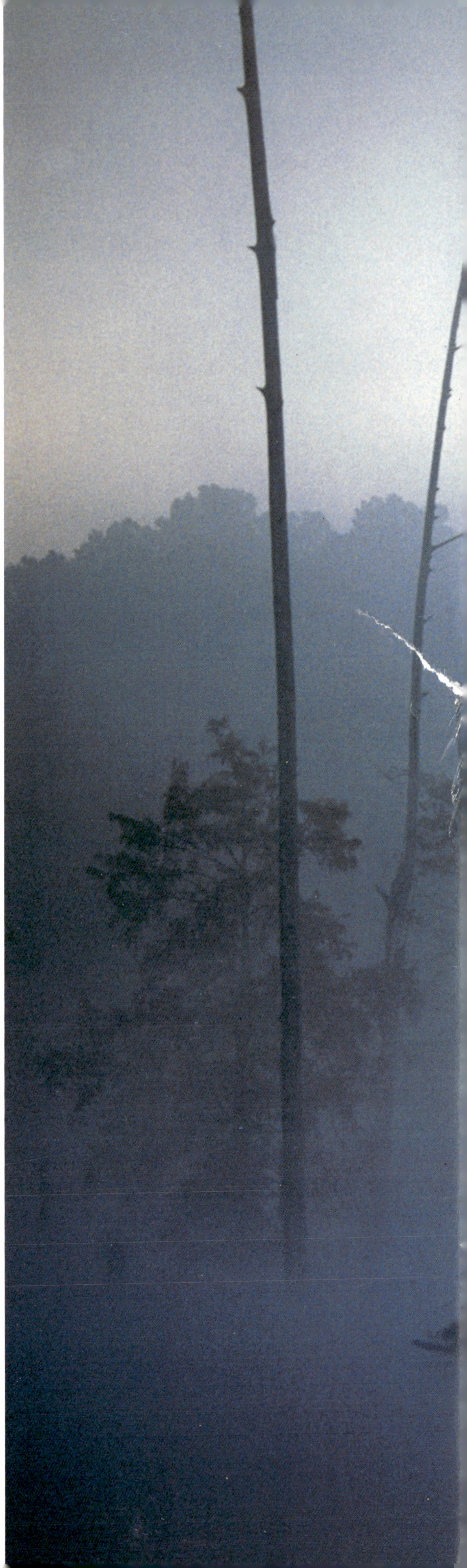

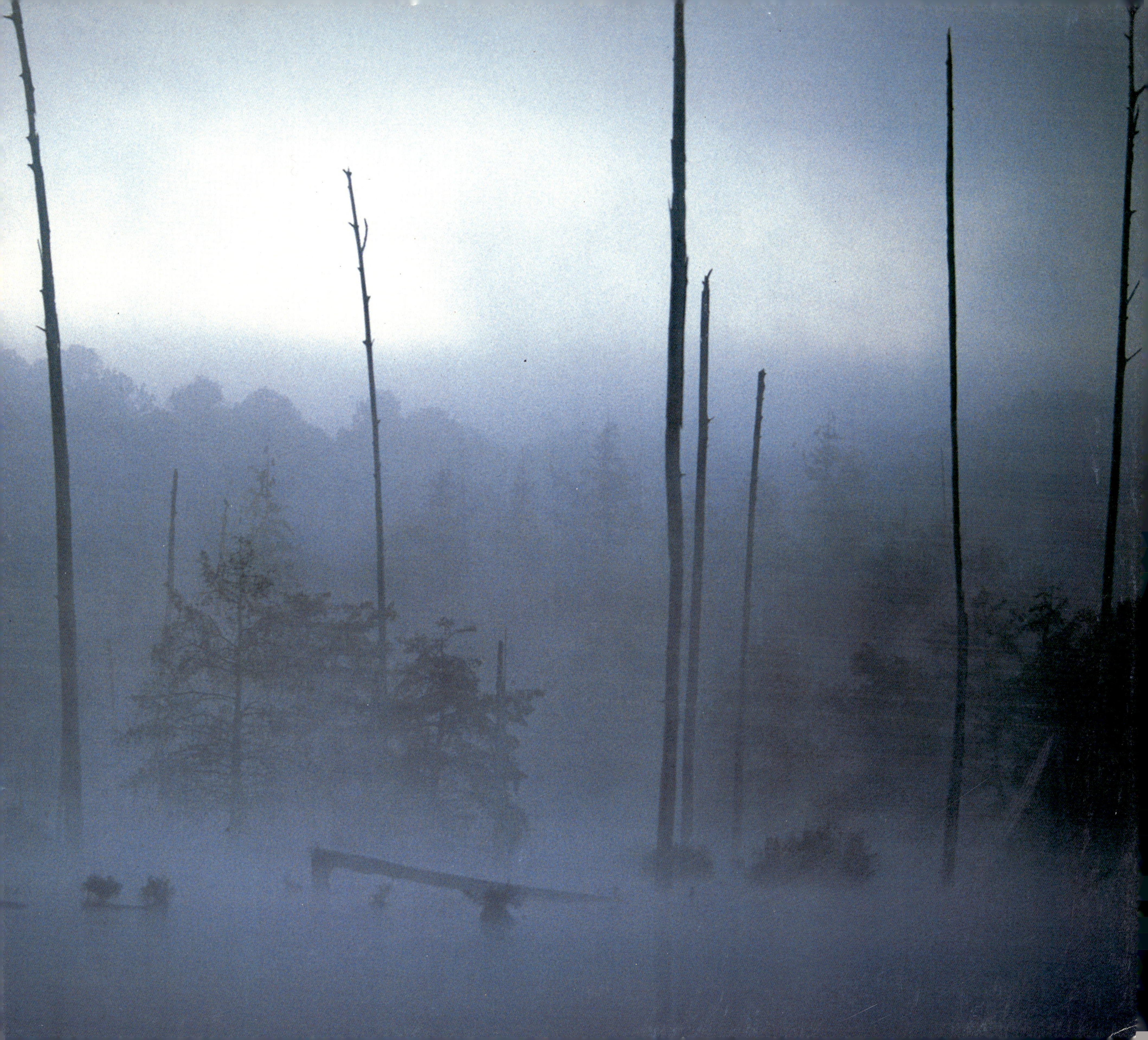

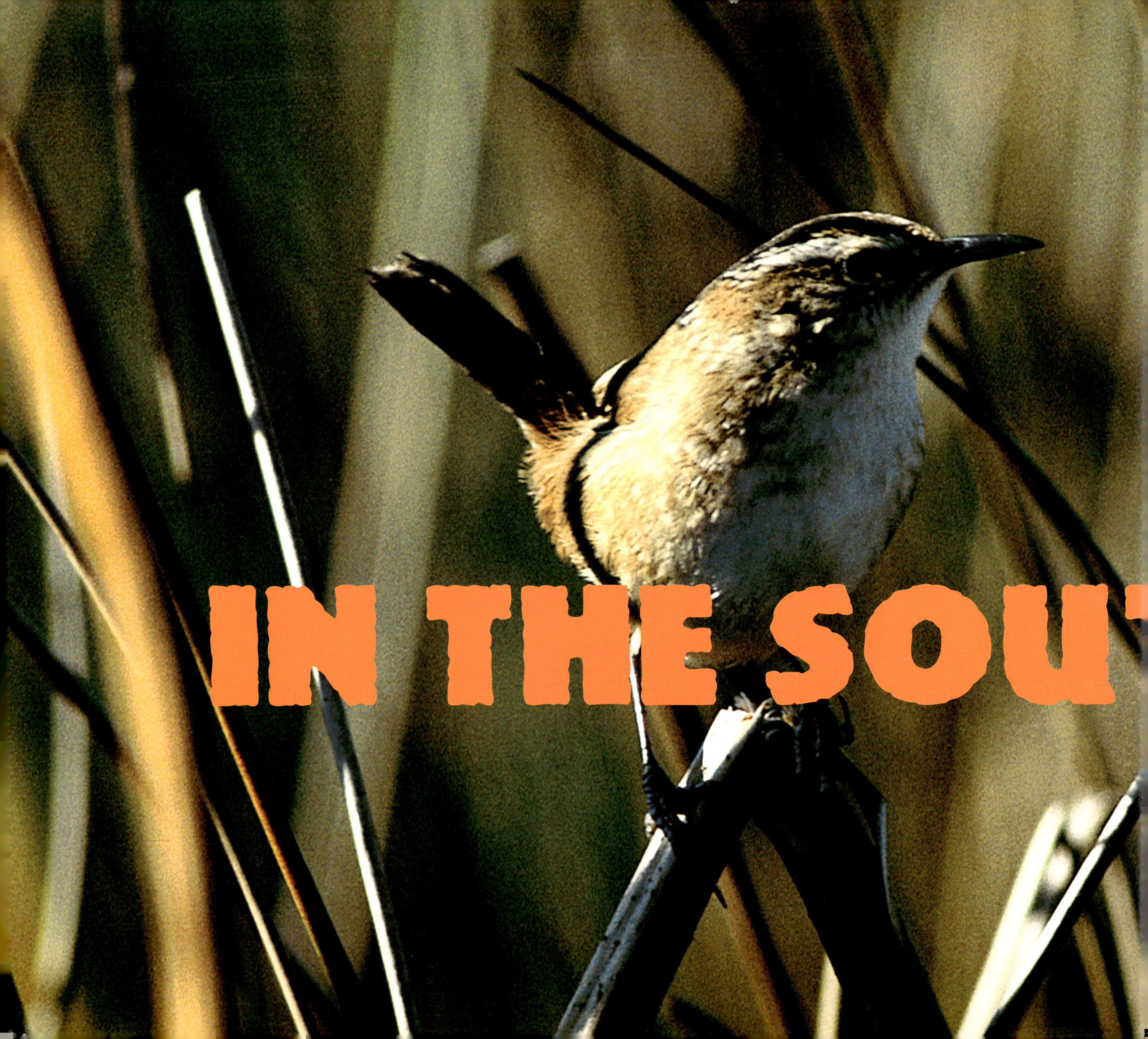

IN THE SOUT

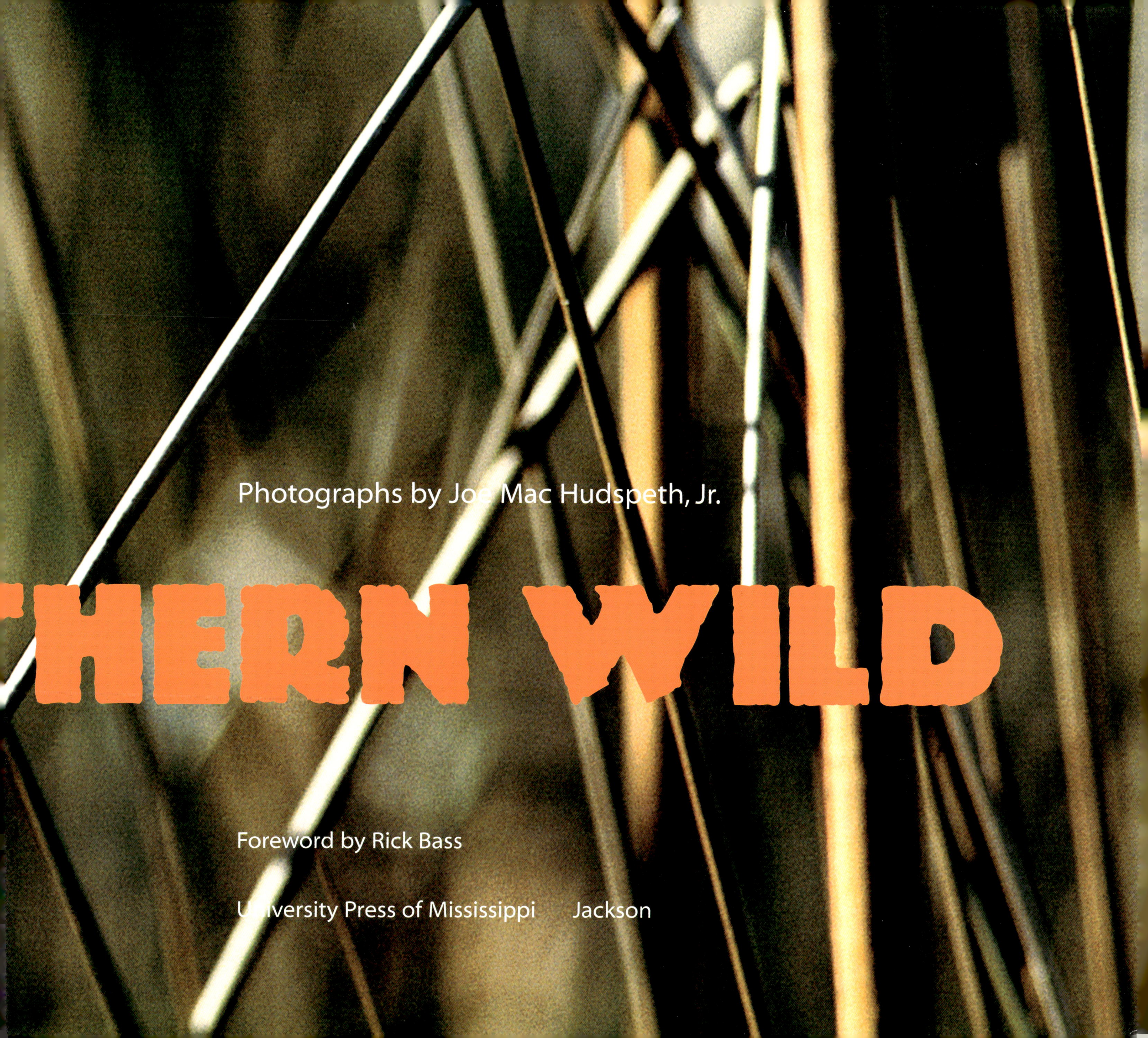

Photographs by Joe Mac Hudspeth, Jr.

THERN WILD

Foreword by Rick Bass

University Press of Mississippi Jackson

Publication of this book was made possible in part by the Lexington Foundation

www.upress.state.ms.us

The University Press of Mississippi is a member of the Association of American University Presses.

Manufactured in China

Designed by John A. Langston

06 05 04 03 4 3 2 1

Library of Congress Cataloging-in-Publication Data

Hudspeth, Joe Mac, Jr.

In the southern wild : wetlands photography / by Joe Mac Hudspeth, Jr. ;

foreword by Rick Bass.

p. cm.

ISBN 1-57806-584-4

1. Wildlife photography—Southern States. 2. Wetlands—Southern States—Pictorial works. 3. Hudspeth, Joe Mac, Jr. I. Title.

TR729.W54H83 2003

779'.32'0975—dc21

2003007780

British Library Cataloging-in-Publication Data available

page i: Sunrise

page ii: Wood duck stretching

page ii-iii: Fog bank

page iv-v: Marsh wren

FOREWORD

I live by the edge of a marsh in the jungle in the mountains in Montana at the edge of the Canadian border. The world's marshes, swamps, fens, and wetlands have always seemed mythic to me, for the life they produce and attract, and their ability to purify the world's ills, and for the explosion of beauty that arises lotus-like from that detritus and rot, as well as the procession of life that is summoned to a marsh from elsewhere.

My marsh in Montana isn't even in the same flyway as Joe Mac Hudspeth's, but I recognize many of Montana's spring and summer residents in these portraits, and am reminded of how all of our vanishing wetlands are still connected, even if tenuously, like the veins and arteries of a single organism. Everywhere, the vital organs—the heart and lungs, and other internal workings of this country's wild heritage—pass from marsh to marsh, with their migrations twining within the conduits of those passages to form a current like that of electricity, and possessing a shimmering vibrance that is not, as we see in Hudspeth's photographs, merely metaphorical.

How elegant is this plan, this design, the whirling, shouting, writhing profusion of life that manifests itself from the organic funk and foundation of a marsh. Such richness is perfect testimony, I think, to the whirling, leaping complexity that lies just below. Of my own marsh, well-meaning friends with backhoes and bulldozers have offered to scallop and dredge the ancient bed of peat—thousands of years of biological investment—and to build dikes and dams and levees, lining the open wound then with an impermeable smear of clay, so that the wound, and the absence, could be converted into a nice pretty lake, a serene sprawl of blue water on which a red canoe might float, and upon which trumpeter swans might swim in graceful figure-eights, luminous at twilight.

While I understand the attraction to the simple aesthetics of a lake, and an absence of mud and mosquitoes, I am disappointed frequently by a suspicion that in our culture there is not yet a sufficient ecological understanding of what an amazement, a miracle, a wetland truly is. And again, I think Hudspeth's photos are of great service in this regard, far exceeding "merely" the aesthetic and the artistic.

When I think of recent environmental legislation, I am chagrined and angered by proposals that seek to devalue or dismiss the importance of the nation's wetlands. Even a cursory examination of various dictators and despots in the Middle East and Africa reveals a common pattern in which it is not merely the human cultures that are despoiled, but the ecological underpinnings of those cultures. Such an examination of history illustrates with shocking clarity, I think, the dangers of our arrogance and avarice toward the environment.

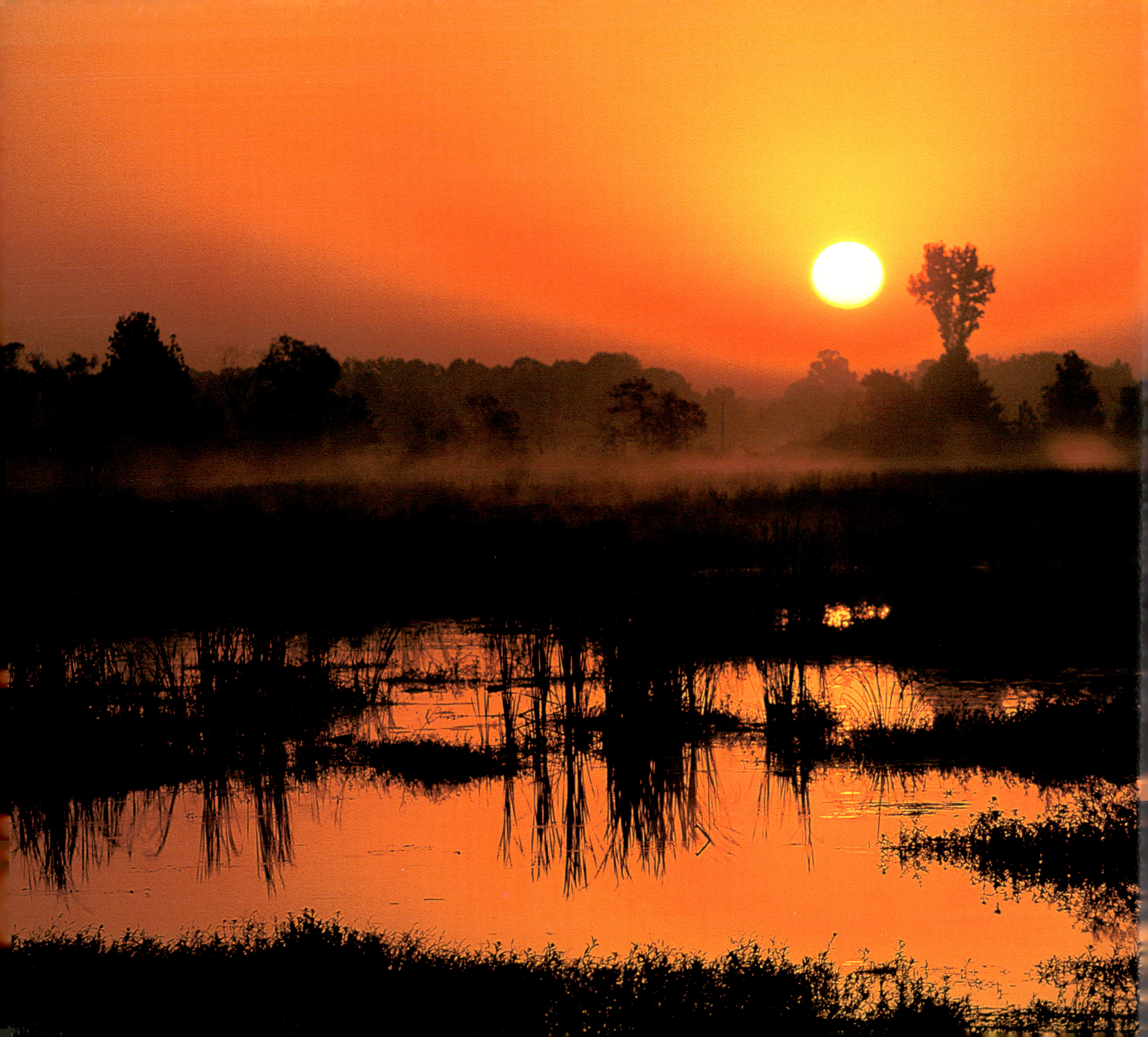

In our own country, the single greatest (and most compromised) biological artery, the Mississippi River, has been cut off completely from fulfilling its chief ecological function, supplying the breath of life of sediment and nutrients to its downstream ecosystems in the high waters of spring. Particularly impacted is the Louisiana coast, which is sinking as a result, vanishing before our eyes as if by theft, and taking with it not just homes and towns but the nation's shrimping industry, protection against inland hurricane surges, and vital habitat for many of the world's birds, including many of those in this book.

In the midst of such loss—ongoing and accruing—it is easy for a lover of wild places to despair, and so again, I am grateful to Hudspeth for the educational content of these photographs, which tell a story, a narrative, matching species to habitat, function to need, and which assert, in their beauty, the fundamental right of "mere" existence. Somehow, they give me hope. Blind hope, and hope without action, is useless, but these photos are somehow of a different kind. They possess the hope of knowledge.

It pleases me to read that Hudspeth's favorite bird might be the wood duck. (I've always felt a little guilty that this most beautiful bird is also one of the most delicious.) I'm reminded also of an assertion by the poet and novelist Jim Harrison that many of the birds of North America are sorely in need of renaming, their present appellations in no way giving due to their astounding brilliance and life habits. The bluebird, the brown thrasher. The wood duck. Such creatures, Harrison points out, demand—and deserve—more of our imagination.

Swamps, particularly in the South, have proved as fecund to that imagination as to the web of life—from Faulkner's *Big Woods* to Larry Brown's swamp classic, *Joe*; from Eudora Welty to Barry Hannah. And again, our wetlands manifest dramatically the elegance for form following function, and the power of paradox, or perceived paradox: accommodating shoulder-to-shoulder an explosion of feather and scale, hue and vibrance, the spiny and the finned, the masked, the webbed, the sleek and the corpulent, the grotesque and the magnificent, the solitary and the social. What force first dreamed—and still dreams—such a continuing elegance of fit? How can any one landscape contain the patience of a rail or heron waiting to spear a frog, even amidst the turmoil of a tornado of geese or a tempest of mallards at the other end of the same swamp? How can such brown muck, such spar-rot mire, produce such relentless flames of color?

I'm grateful to Hudspeth for capturing these marsh-flames, as well as the tones and shadows that add to our understanding of these imperiled ecosystems' mystery and complexity. Wetlands are vanishing quickly in this country, and around the world, but I have to believe in hope, and in the possibility that images as vivid and powerful as these will help remind us of our many blessings, and of the incumbent responsibilities not just to celebrate but to safeguard these blessings.

Rick Bass
Yaak, Montana
March 2003

Sunrise

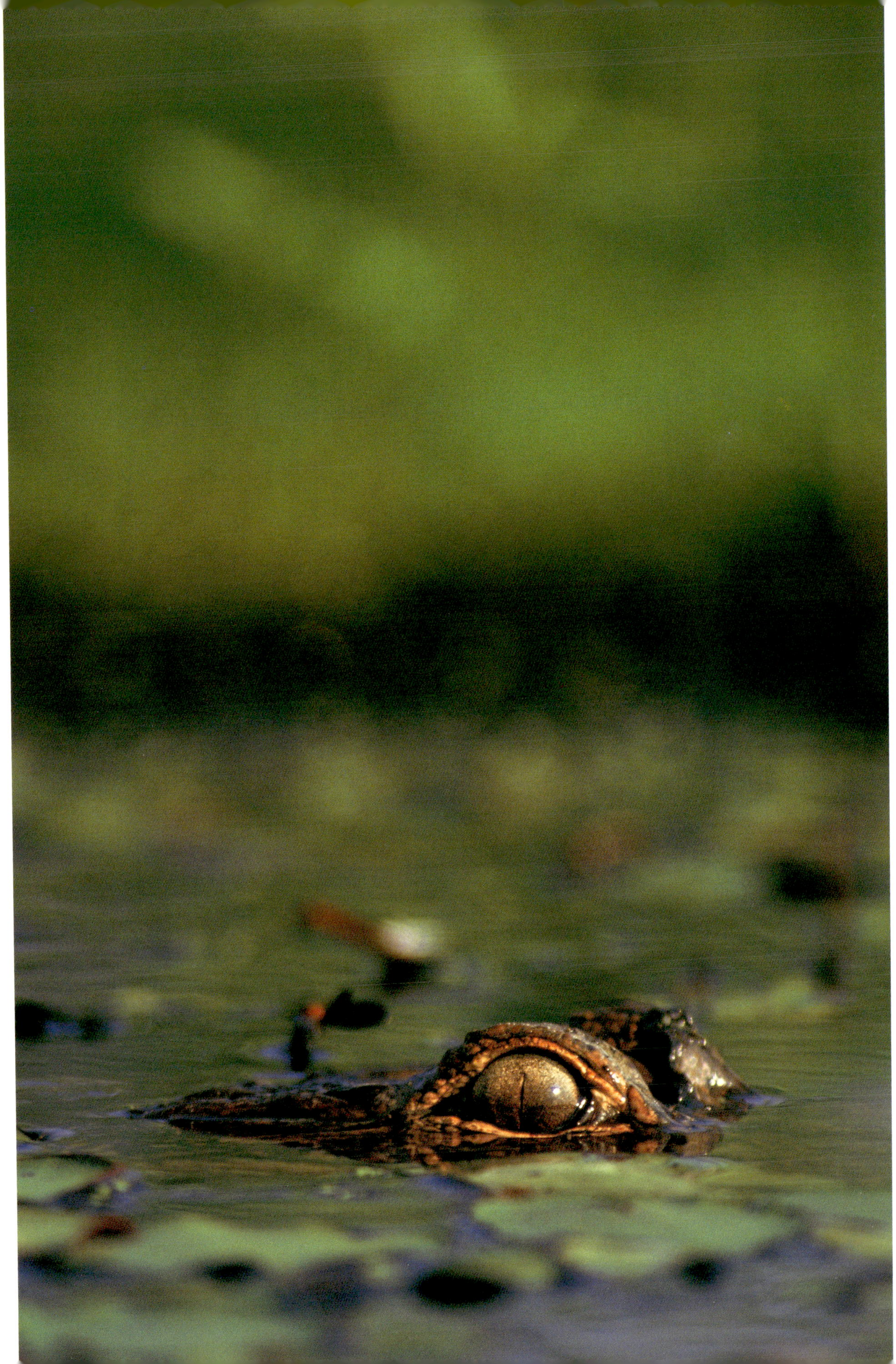

American alligator

A VIEW FROM THE BLIND

I grew up hunting and fishing in the hills of northern Mississippi. On my trips into the woods, I always carried a Kodak 110 Instamatic to take photos of the deer my friends and I harvested. One frigid January morning as I was returning from a hunt, a slight movement in a honeysuckle thicket caught my attention. Moving in for a closer look, I discovered a screech owl sunning himself. When this little fellow allowed me to get within two feet of him, I took my very first wildlife photograph. At that time, I had never heard of shutter speeds, f-stops, or aperture, and I did not know that my camera would not focus at that close range. This experience, however, stoked a fire that has burned within me ever since.

Another ten years passed before I saved enough money to buy my first 35 mm camera, an automatic with 100–300 mm zoom, 90 mm macro, and 28 mm wide-angle lens. The zoom lens, I was sure, would let me photograph wood ducks and mallards from the window of my car without getting my feet muddy. I rode around Pipe Line Road on Ross Barnett Reservoir and took photograph after photograph of waterfowl. I believed in my heart that the ducks in the final prints would be ten times larger than they were in the viewfinder. Of course, this did not happen. Discouraged, I put all my equipment into the case and stashed it in the closet.

Two years later, my fiancée surprised me on my birthday with a simple 70–210 mm macro lens. Motivated once again to photograph wildlife "up close," I decided to take a different approach. I bought and studied books on wildlife photography. The 70-210 macro lens reduced me to stalking smaller subjects such as frogs, turtles, lizards, and butterflies, but photographing these creatures honed my skills. Next I targeted sunrises, sunsets, wild flowers, spider webs, and fall leaves.

With the purchase of a big 300 mm telephoto lens, I turned my attention to the wood duck, in my opinion, the most beautiful of all ducks. But I soon realized that even with the big lens I had to be less than twenty feet from the ducks to get the full-frame photographs that I so desperately wanted. To get close to my subjects, I designed a lightweight blind, a PVC-pipe frame set in knee-deep water near an old beaver dam. I covered the frame with Mossy Oak's camouflage material and surrounded it with tree limbs stuck in the mud. Now, or so I thought, I was ready.

After a week of waiting, I discovered one big problem—the ducks coming in at the crack of dawn would always land in the same spot, fifty yards away from me. I knew they weren't afraid of my blind because every now and then a duck would swim by only a few feet away. They just liked it better where they were. I moved my blind closer to where the

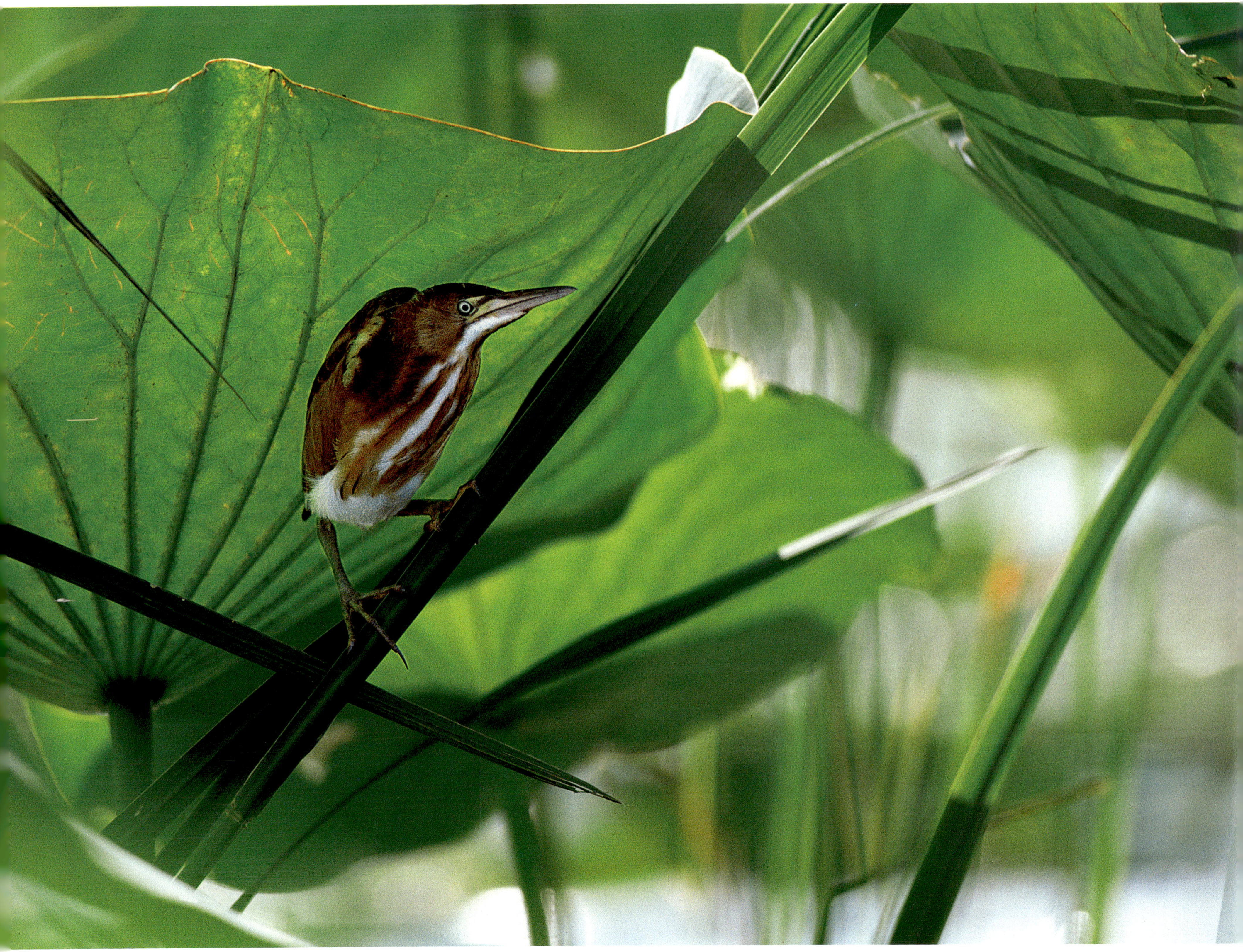

Least bittern (Winner of the 1993 Award for Excellence in Calendar Photography by the Roger Tory Peterson Institute of Natural History)

ducks congregated and stayed away for a couple of weeks so they could get comfortable with the blind.

The first morning back in the blind, I watched the beaver dam come alive at 5:50 A.M. with at least twenty ducks arriving on cue and landing mere feet away. One actually came to rest on the top of my blind. The wood ducks fed and preened for the next hour and a half while I waited for enough sunlight to capture them on film. And capture them, I did. That morning I took ten rolls of film, quite an accomplishment since I had only taken a total of three rolls of film the whole previous year.

As my photographs improved, I began submitting them for publication. Many long months later, quite unexpectedly I received in the mail two magazines featuring my photographs, one on the back cover and the other on the front cover. It was then that I said, "I can do this."

Patience and perseverance have had much to do with my success as a wildlife photographer, but often it's just a matter of being in the right place at the right time. One summer a few years ago, I had been out in my blind unsuccessfully trying to photograph wood ducks. On my drive home I noticed something out of place under a lotus leaf about seventy-five yards off shore. High winds hit me as I stepped out of my car to get a better look. With my binoculars I located and identified an immature least bittern grasping a leaf and riding out the gale. Least bitterns are usually very secretive and unapproachable, and I knew that the odds of getting close enough to photograph this one were against me. As I put my waders on, I noticed that the "prime time" morning sunlight had been replaced by harsh overhead light. Viewed from the shore, the lotus leaf completely shaded the bittern. My plan was to wade past the bird in the hope that the sun would light him from the other side. As I approached I started shooting. I had to time my shots between gusts of wind that blew cattails in front of my subject. In these blustery conditions the camera's light meter was very erratic in trying to determine exposure. The least bittern was shadowed by the lotus leaf while the rest of the scene was bathed in bright sunlight. As I approached to within thirty feet of the bird, I took twenty images before he finally flew away.

The photographs from that roll of film were published in magazines around the country. One that appeared in the Nature Conservancy's 1993 calendar was selected from over two thousand wildlife images to win the Award for Excellence in Calendar Photography by the Roger Tory Peterson Institute of Natural History.

After several years of photographing the native wildlife of Mississippi and surrounding states, I took a trip to Yellowstone and there met professional photographers whose work I knew and respected. National parks have been protected habitats for years, and the creatures there are accustomed to the presence of people. For this reason these areas attract wildlife photographers. While there I photographed elk, big horn sheep, antelope, and coyotes.

When I got home and had my slides processed, I was excited with the results. I called a photo editor who had published one of the least bittern photographs from the year before. I told him I had some amazing new material, and at first, he was eager to see it. But when he heard that I had just gotten back from Yellowstone, there was a long pause at the other end of the line. He finally said, "Well, hurry up and get them to me before all the other photographers who were out there, standing next to you, photographing the same elk you were, get their film processed." My heart sank. He was speaking the truth. I remembered an instance when I had finished lunch and was sitting around relaxing with four other photographers. All of a sudden a coyote appeared chasing a vole. The five of us started photographing the coyote as it jumped into the air and tried to catch the vole. Several minutes later I became aware of the sound of power winders going off behind me. Turning around, I saw about fifty photographers lined up—some kneeling, some standing—photographing the same scene.

While animals in the southern wilds are more camera shy than those at Yellowstone, the woods and water teem with wildlife. I have spent many hours photographing blue-winged teals and alligators on Ross Barnett Reservoir outside of Jackson, wood storks and turtles at the Noxubee Refuge near Louisville, anhinga and snowy egrets at Tara Wildlife on Eagle Lake, and wood ducks and great blue herons at Springdale Refuge and Sardis Reservoir, close to my childhood home, Oxford. On certain private lands where wildlife is not hunted or harassed as much as on public land, deer and turkey have allowed me close enough to get some great photographs.

Birds of many species are everywhere you look. I knew this when I first started taking photographs in the wilds, but I was not very knowledgeable about bird identification and behavior. On my own I learned that if I set a tree limb close to my blind a certain bird would land on it and pose for me. But I had to buy a bird book before I could identify that bird as a prothonatary warbler. The beautiful wood duck, perhaps my favorite subject, is native and can be photographed year round. Around the same time that mallards, gadwalls, and other migratory ducks head north, a new group of birds begin to arrive in the southern marshes. Purple gallinules, common moorhens, least bitterns, and green herons all spend the spring and summer in central Mississippi nesting and raising their young before heading south in late summer and early fall.

In recent years as my photography has attracted some attention, I am frequently asked what expeditions I have planned for the future. While I have visited other wildlife areas around the country, my favorite photographs have been taken near the hunting grounds and fishing spots of my youth. I expect that in the future I will see what more can be found in my view from the blind.

Joe Mac Hudspeth, Jr.

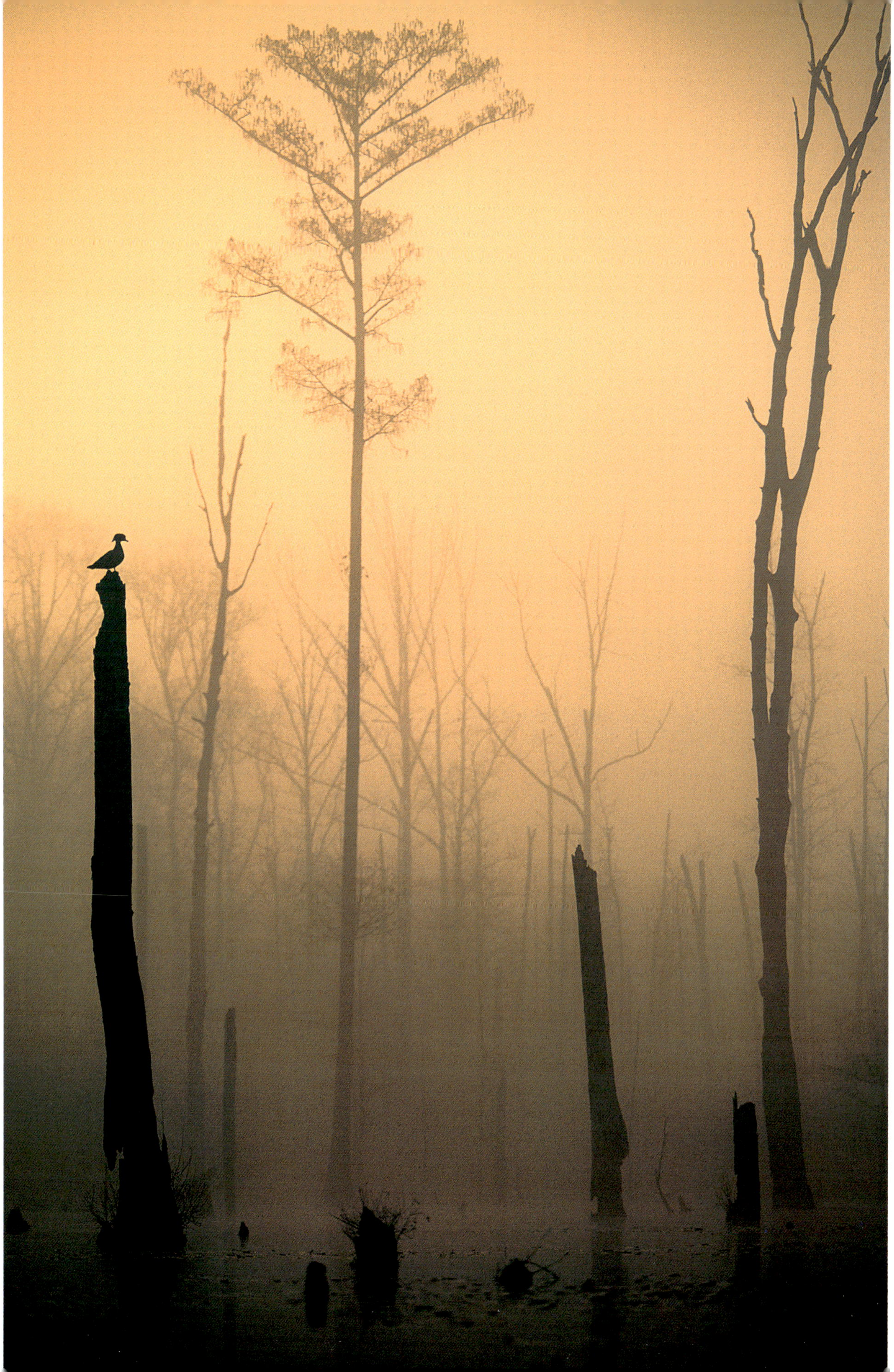

Wood duck in fog bank

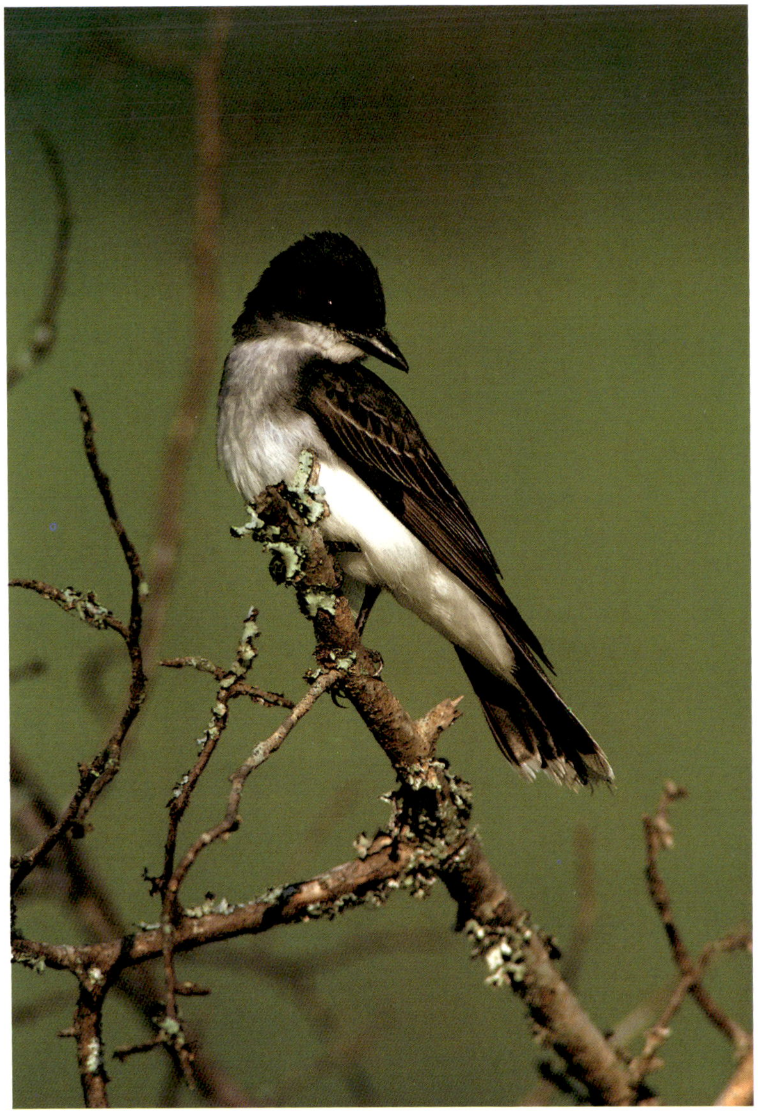

Eastern kingbird

Spider webs in fog

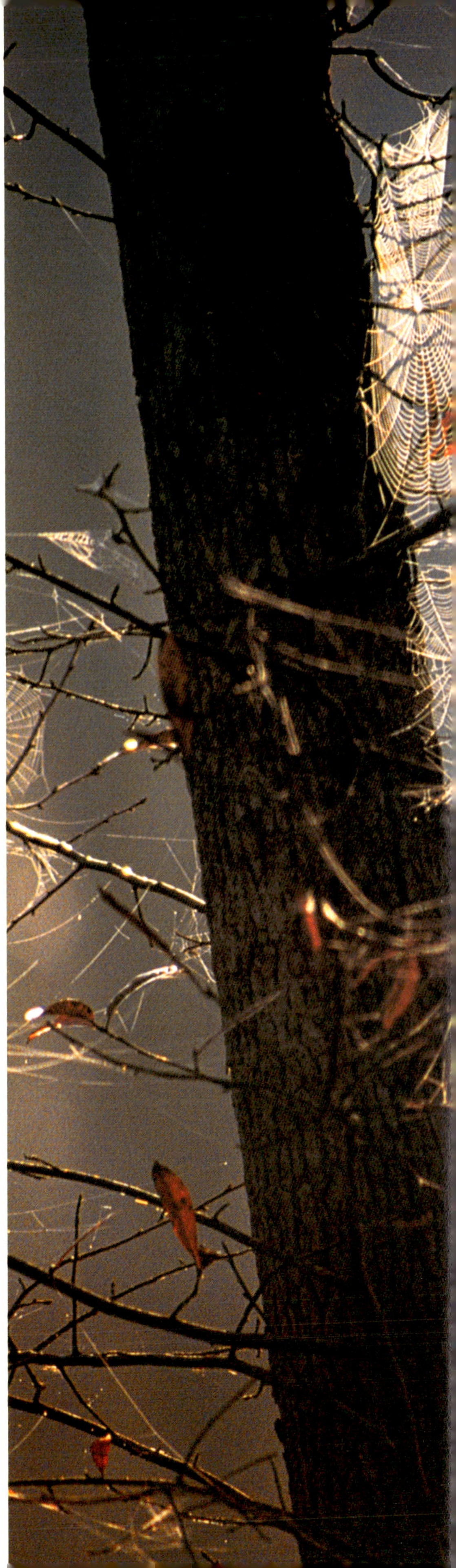

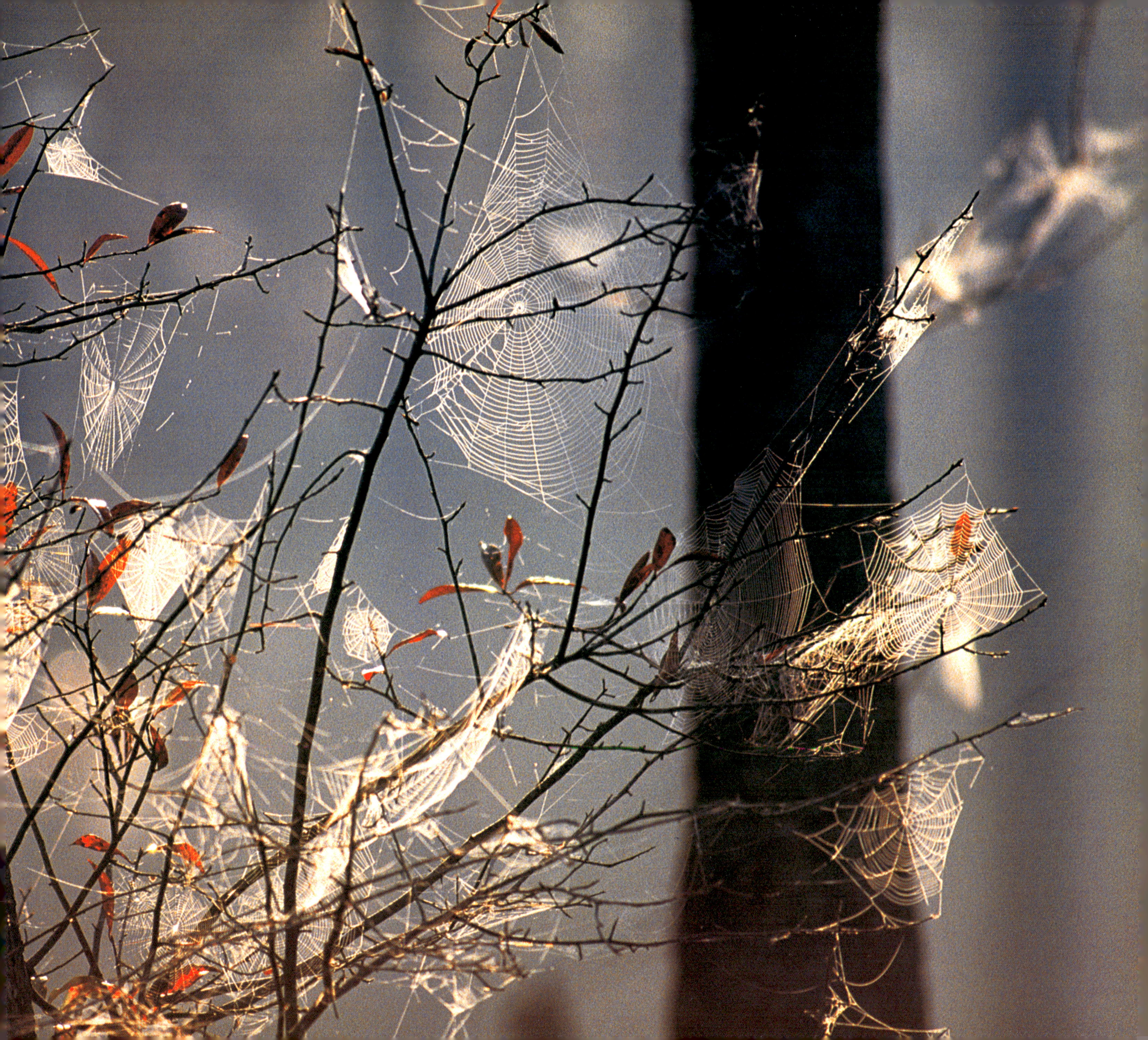

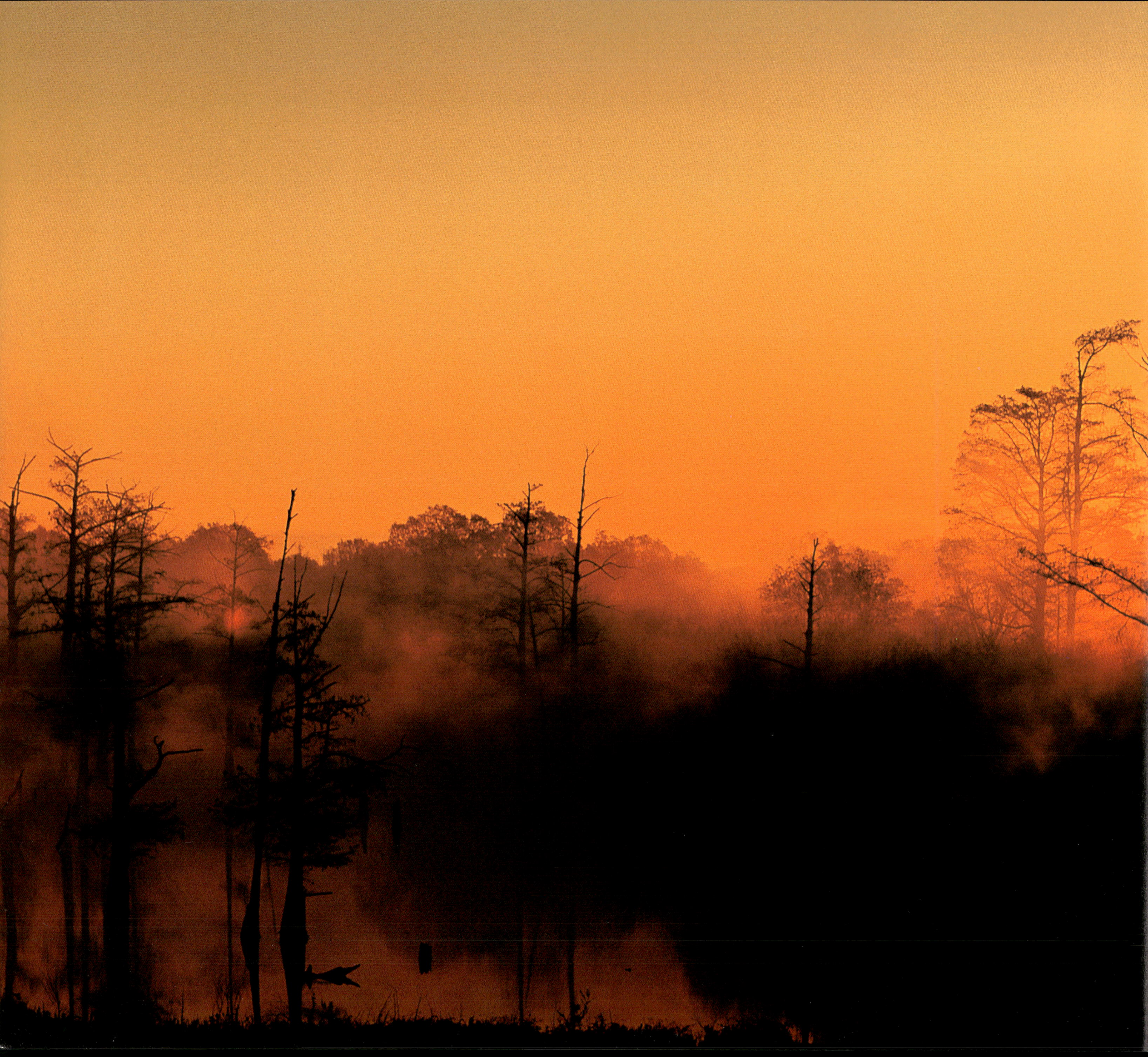

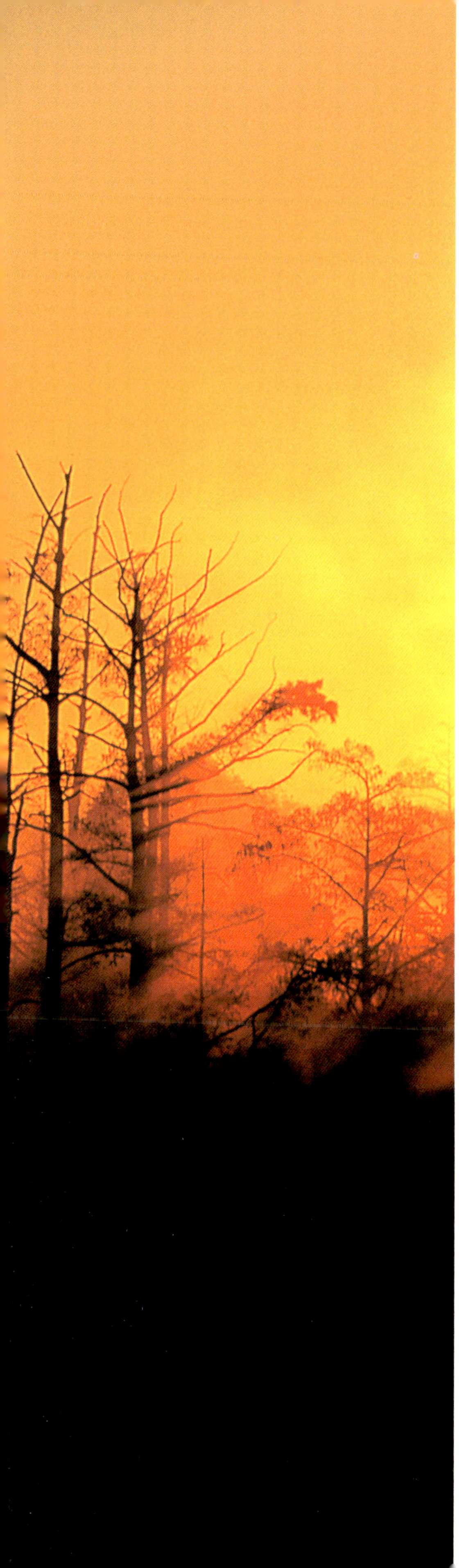

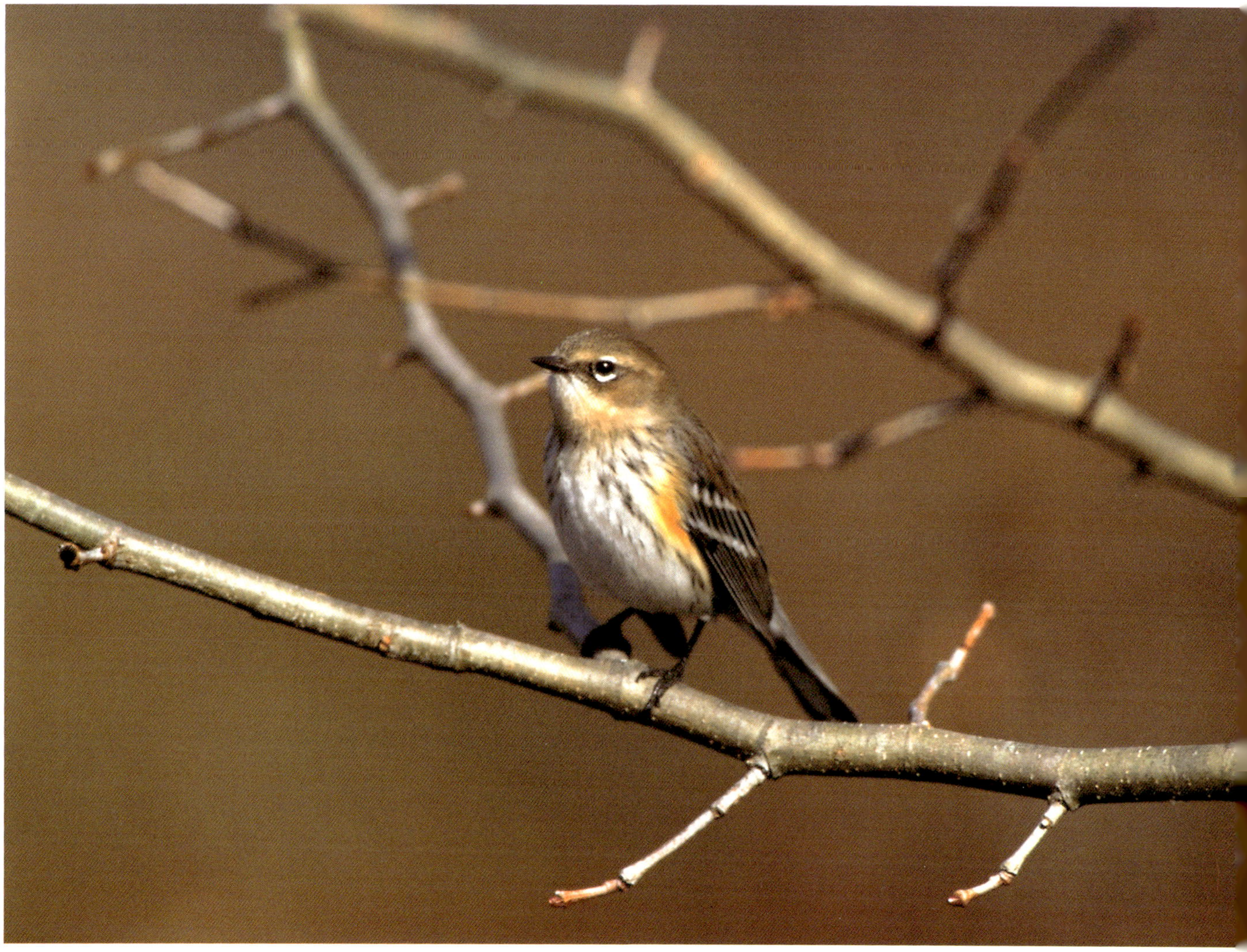

Yellow-rumped warbler

River bottom at sunrise

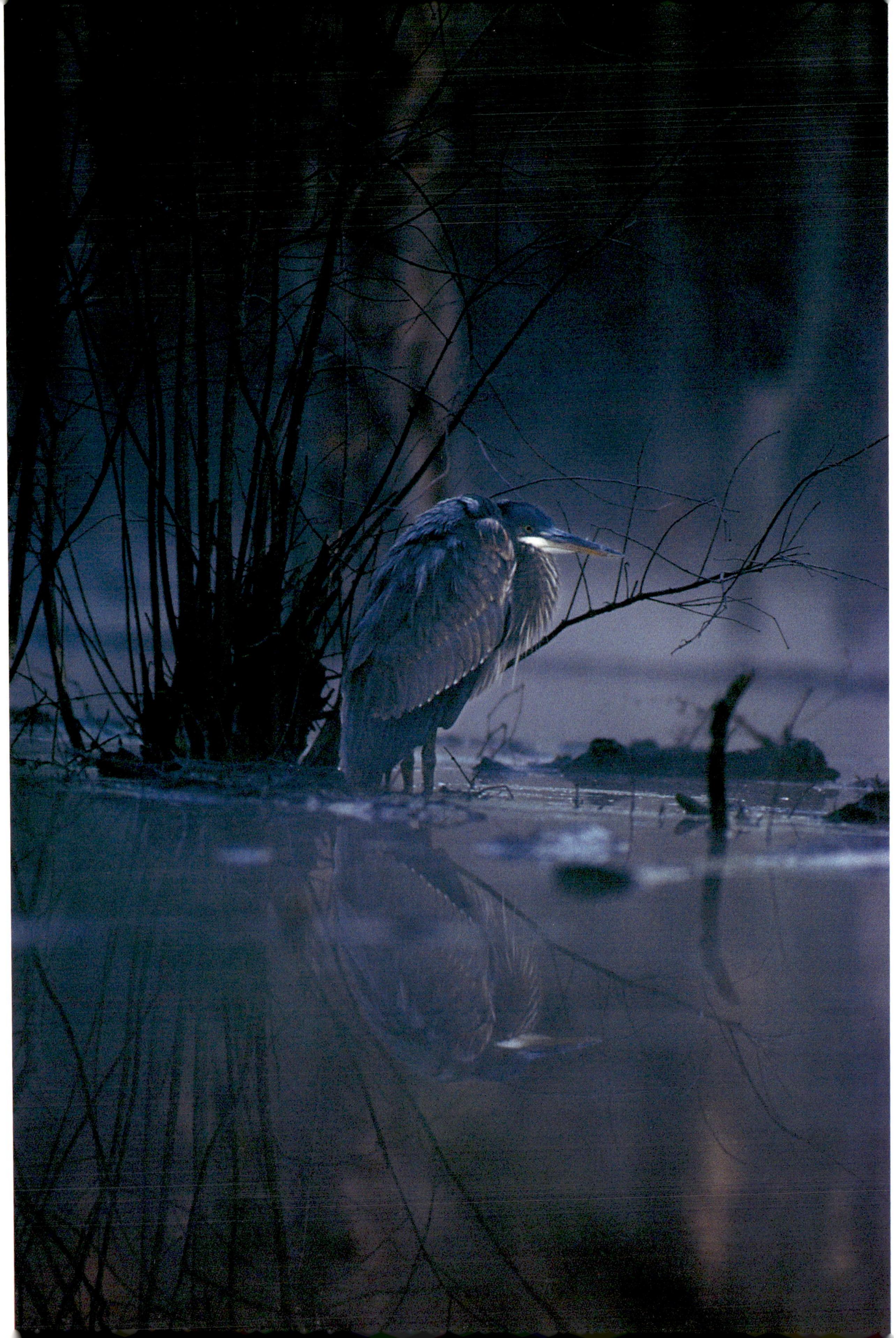

Great blue heron

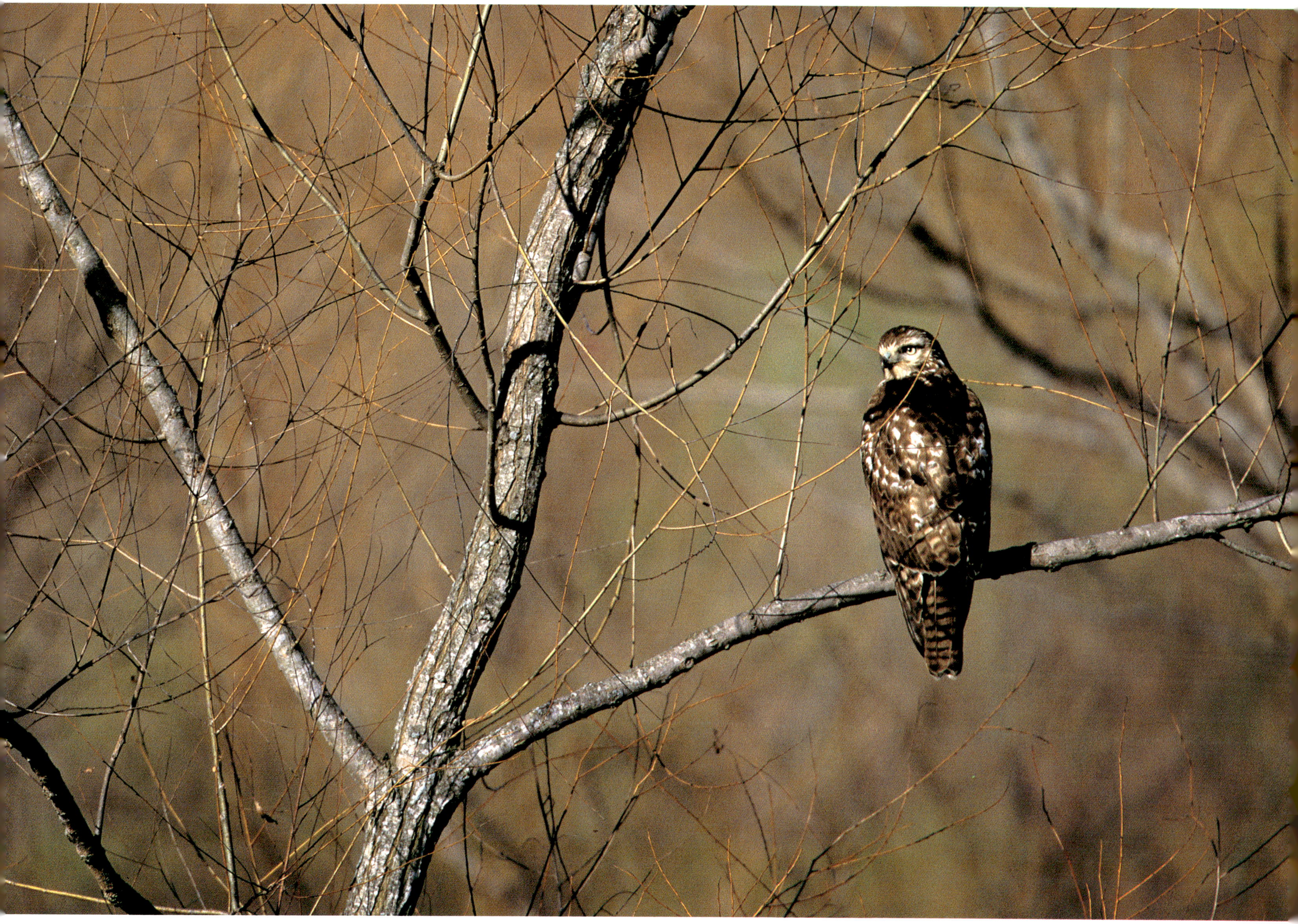

Immature red-tailed hawk

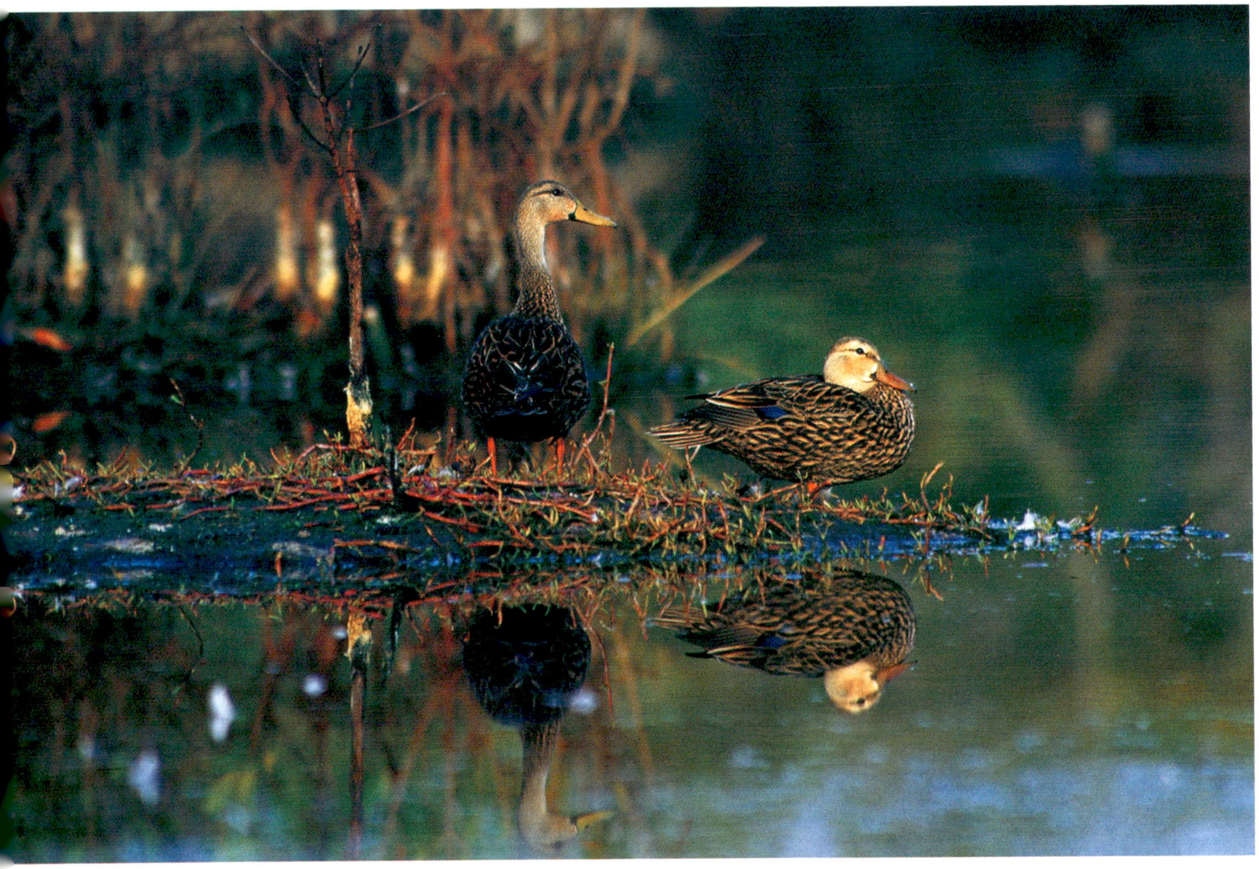

Mottled ducks

Hooded merganser

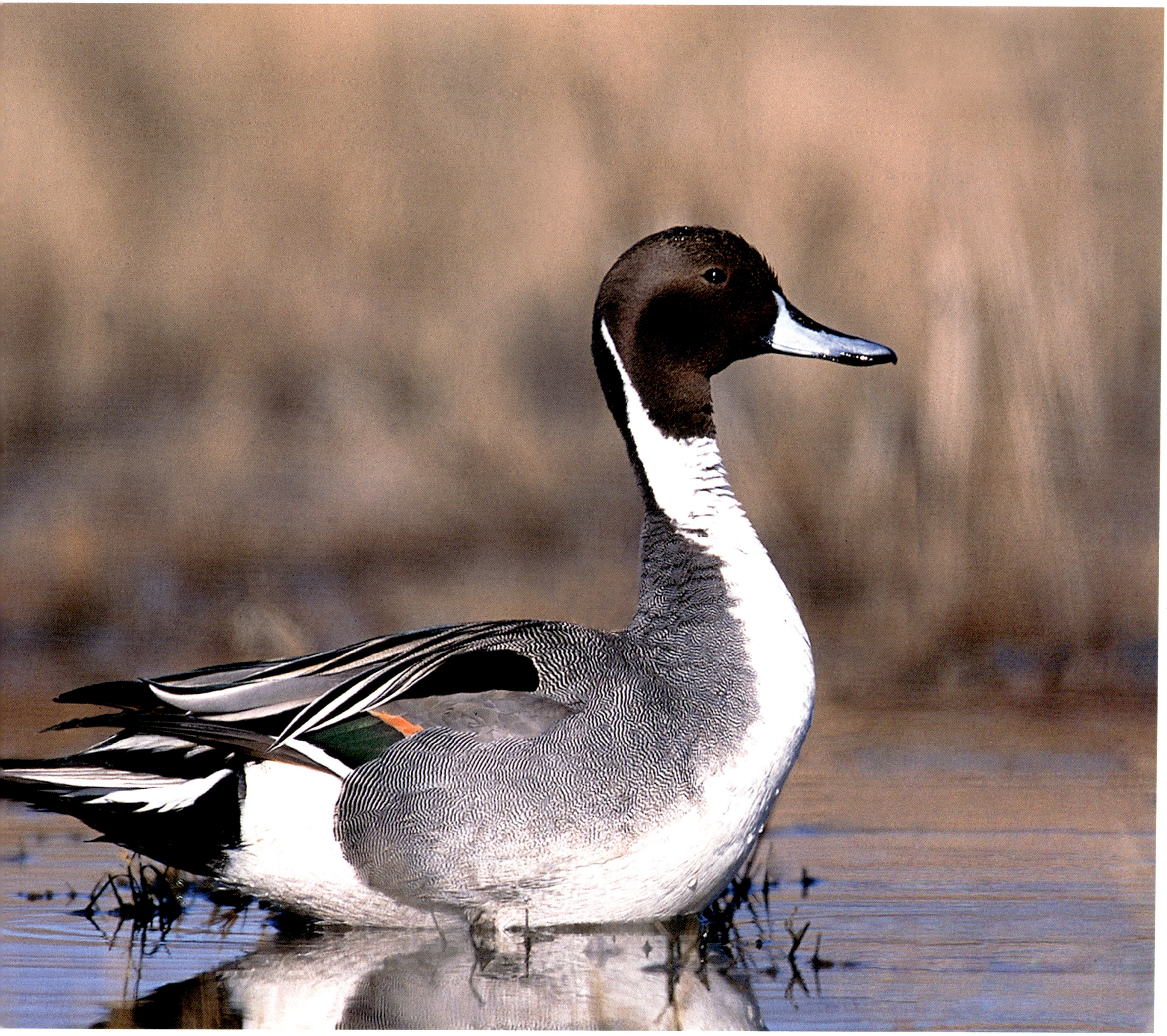

Pintail

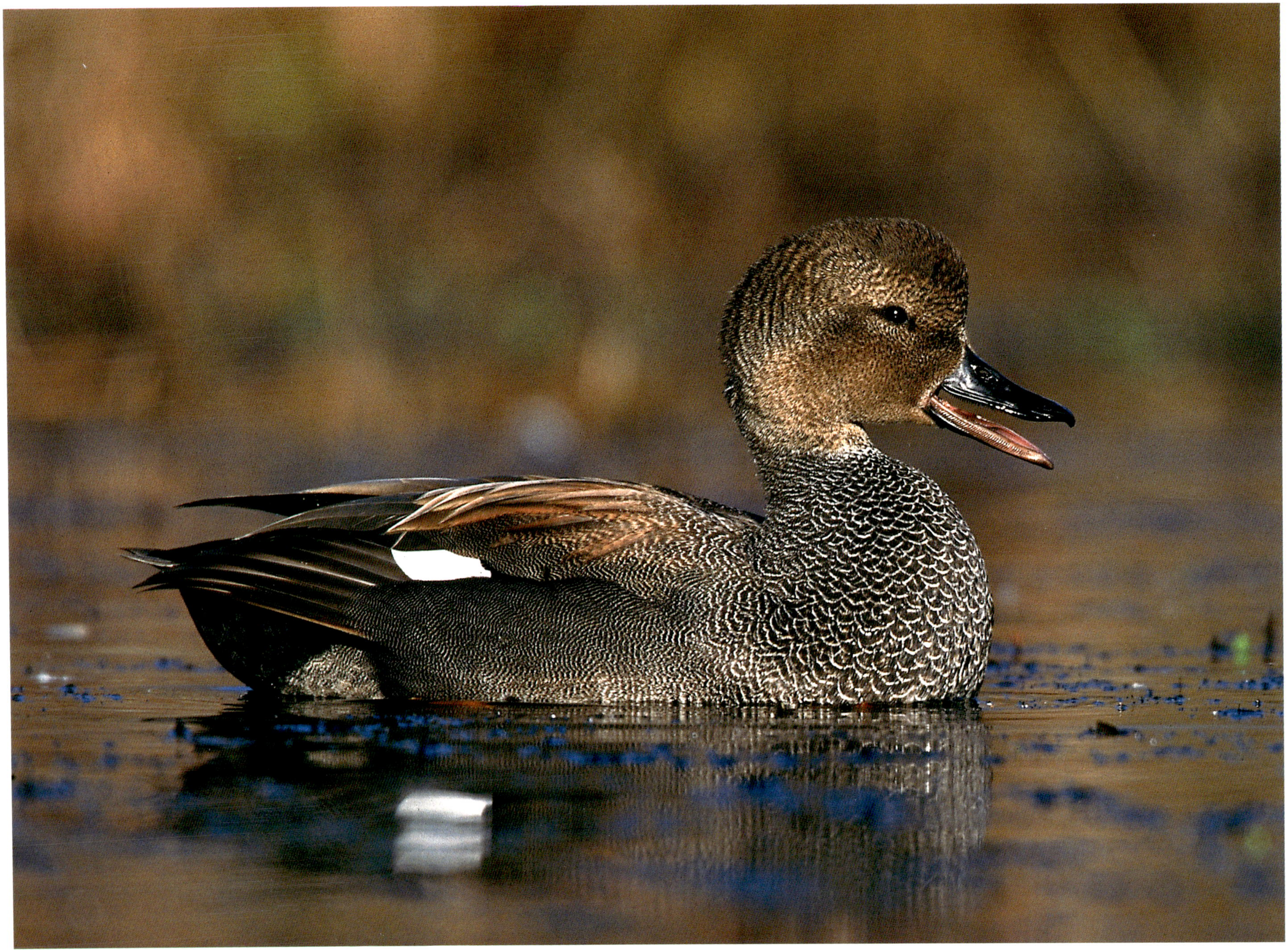

Gadwall

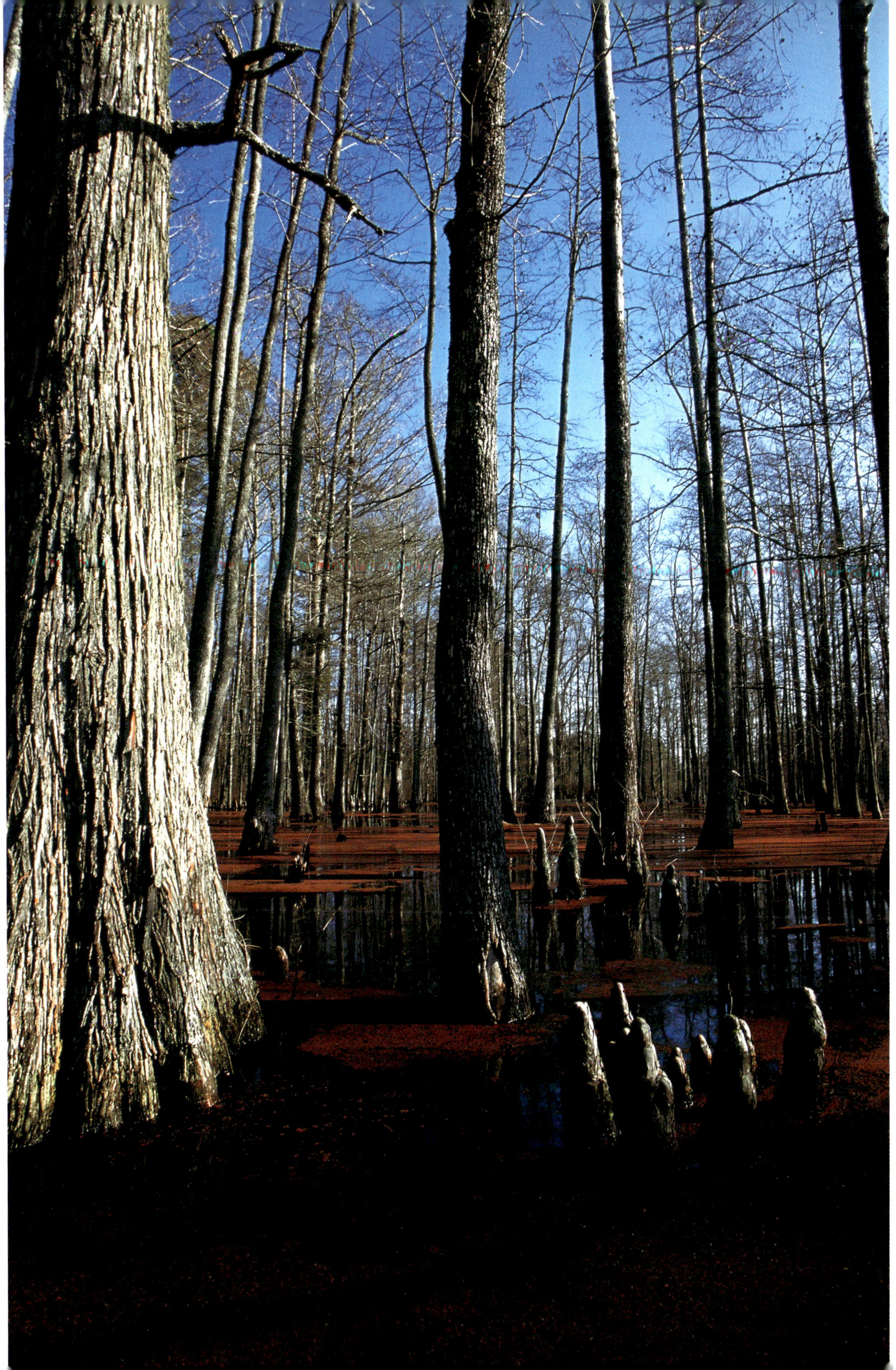

Cypress break

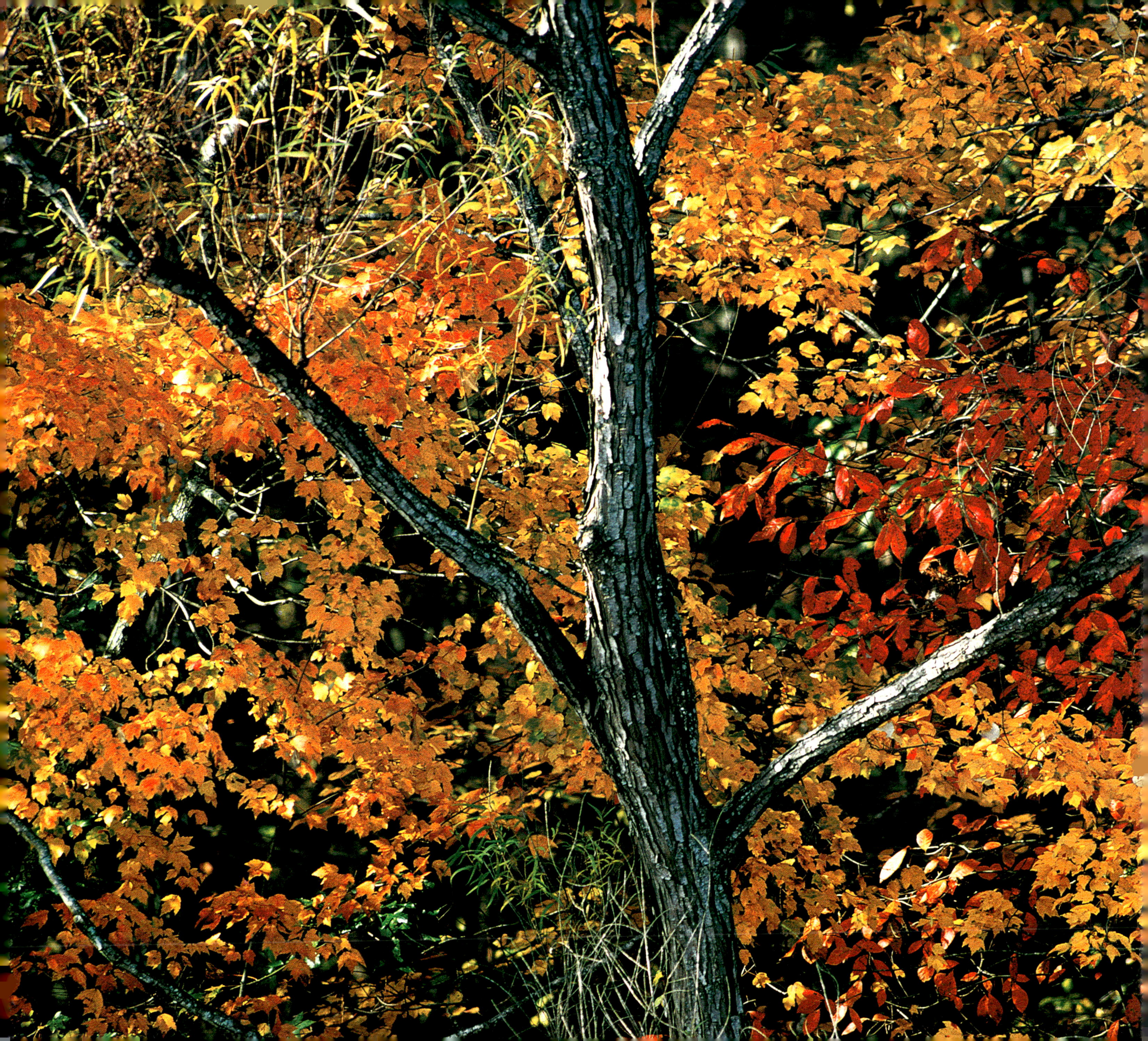

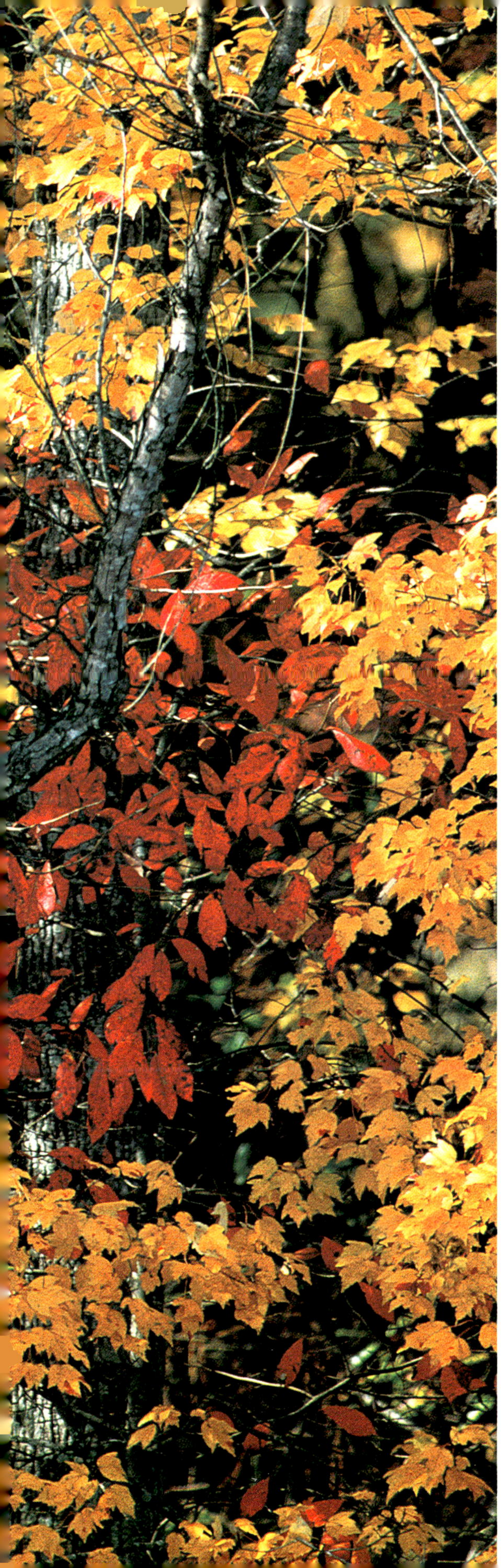

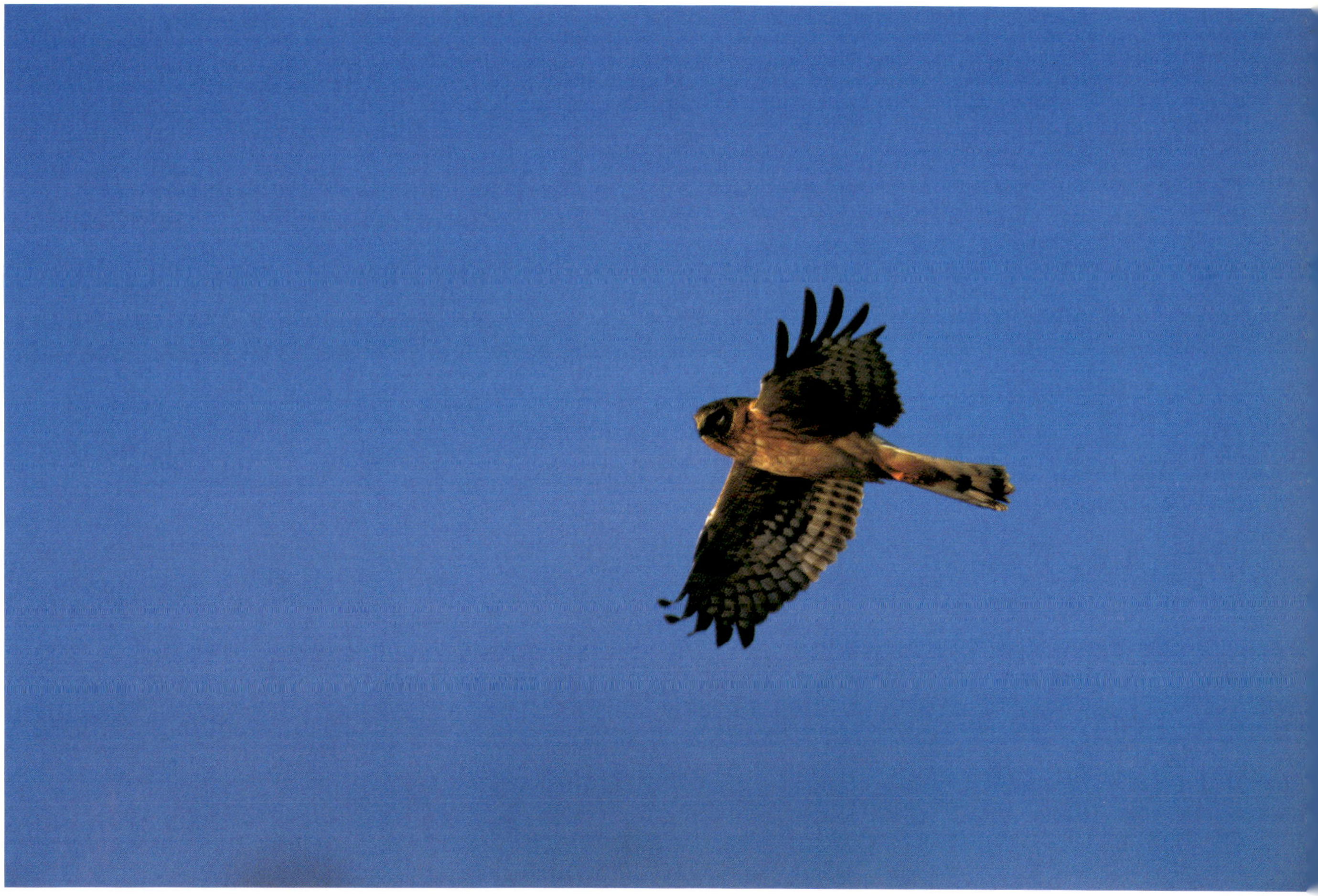

Northern harrier

Fall colors

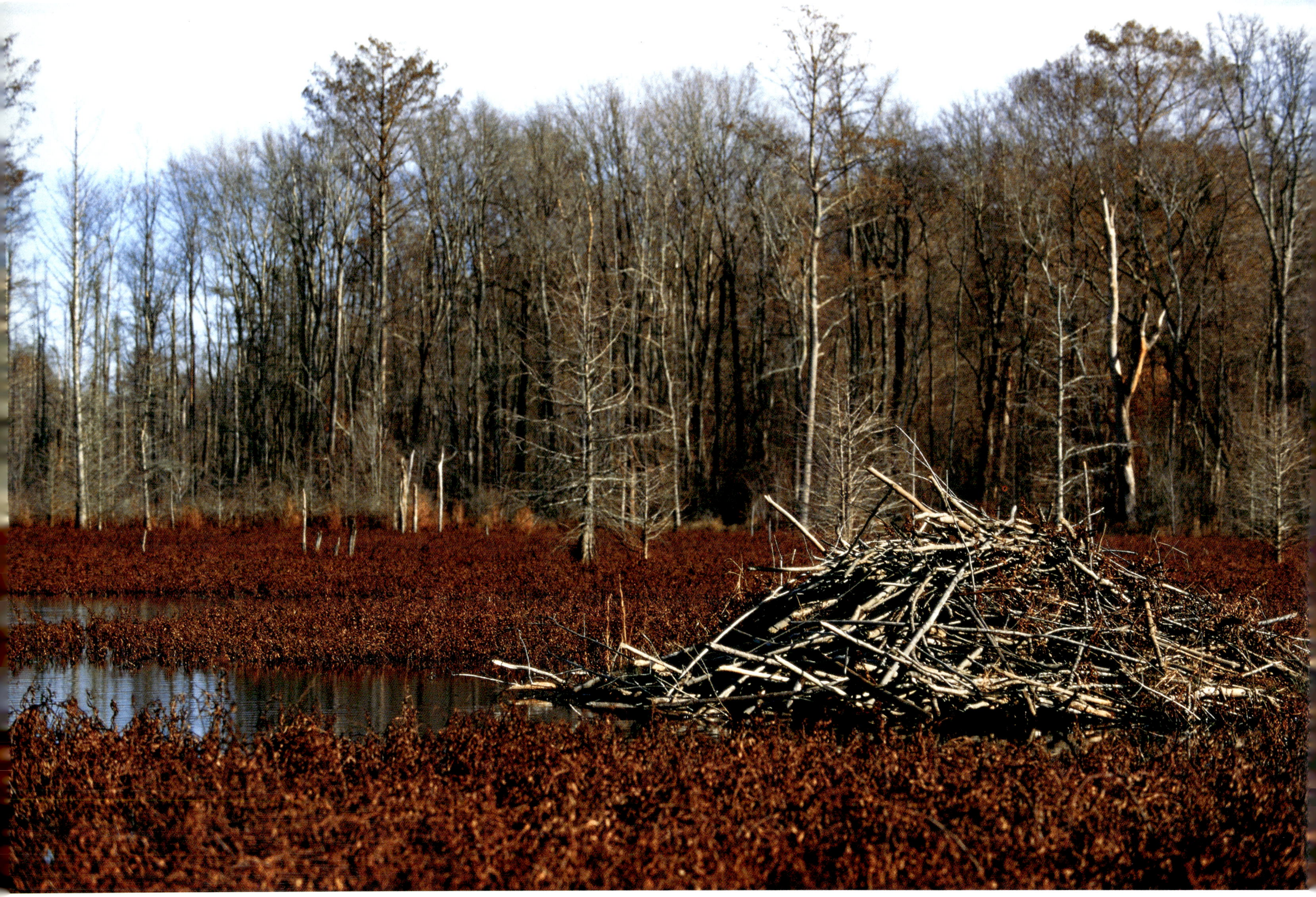

Beaver house

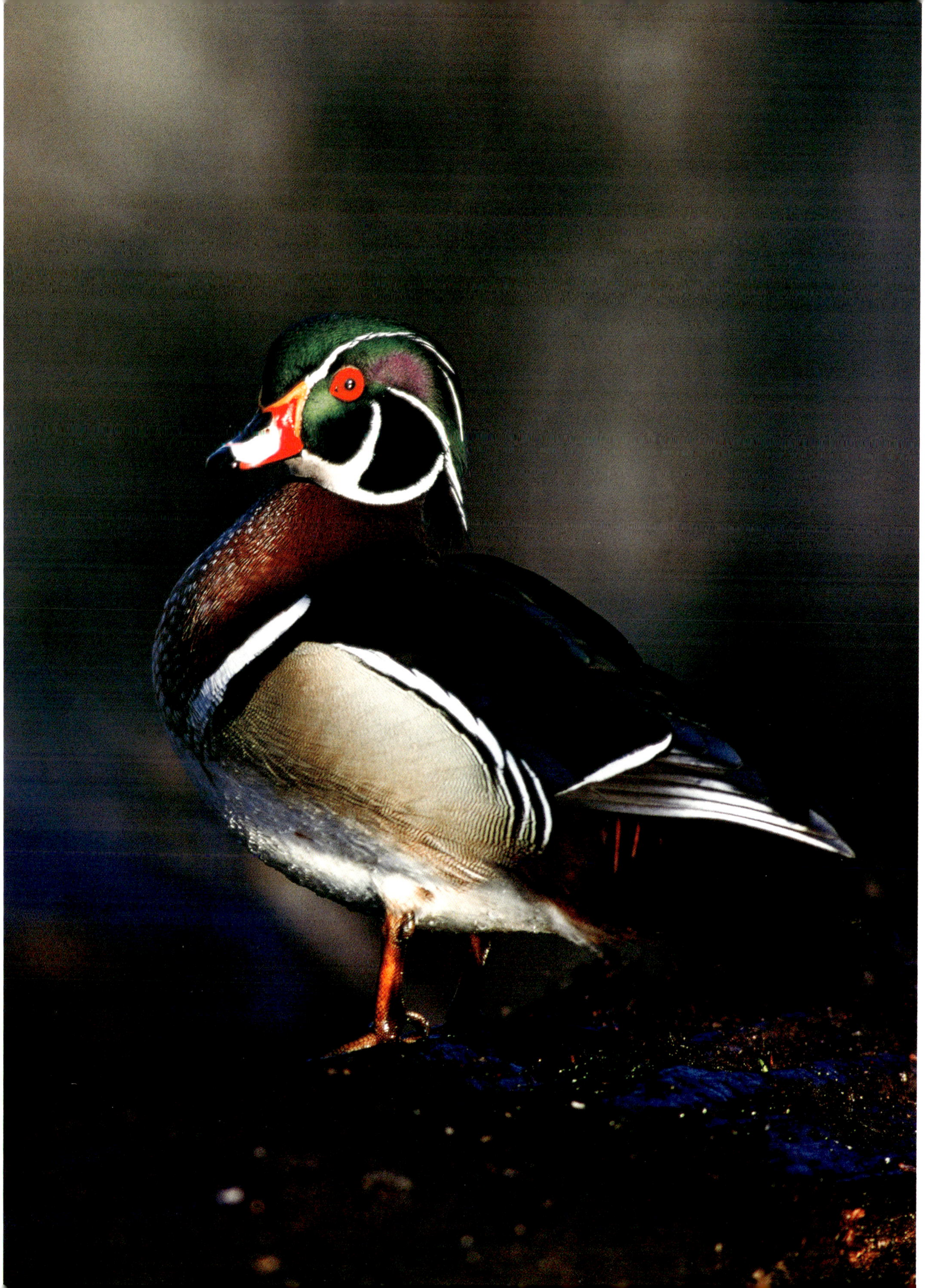

Wood duck

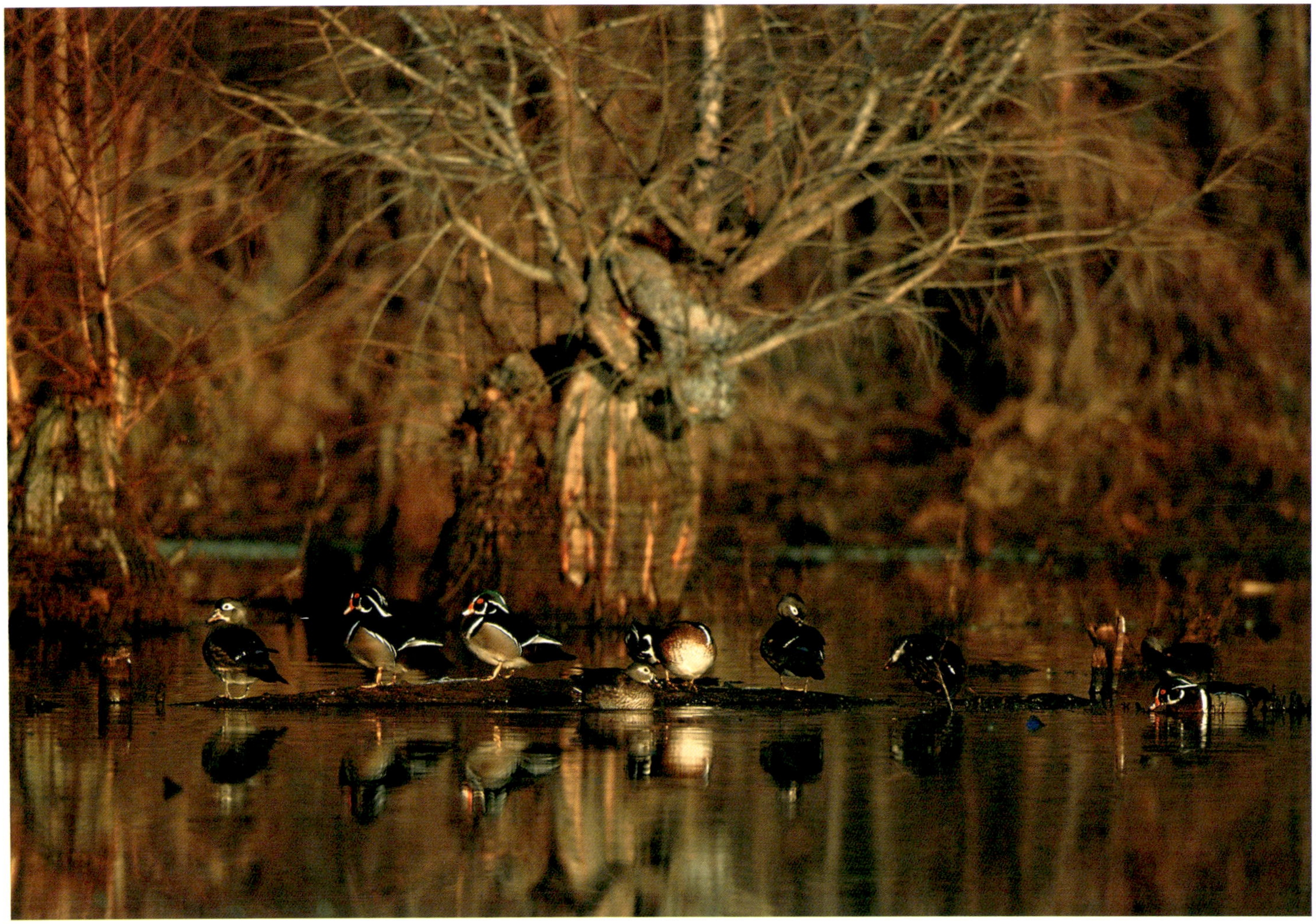

Wood ducks

Wood duck

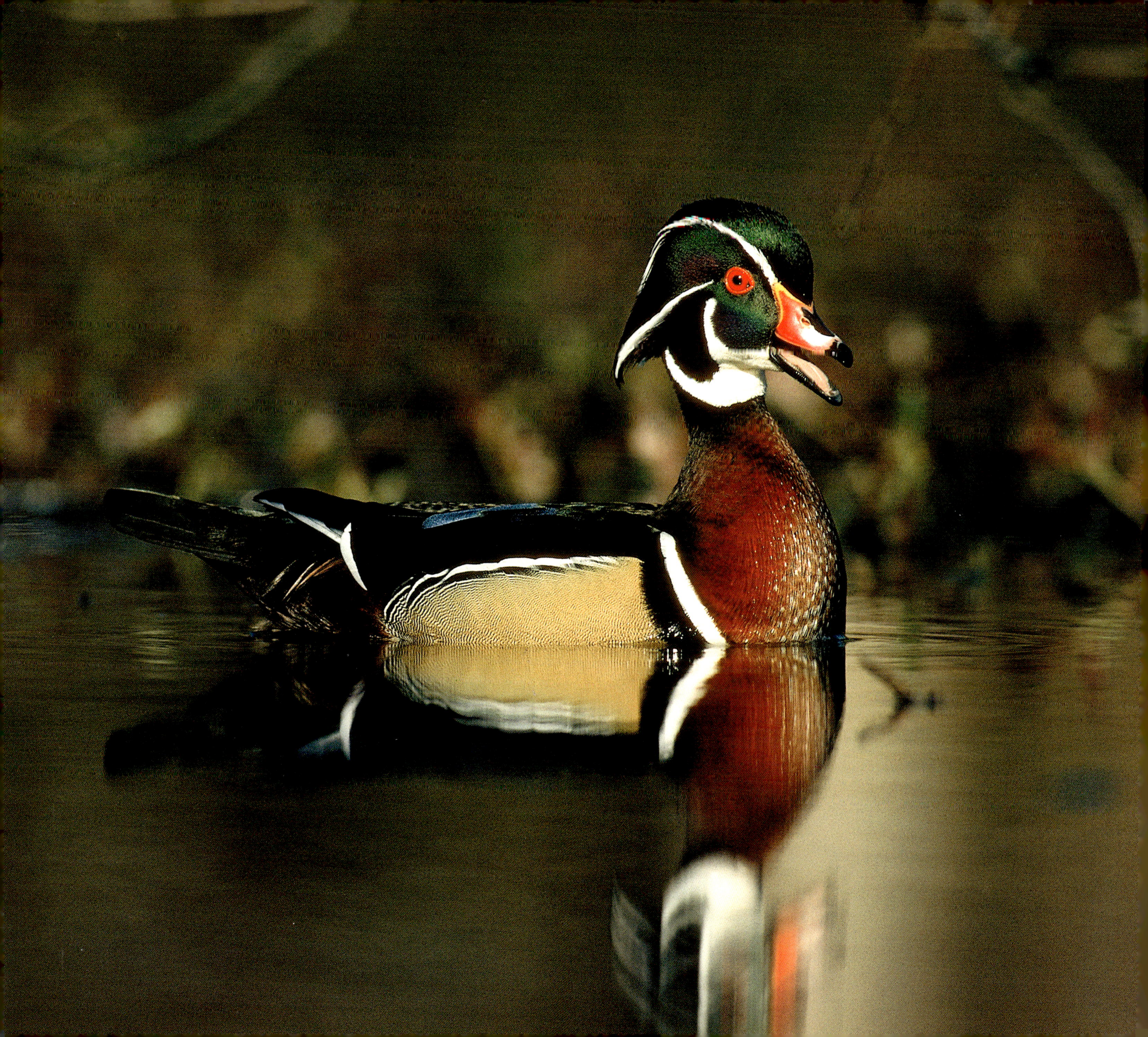

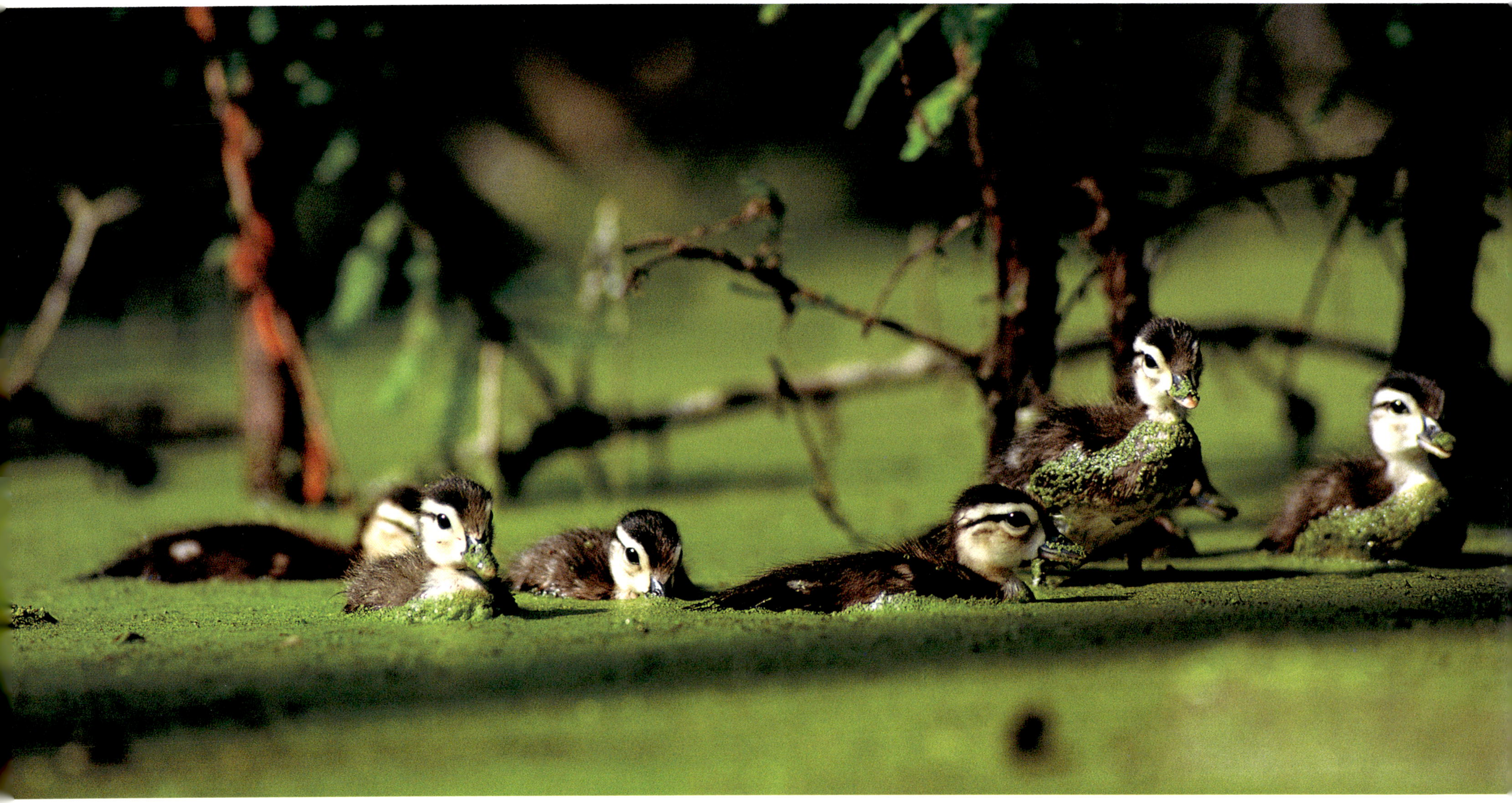

Immature wood ducks in duck weed

Wood ducks preening

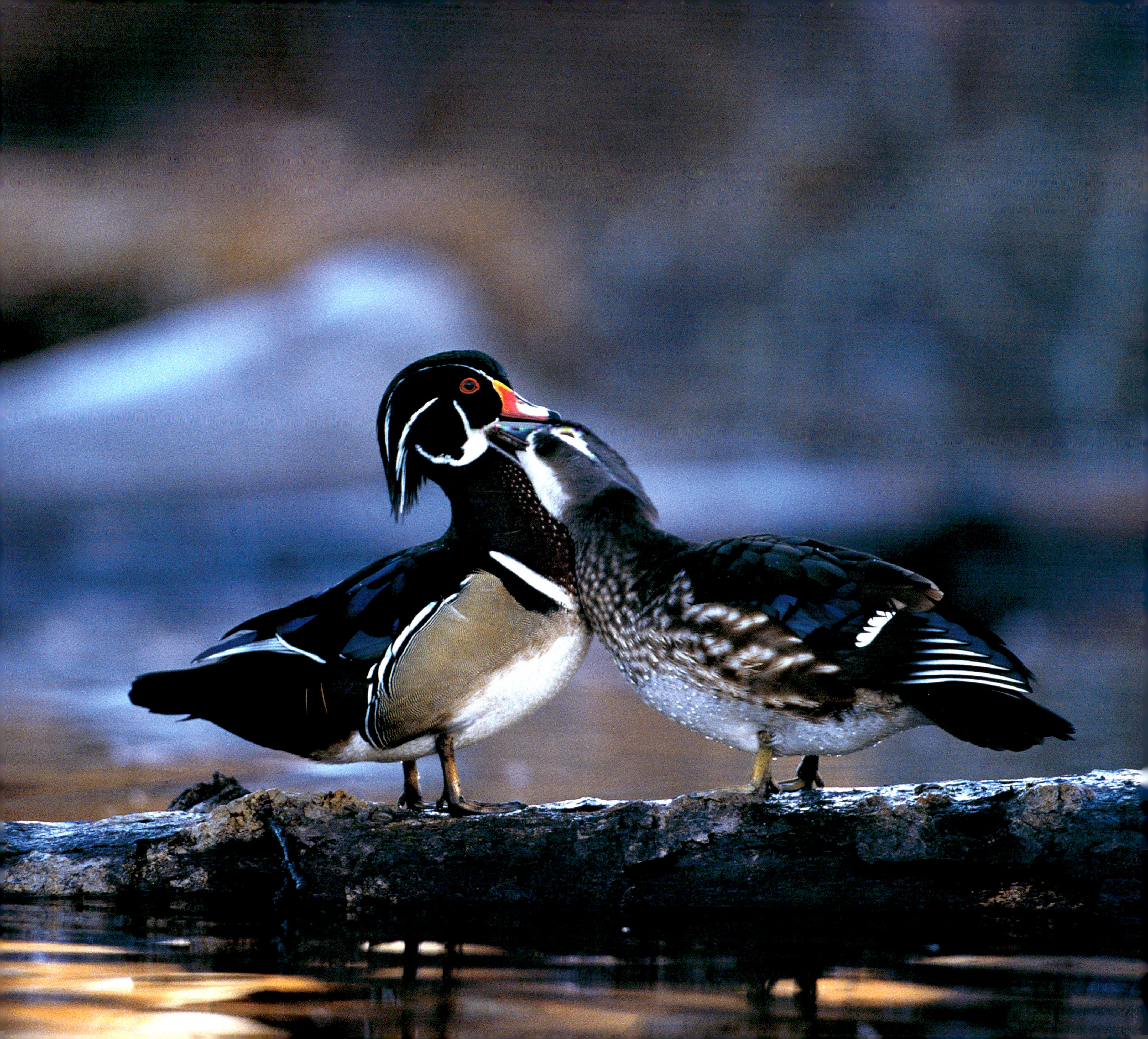

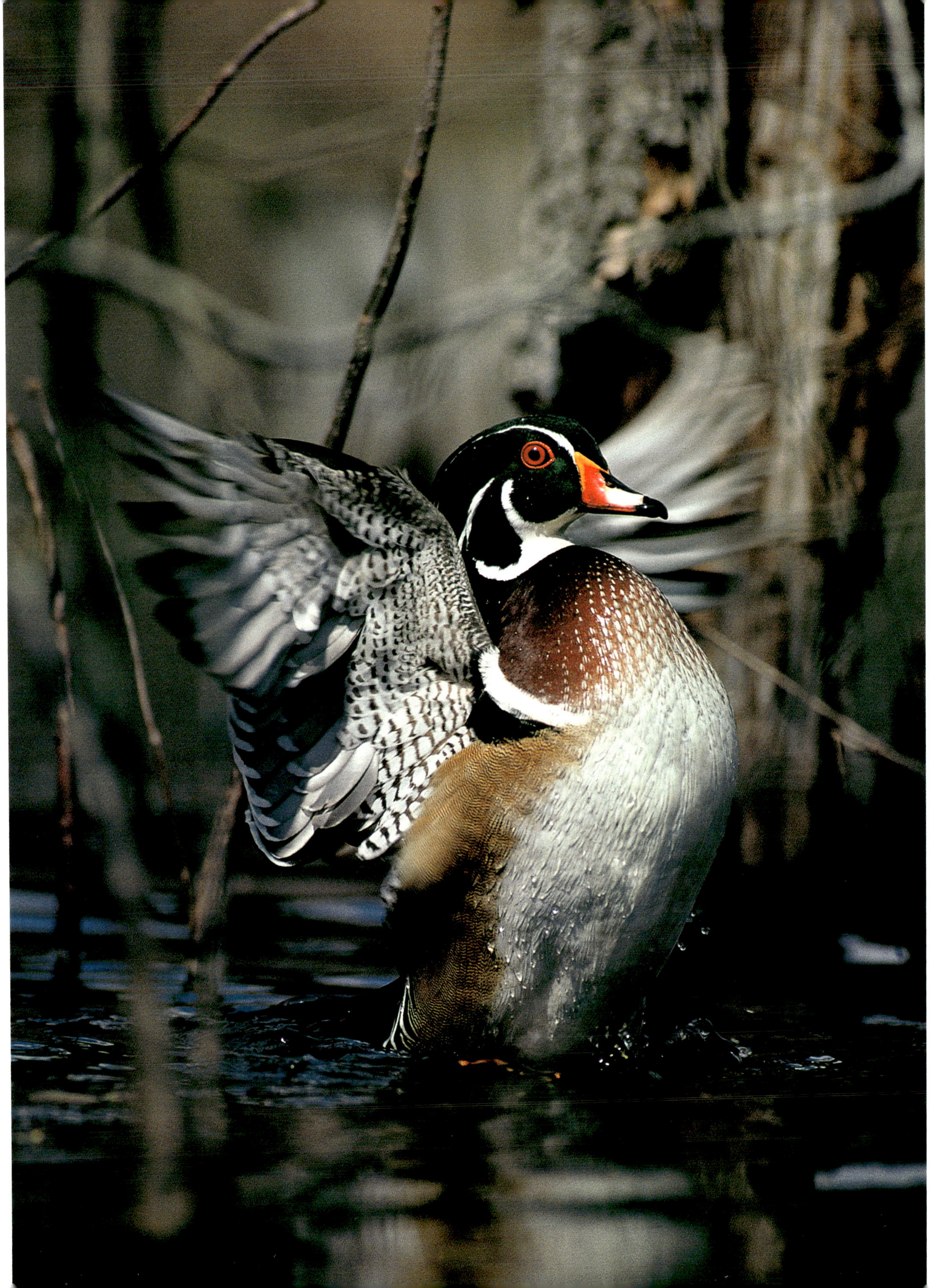

Wood duck

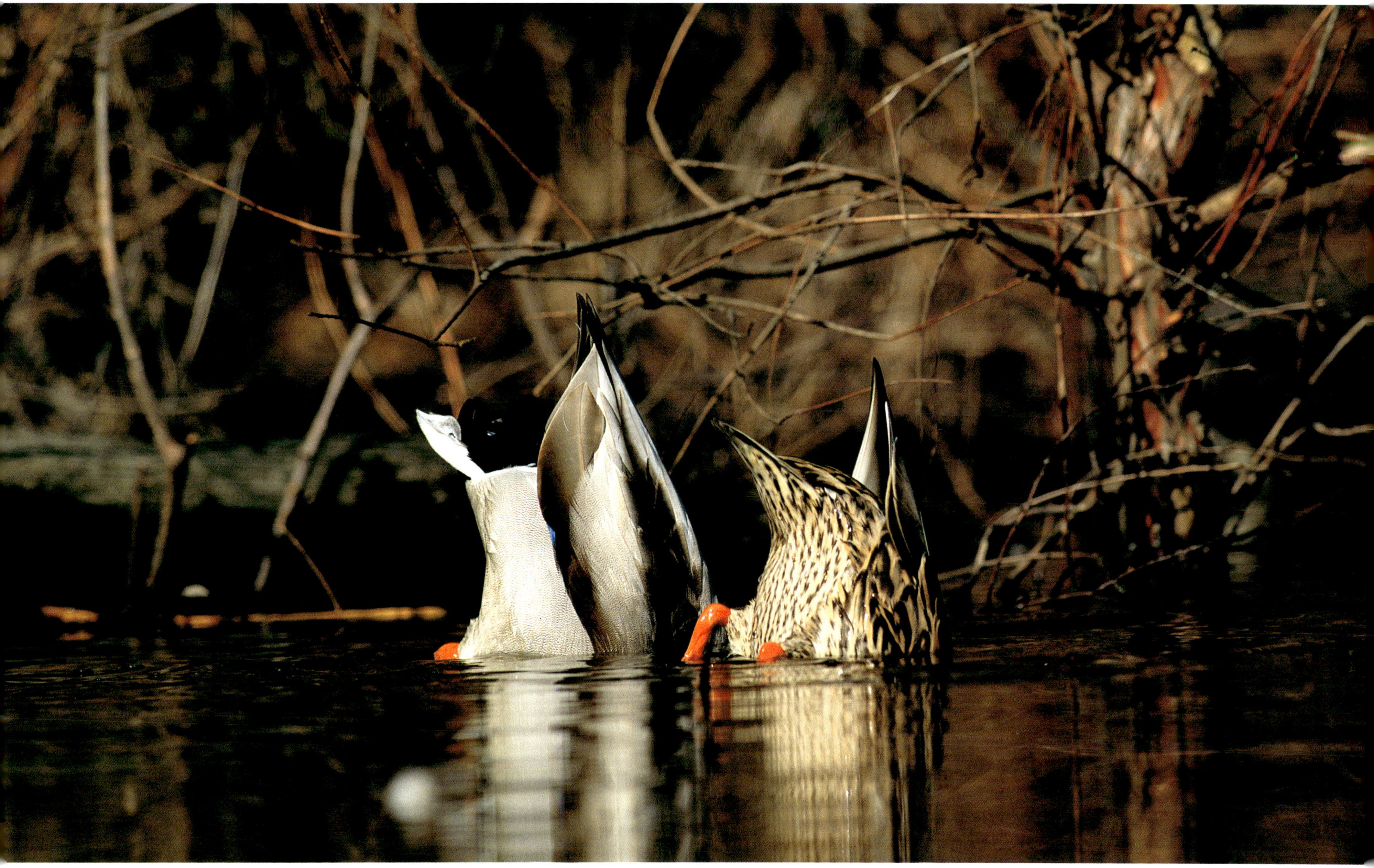

Feeding mallards

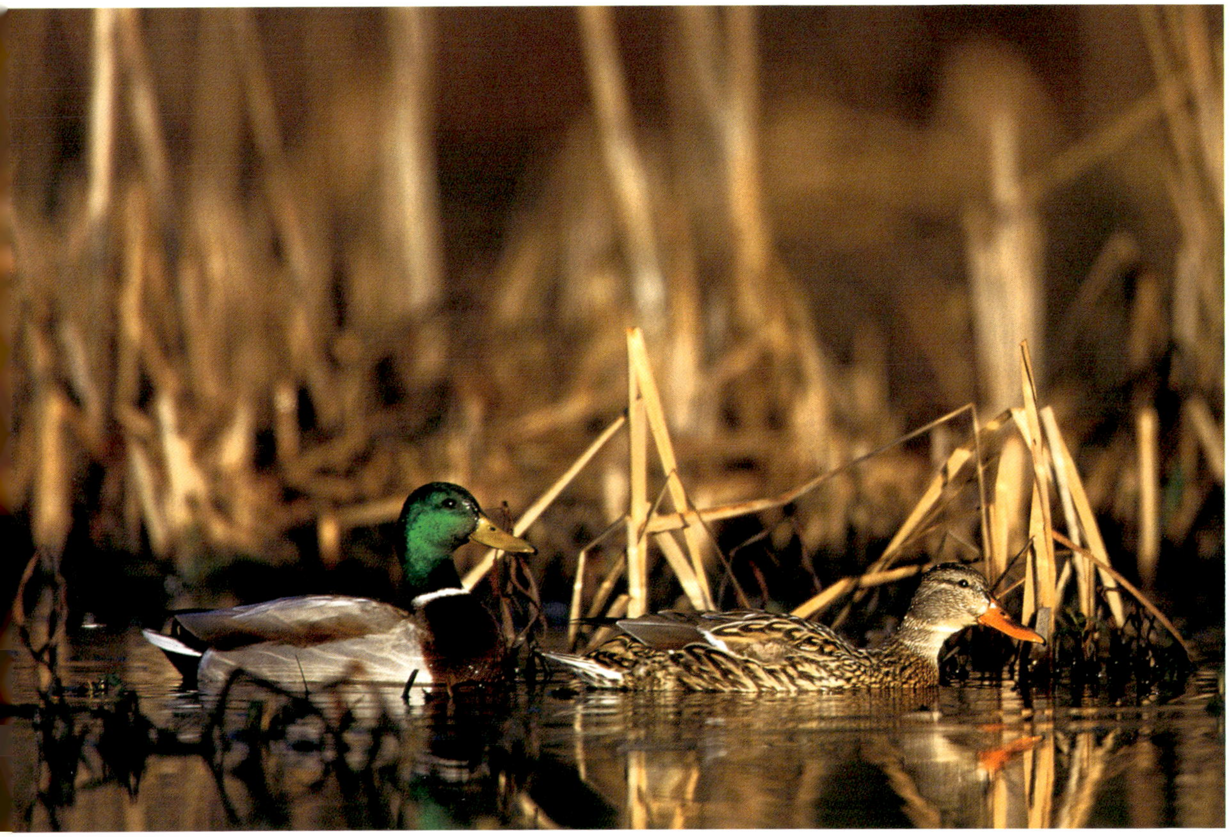

Mallard drake and hen

Mallard flock in flight

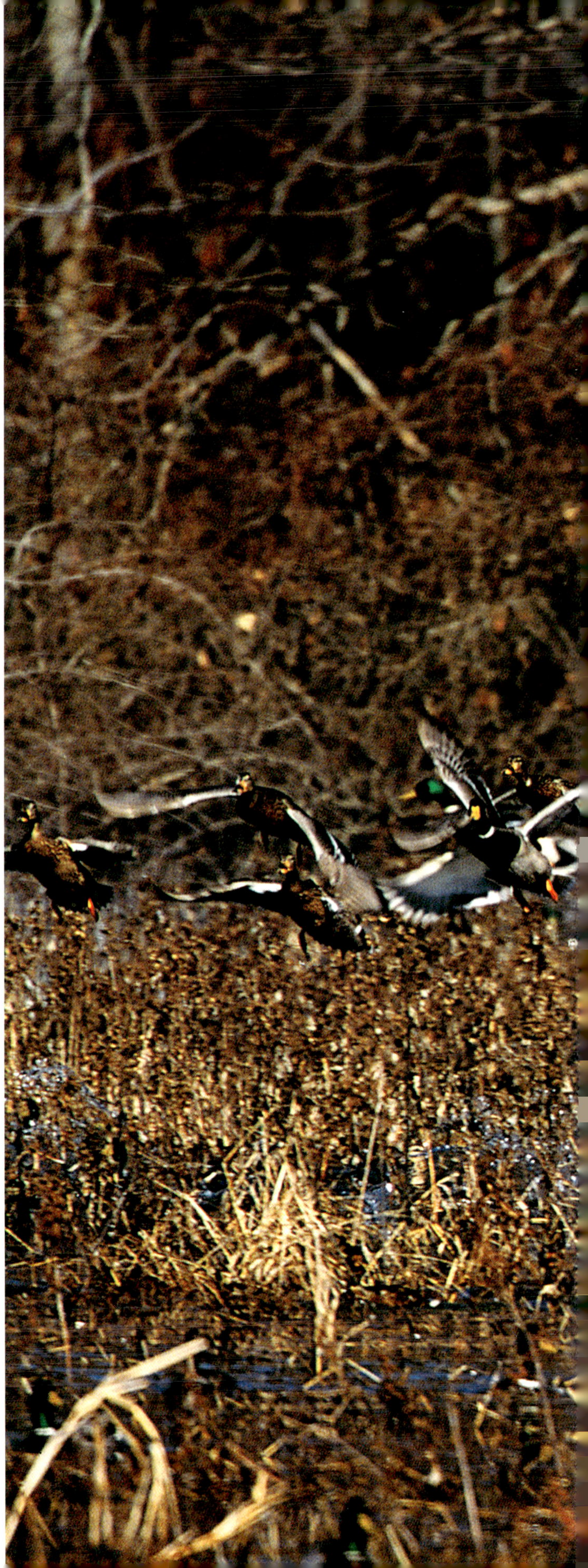

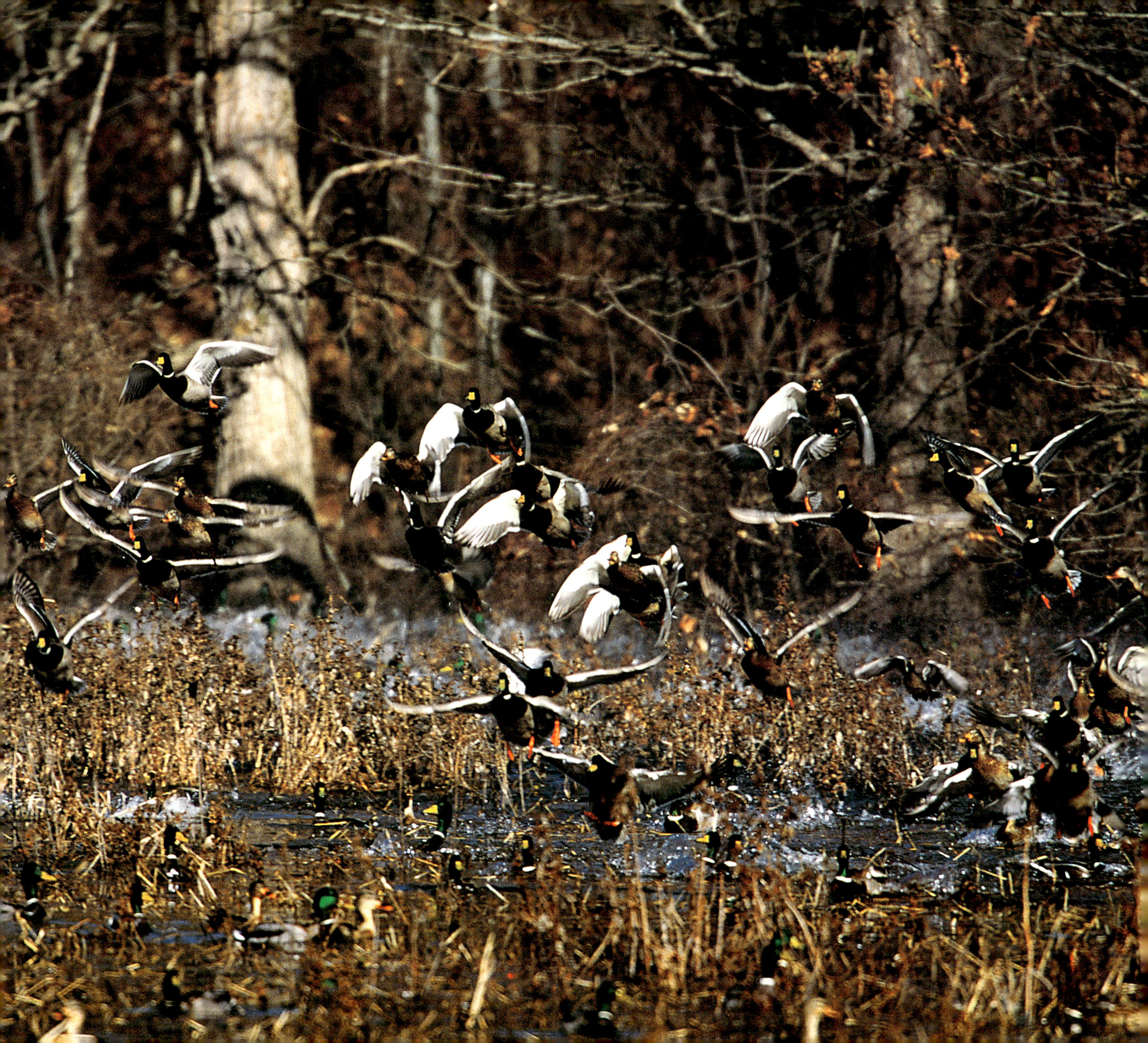

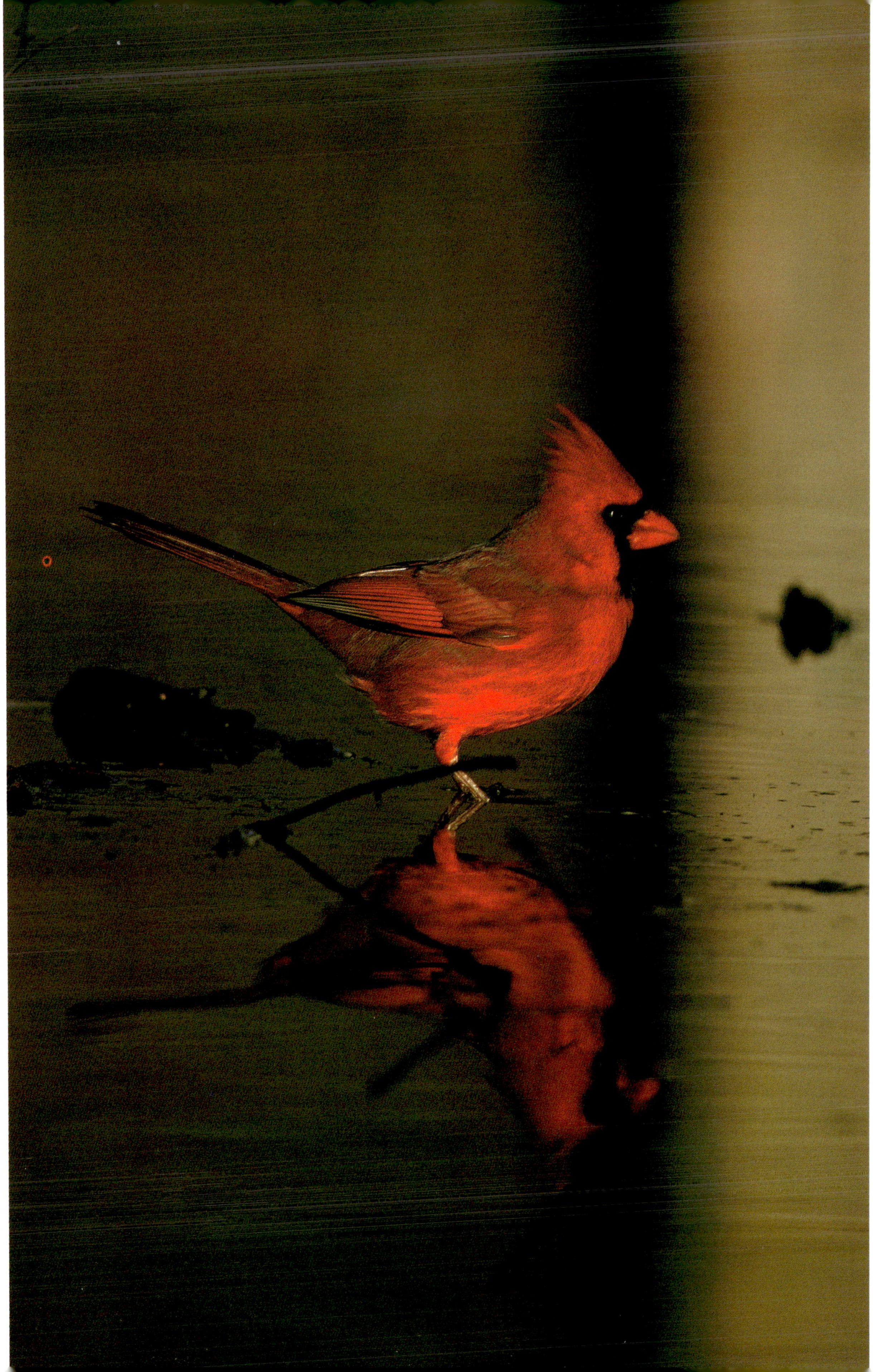

Cardinal

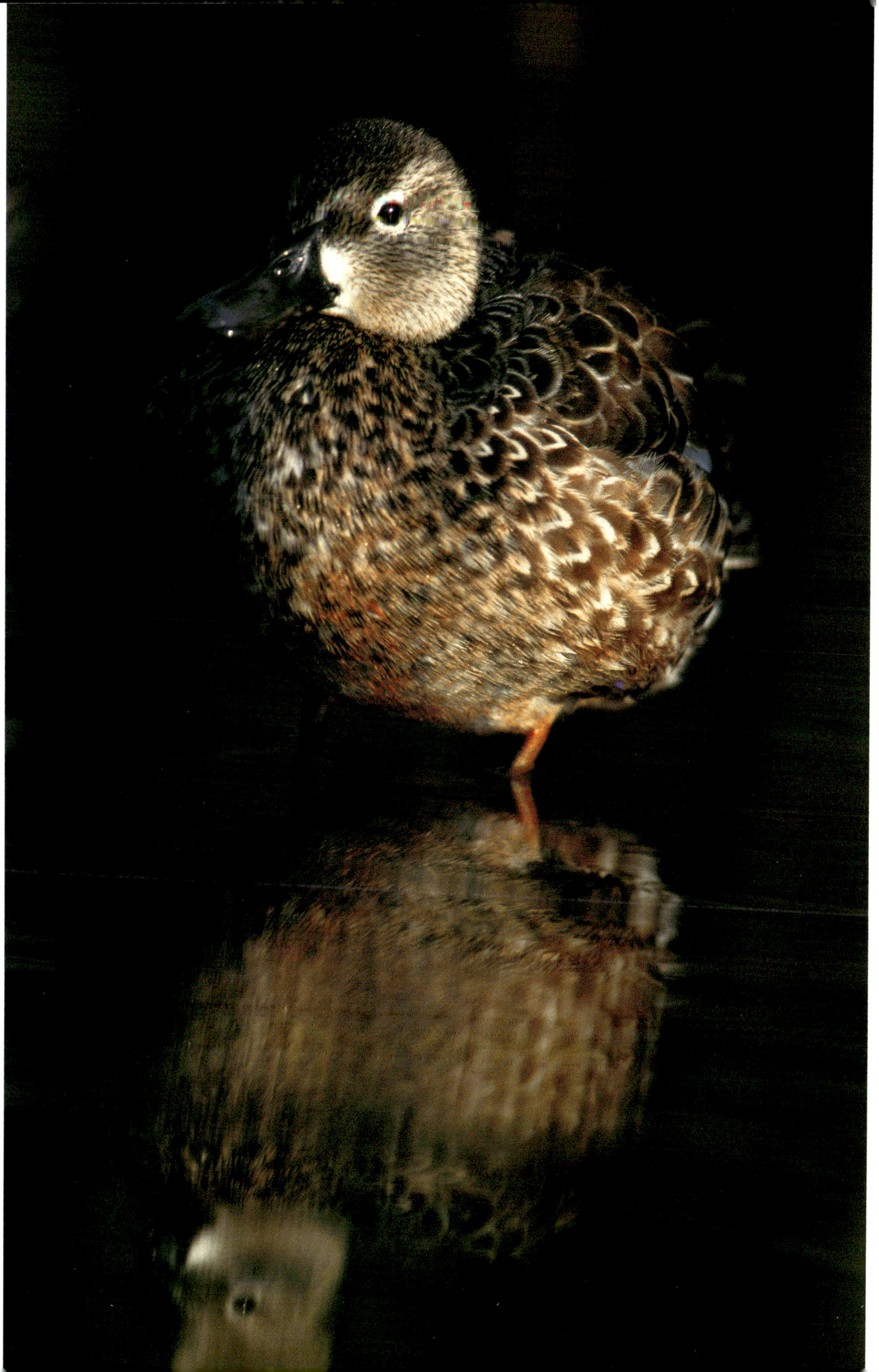

Blue-winged teal

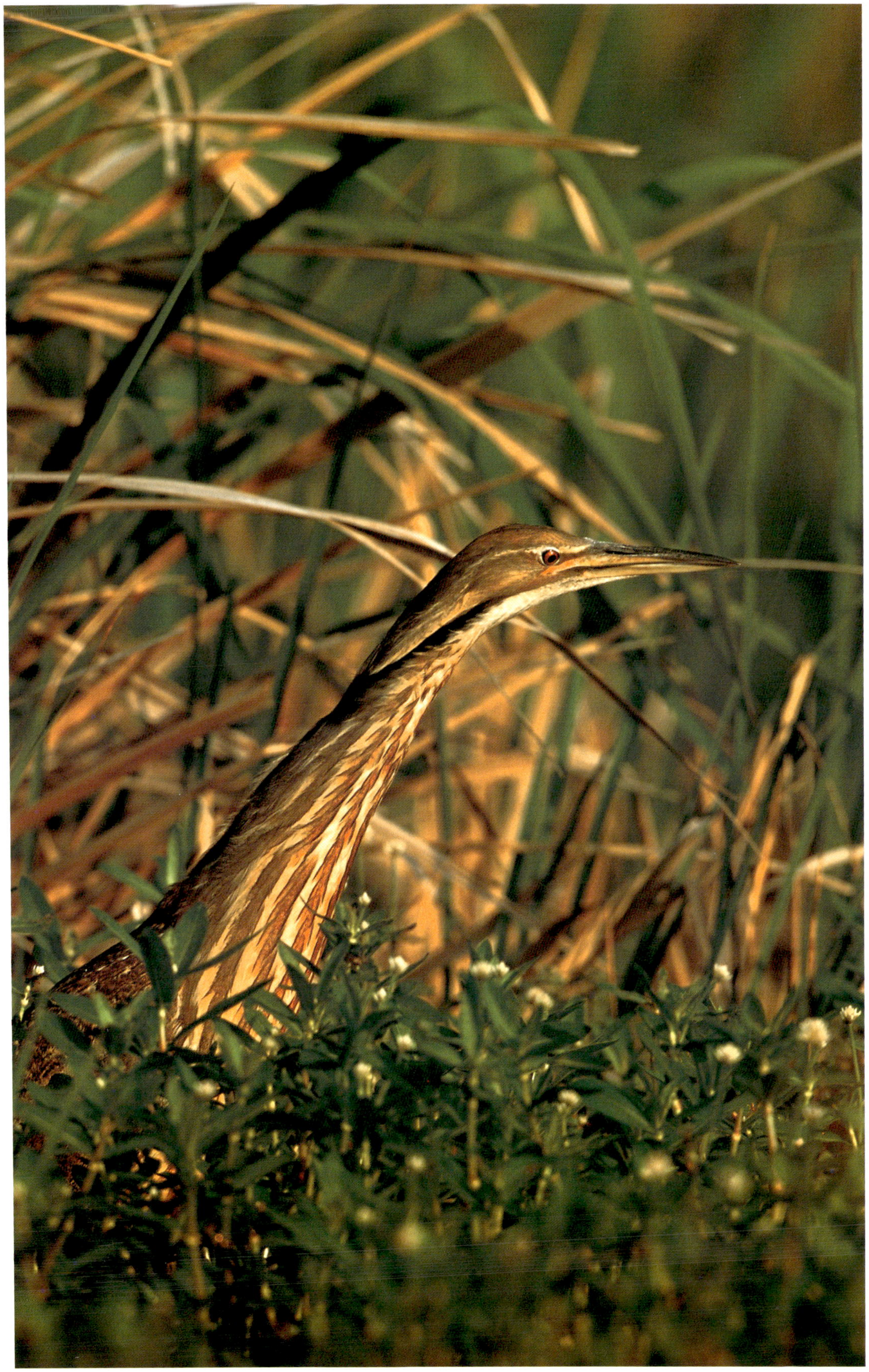

American bittern

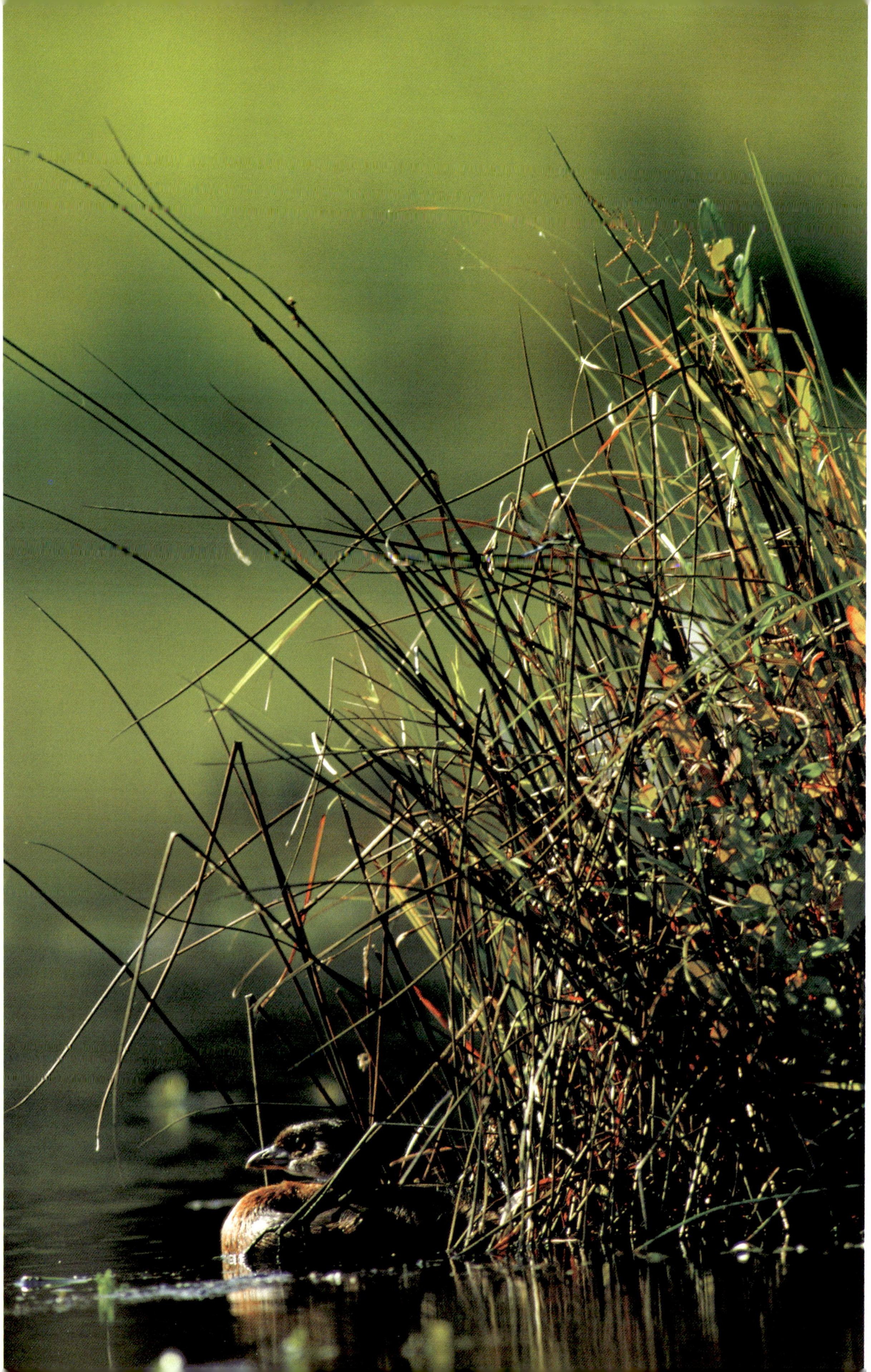

Pied-billed grebe

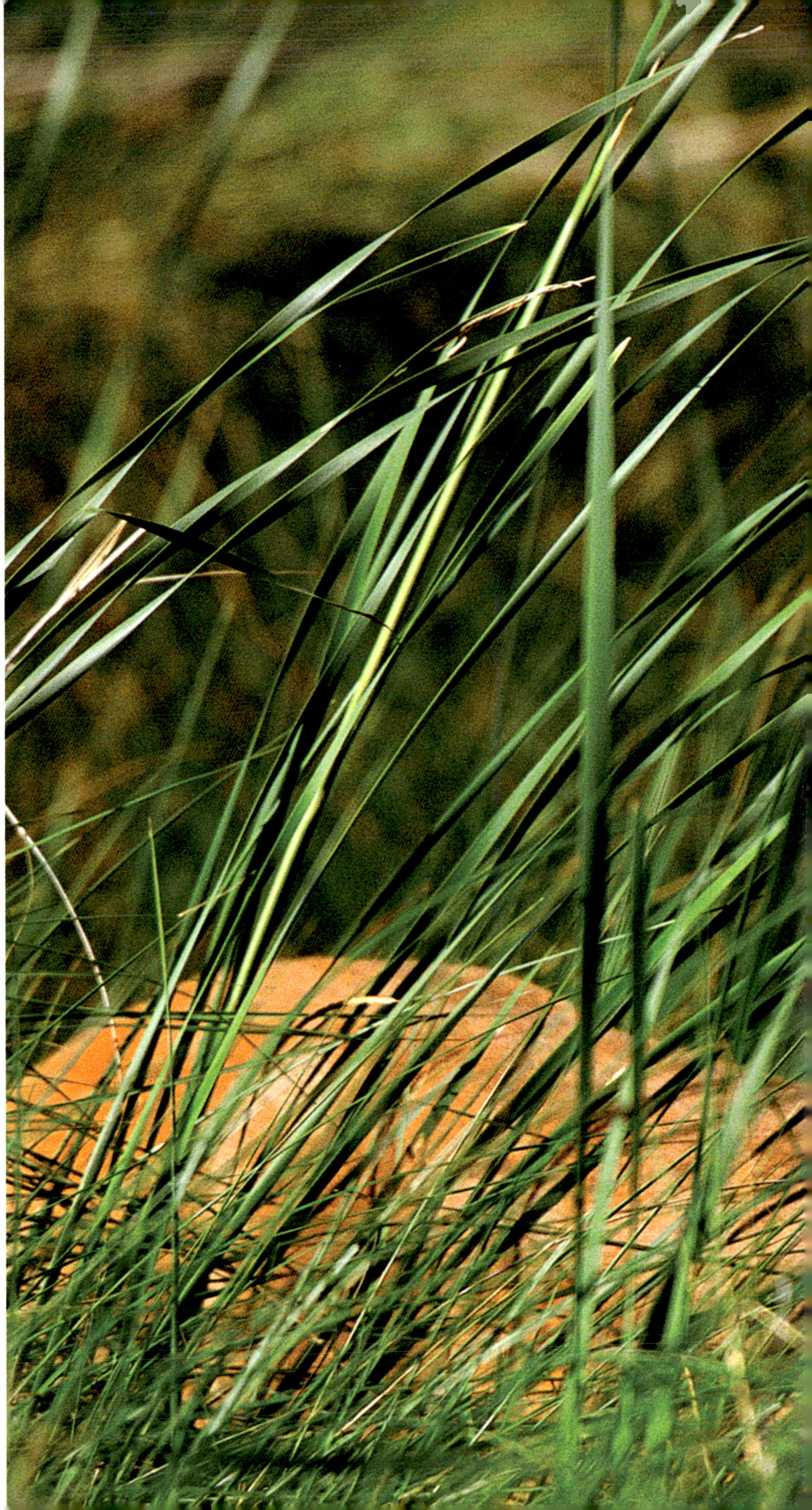

White-tailed deer

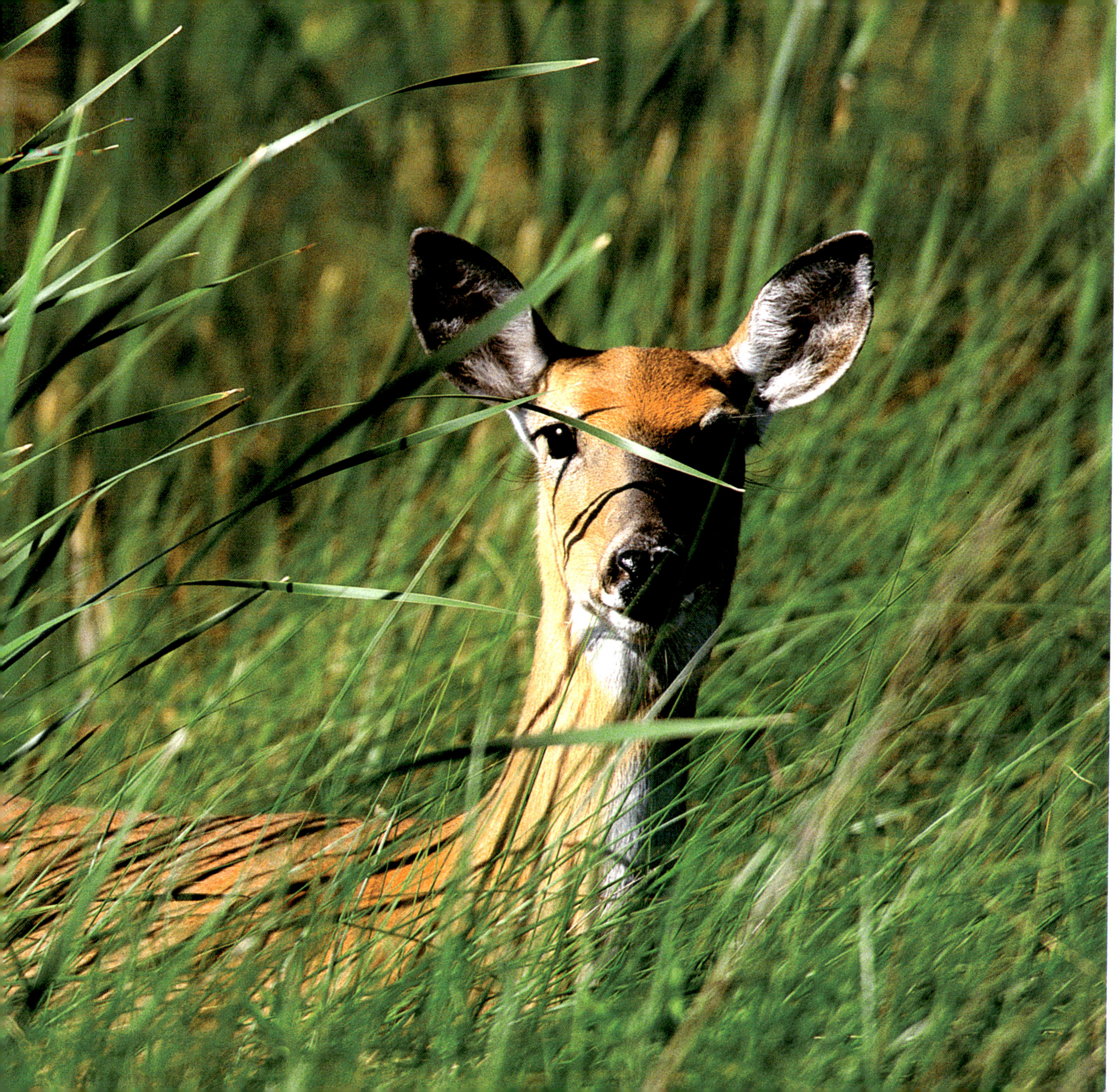

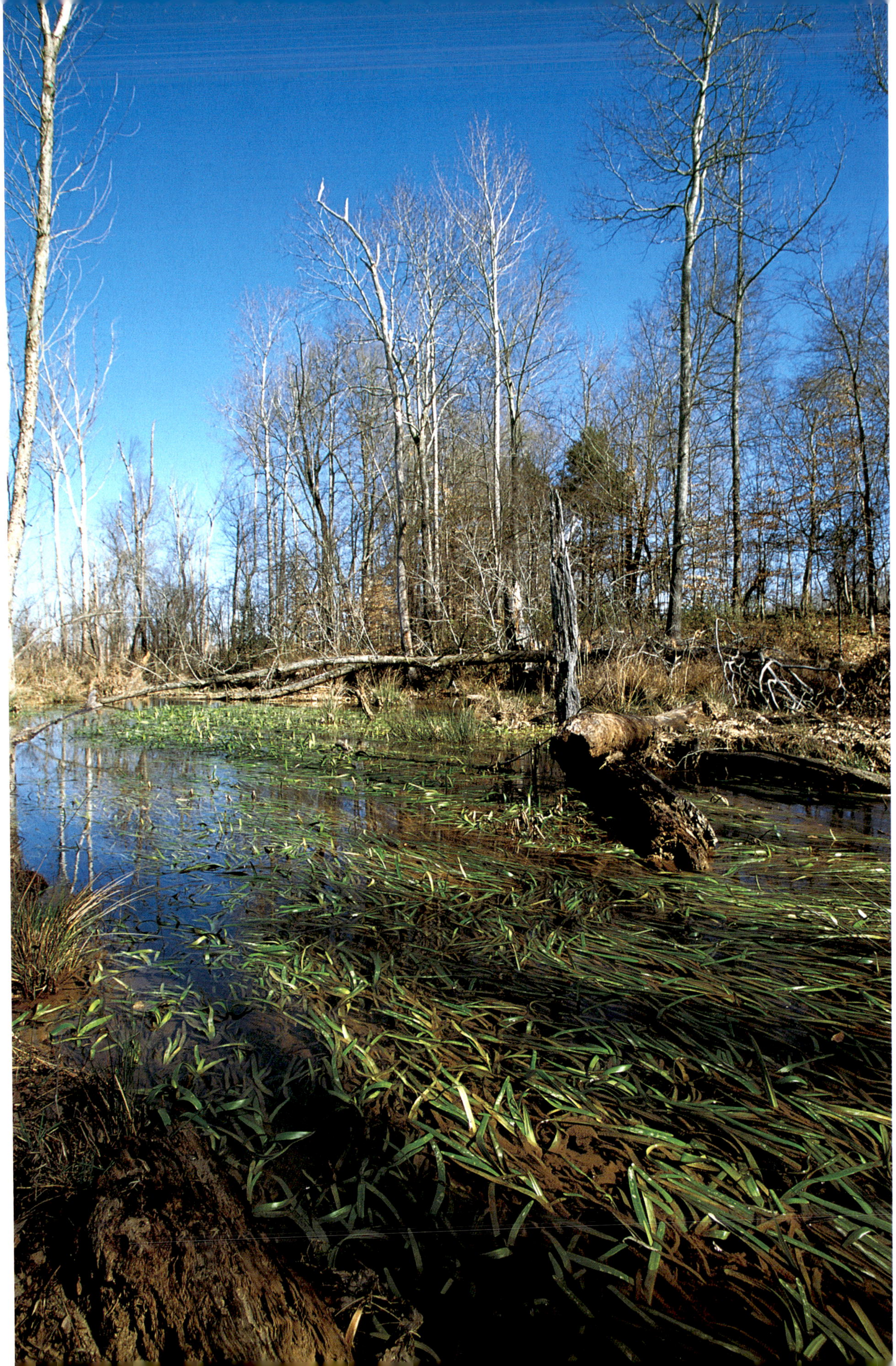

Spring rains runoff

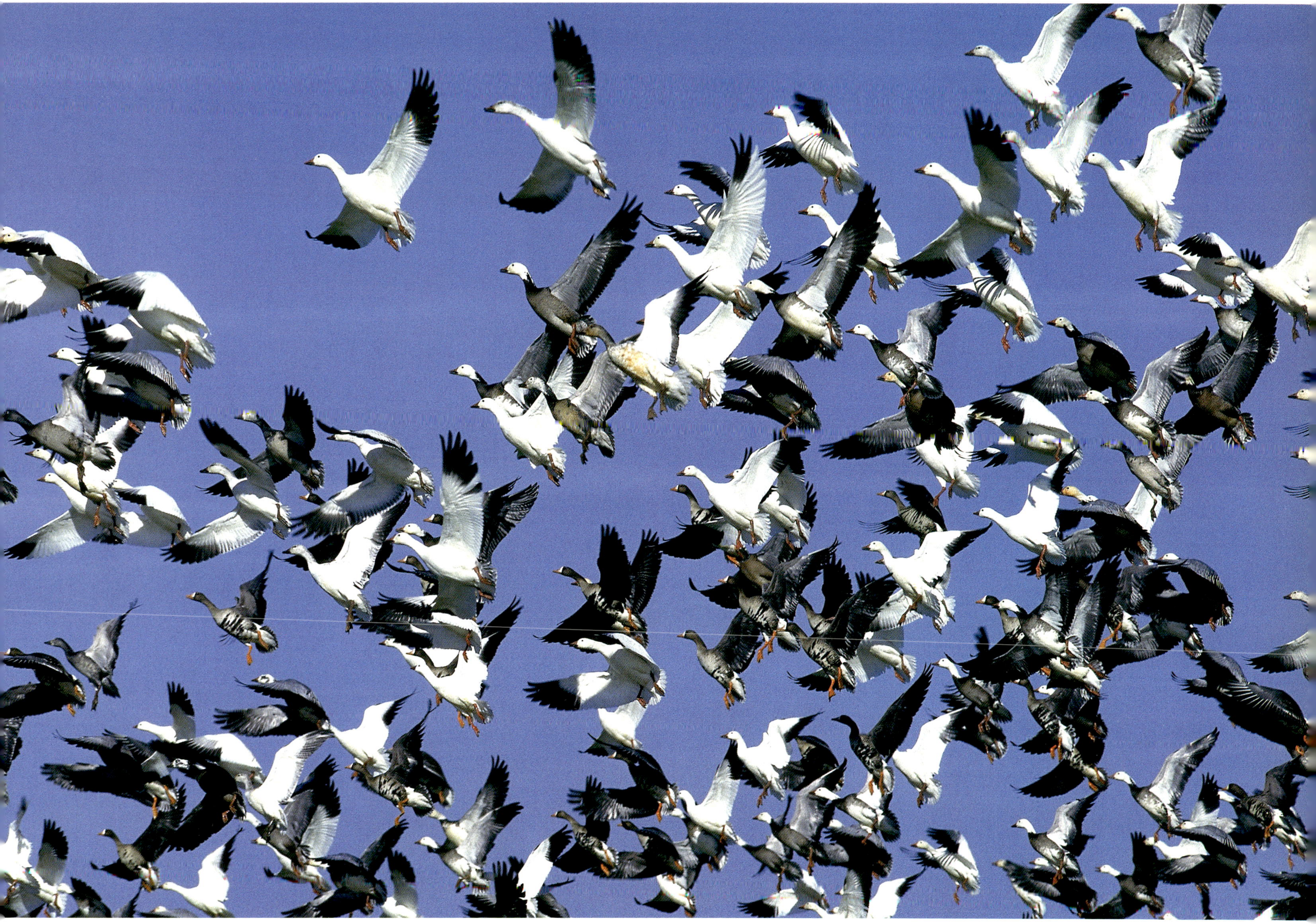

Snow geese and speckle belly geese

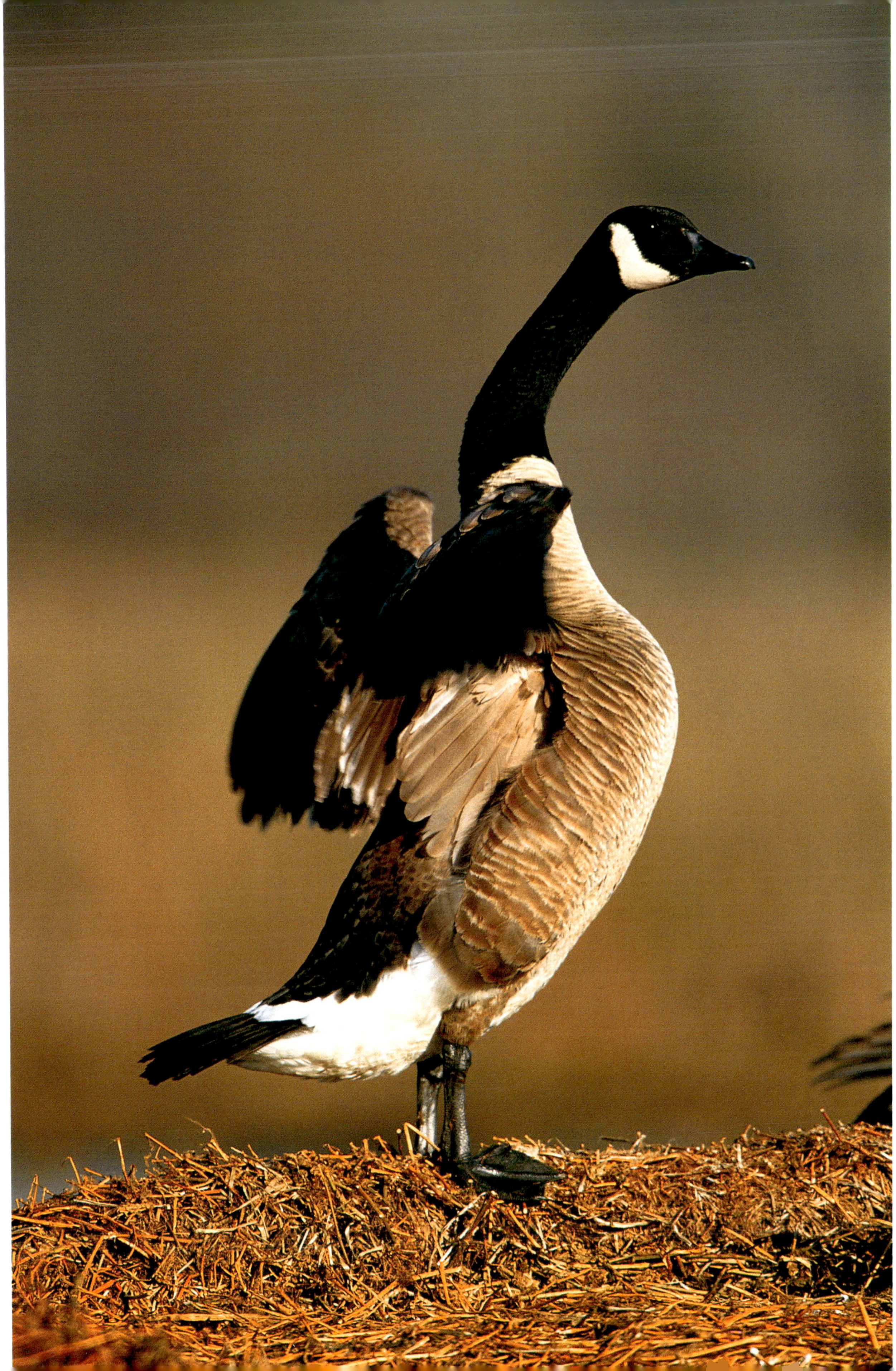

Canada goose

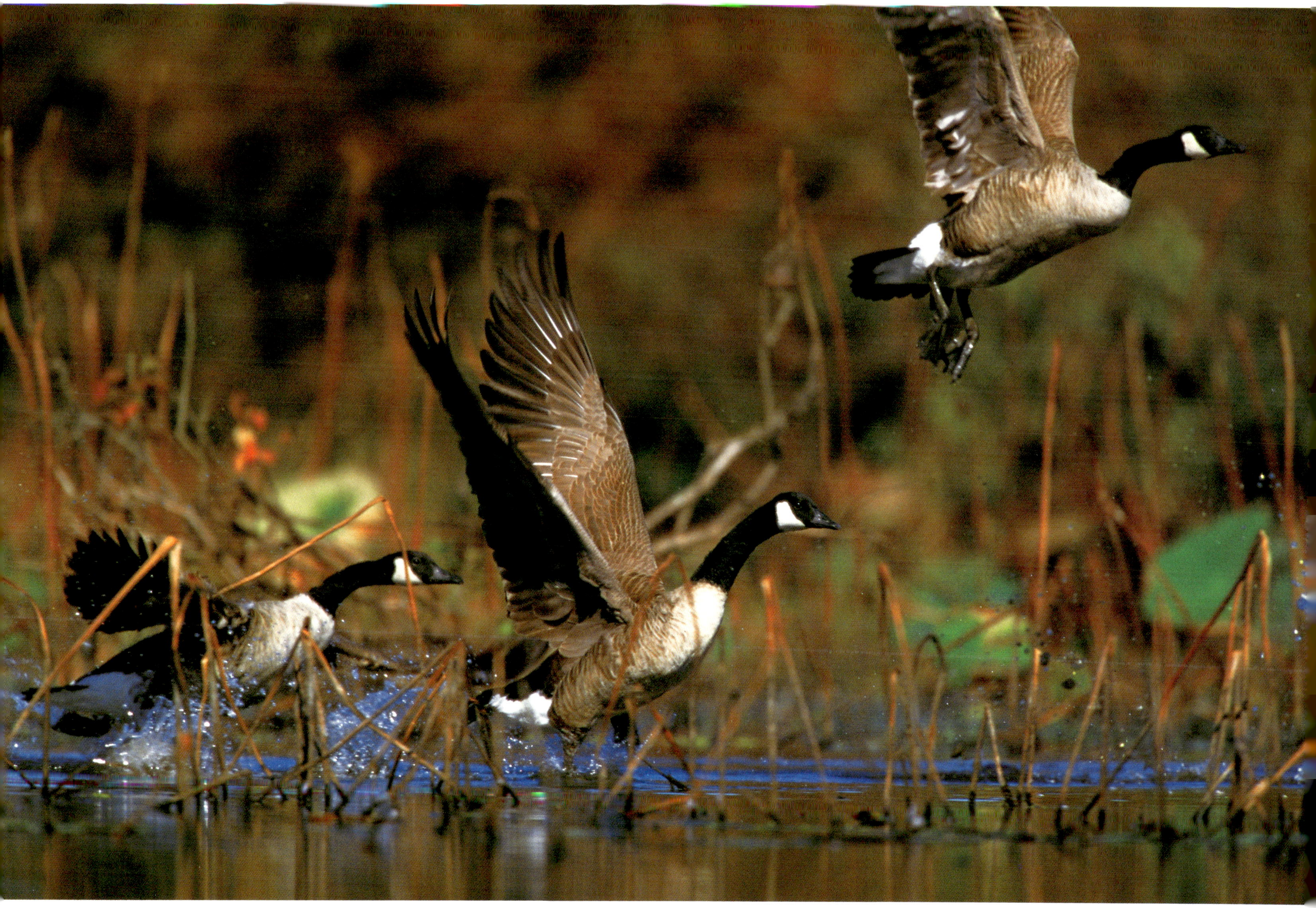

Canada geese

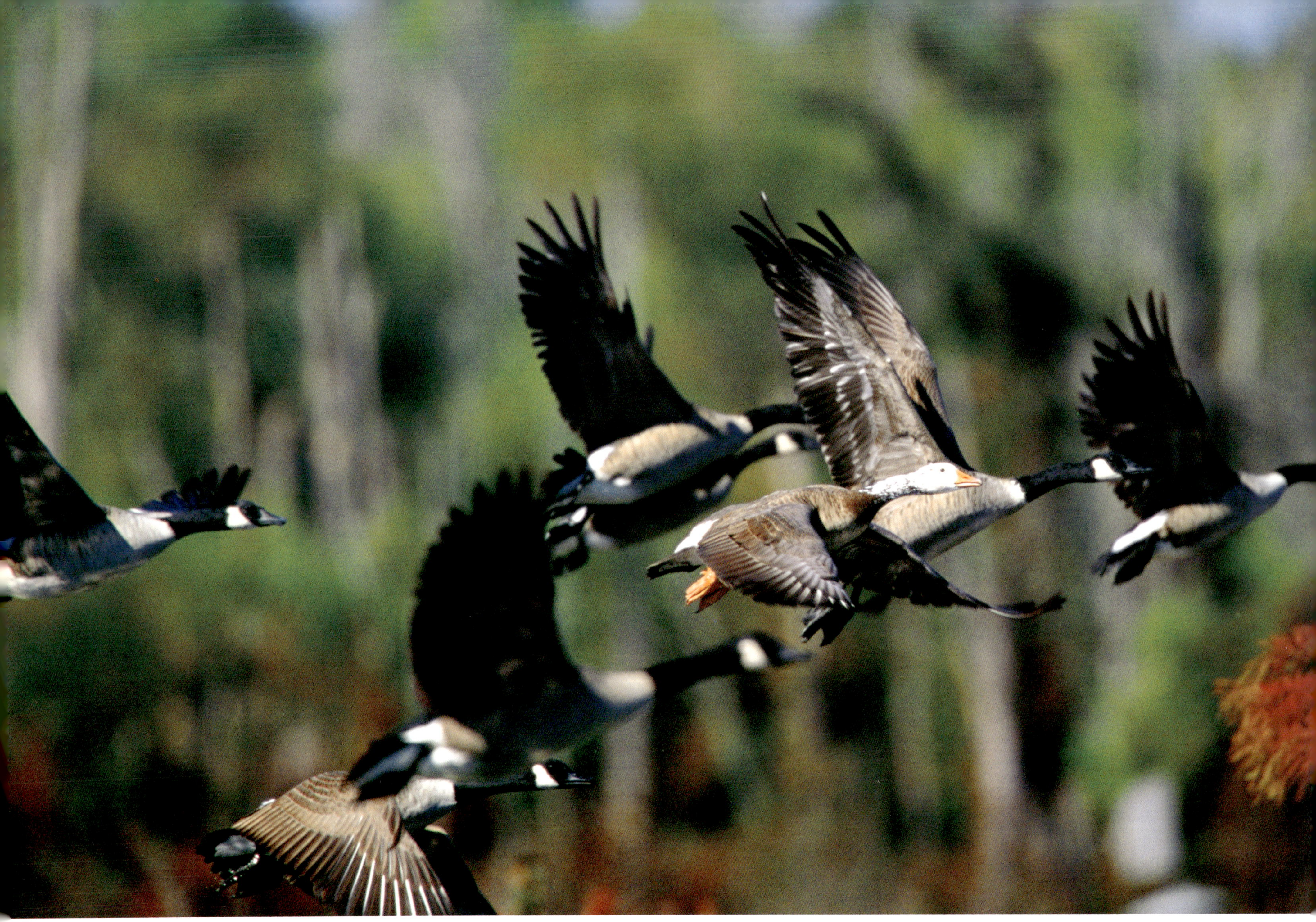

Snow goose with Canada geese

White-tailed deer

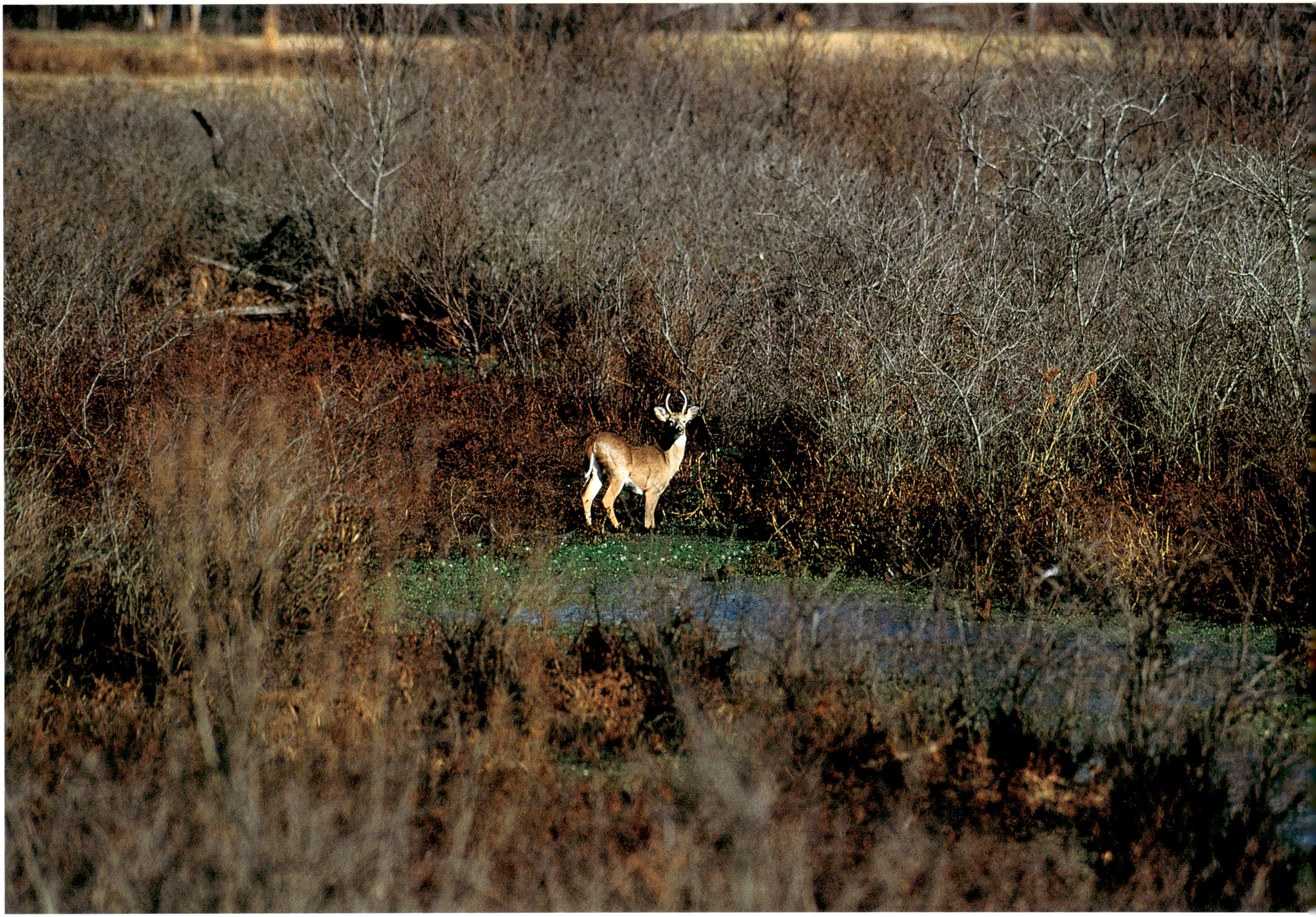

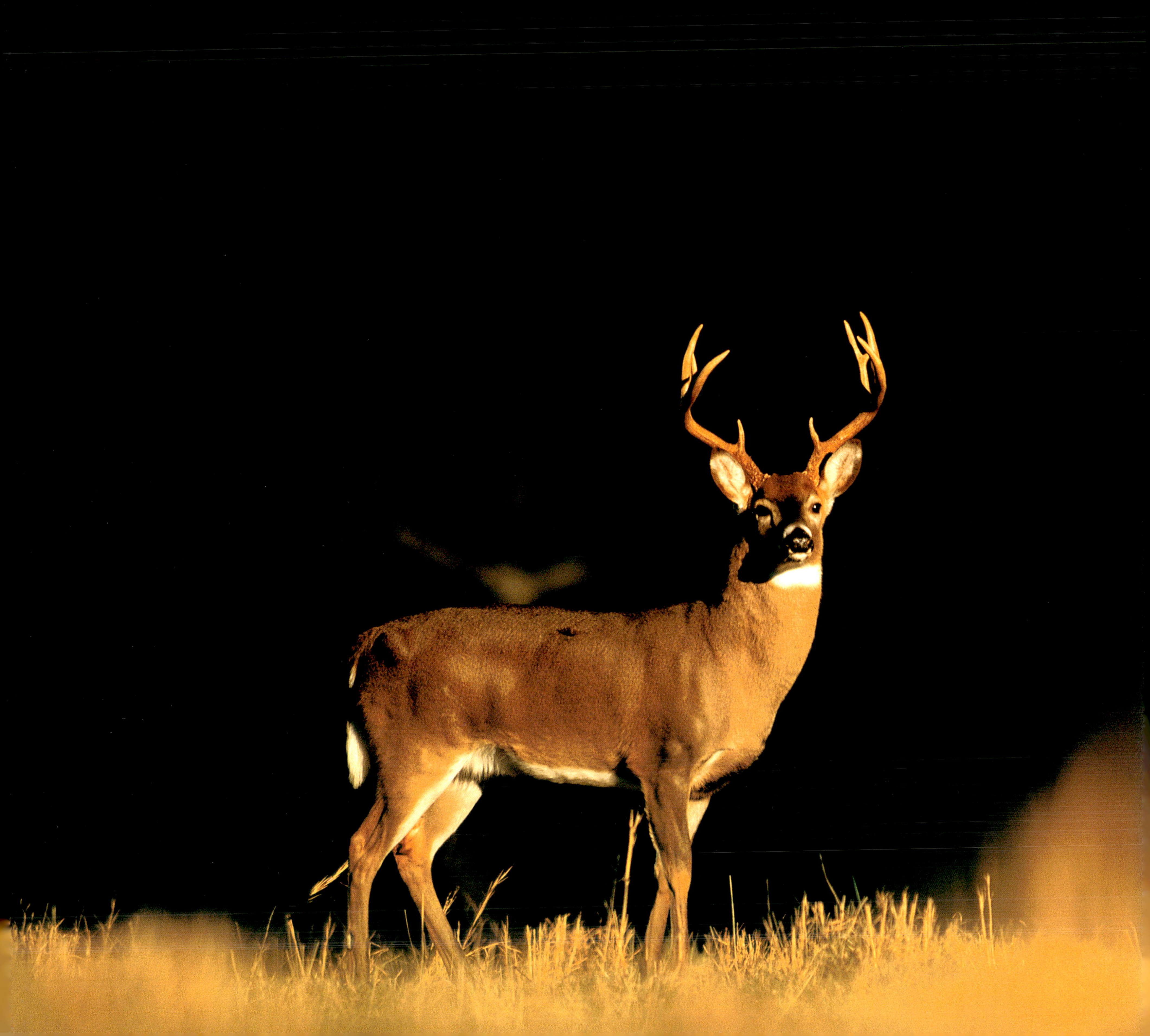

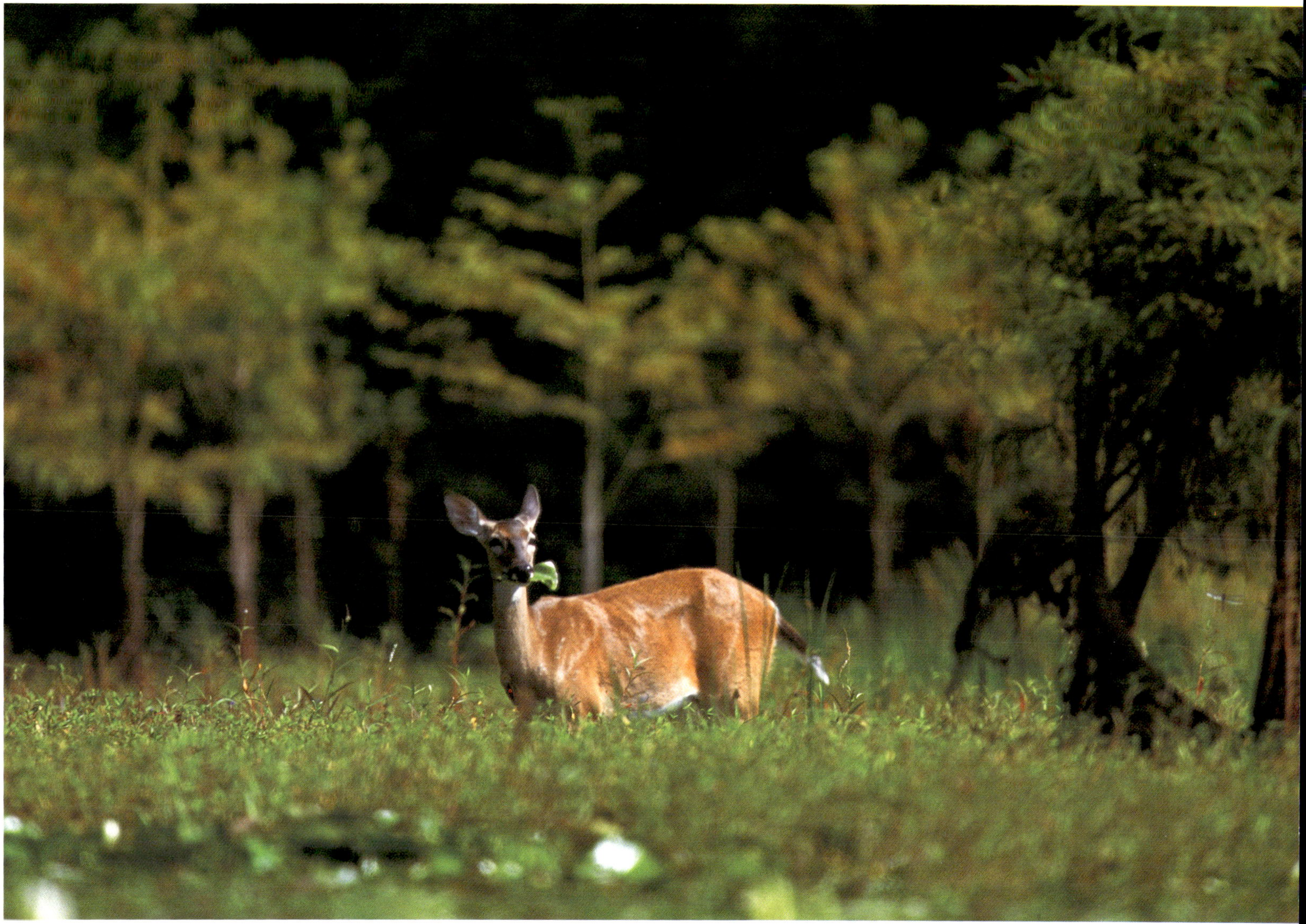

White-tailed deer

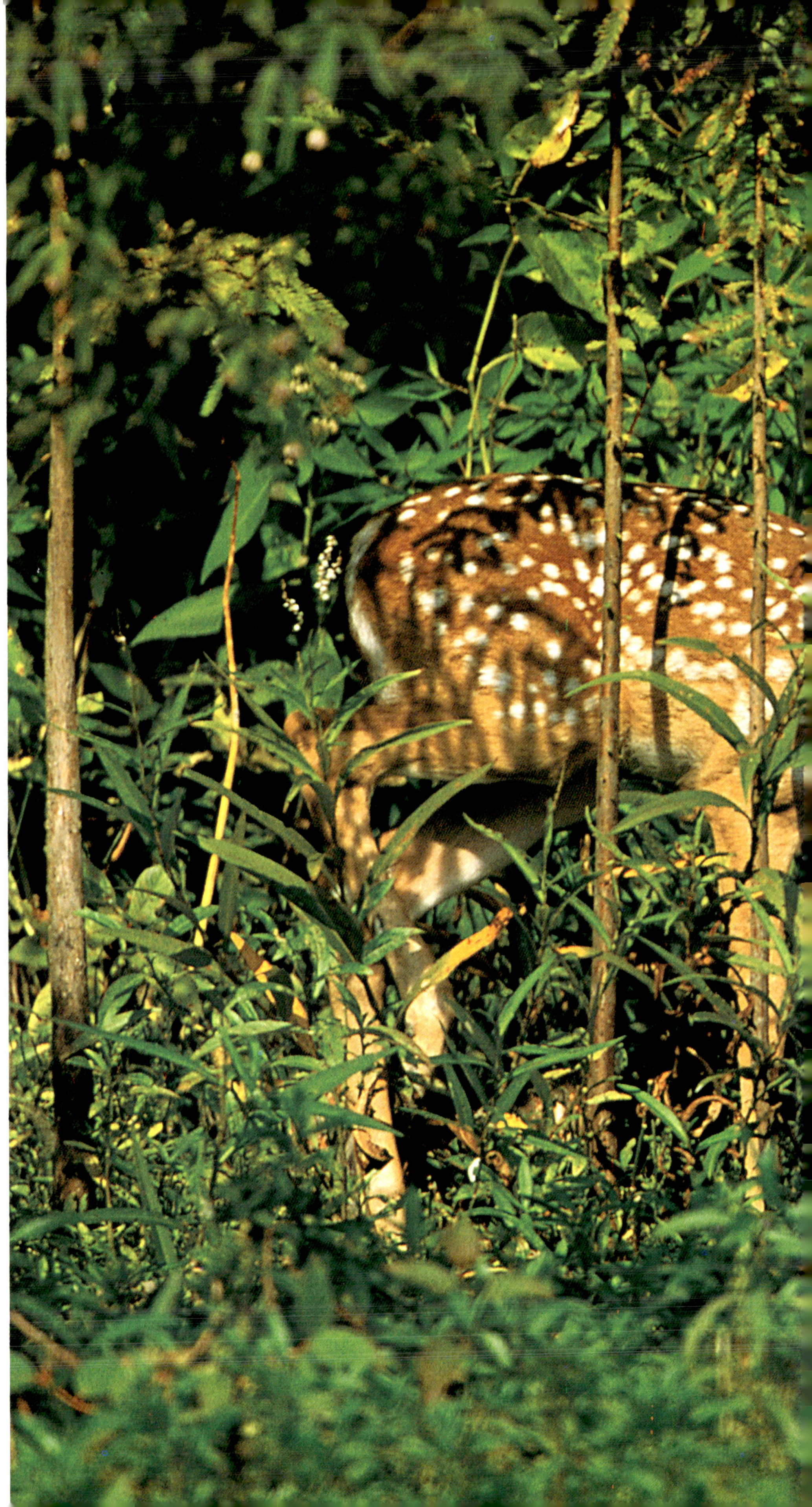

White-tailed deer fawns

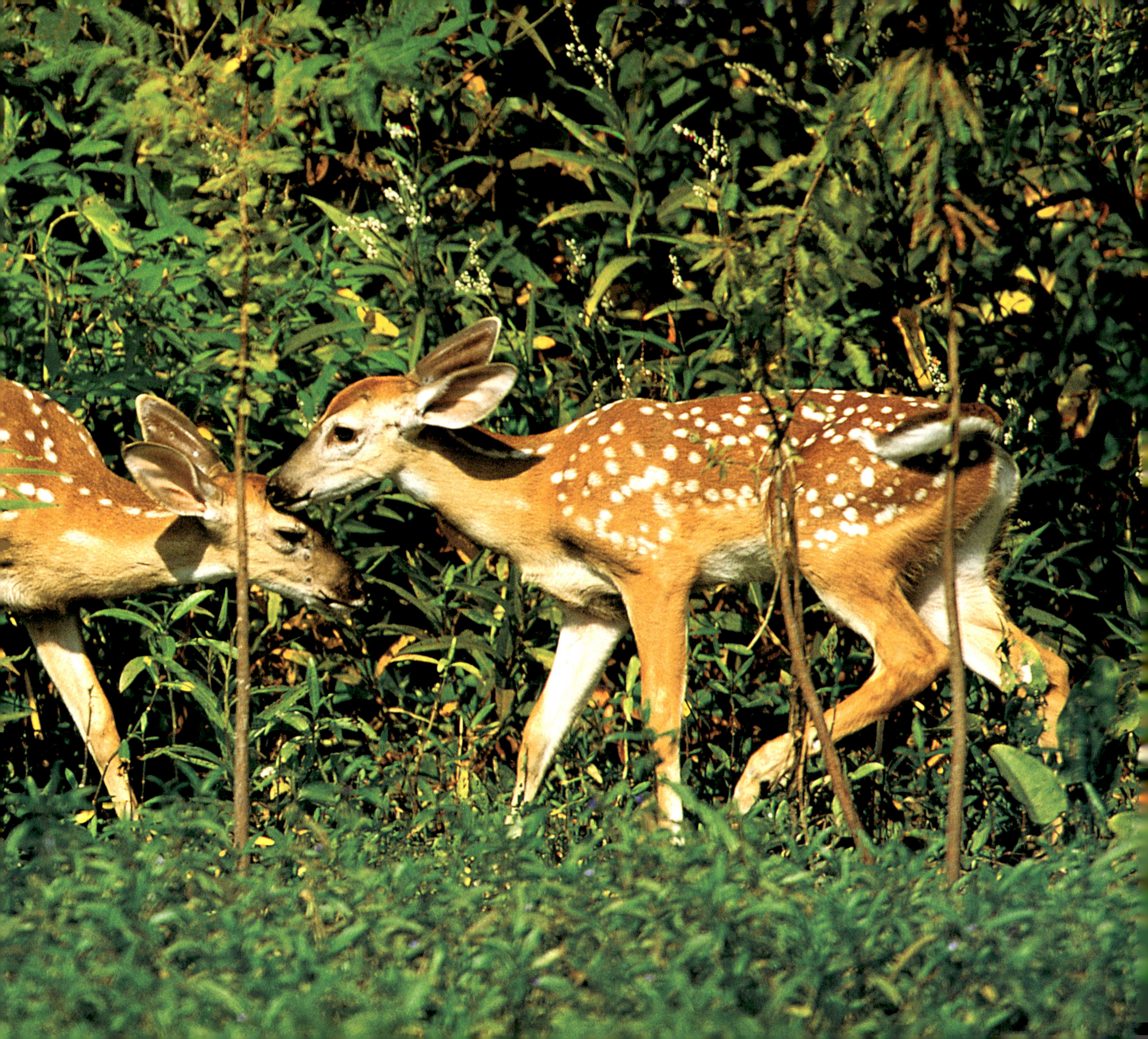

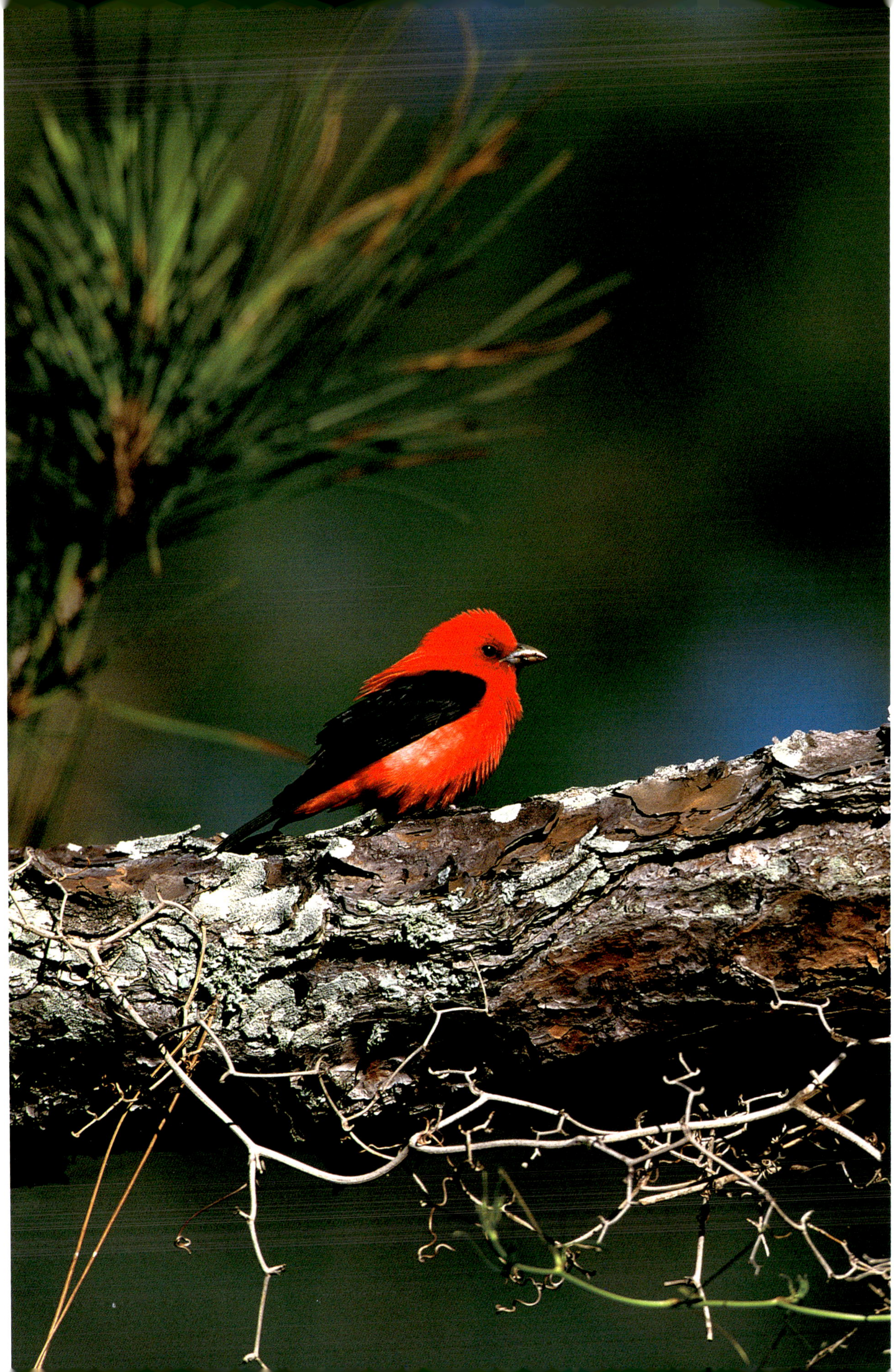

Scarlet tanager

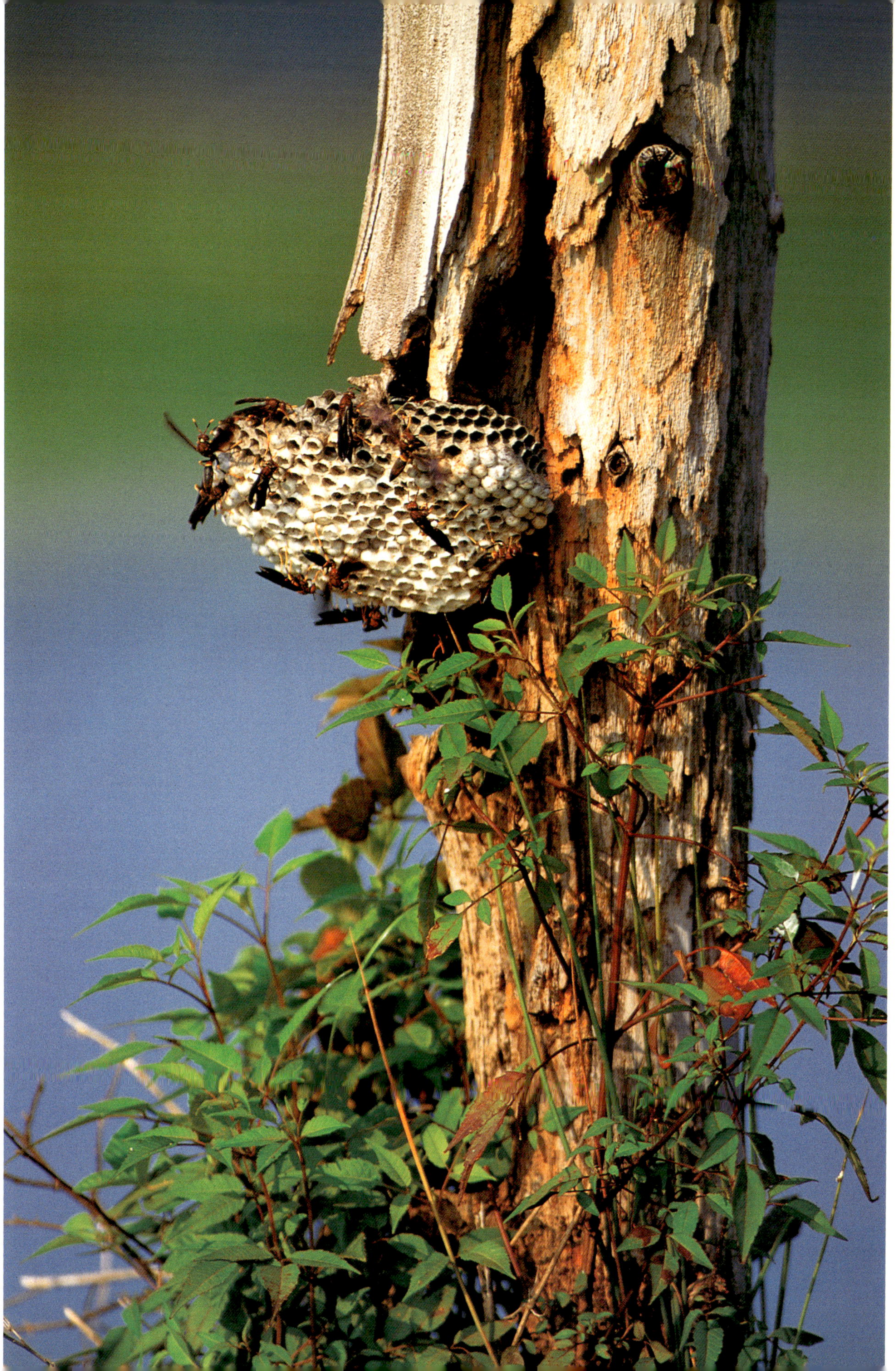

Paper wasp nest

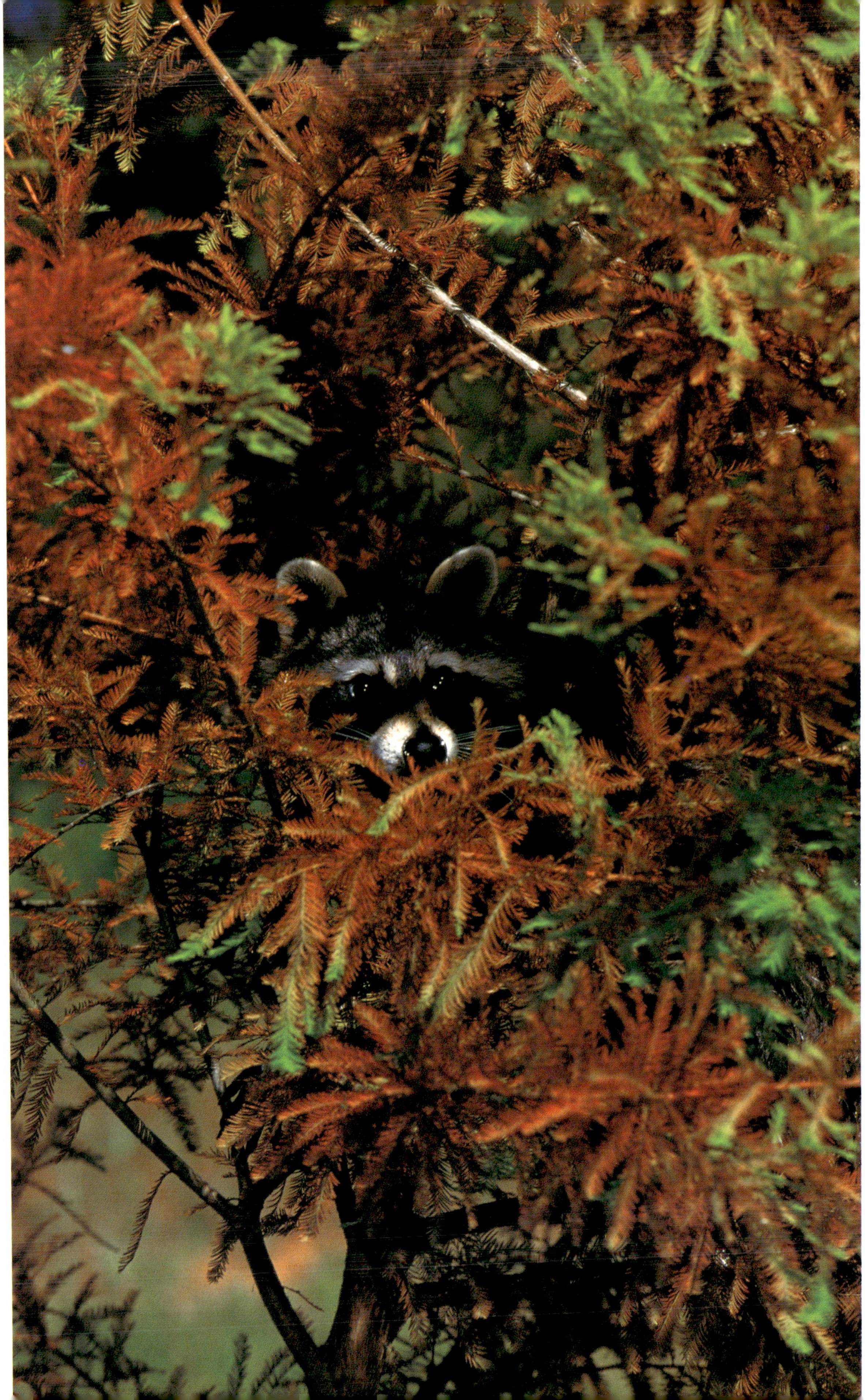

Raccoon in cypress tree

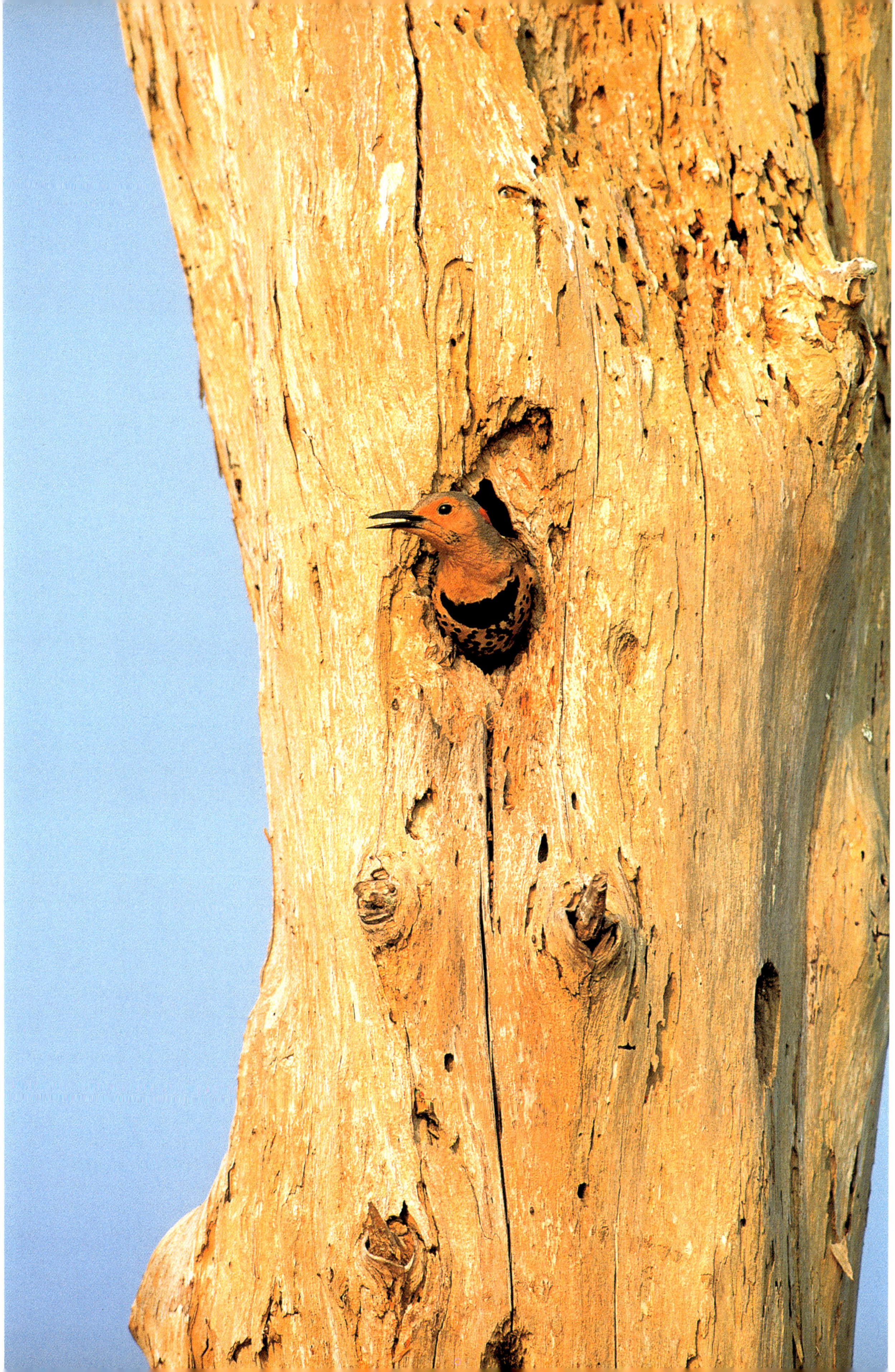

Northern flicker

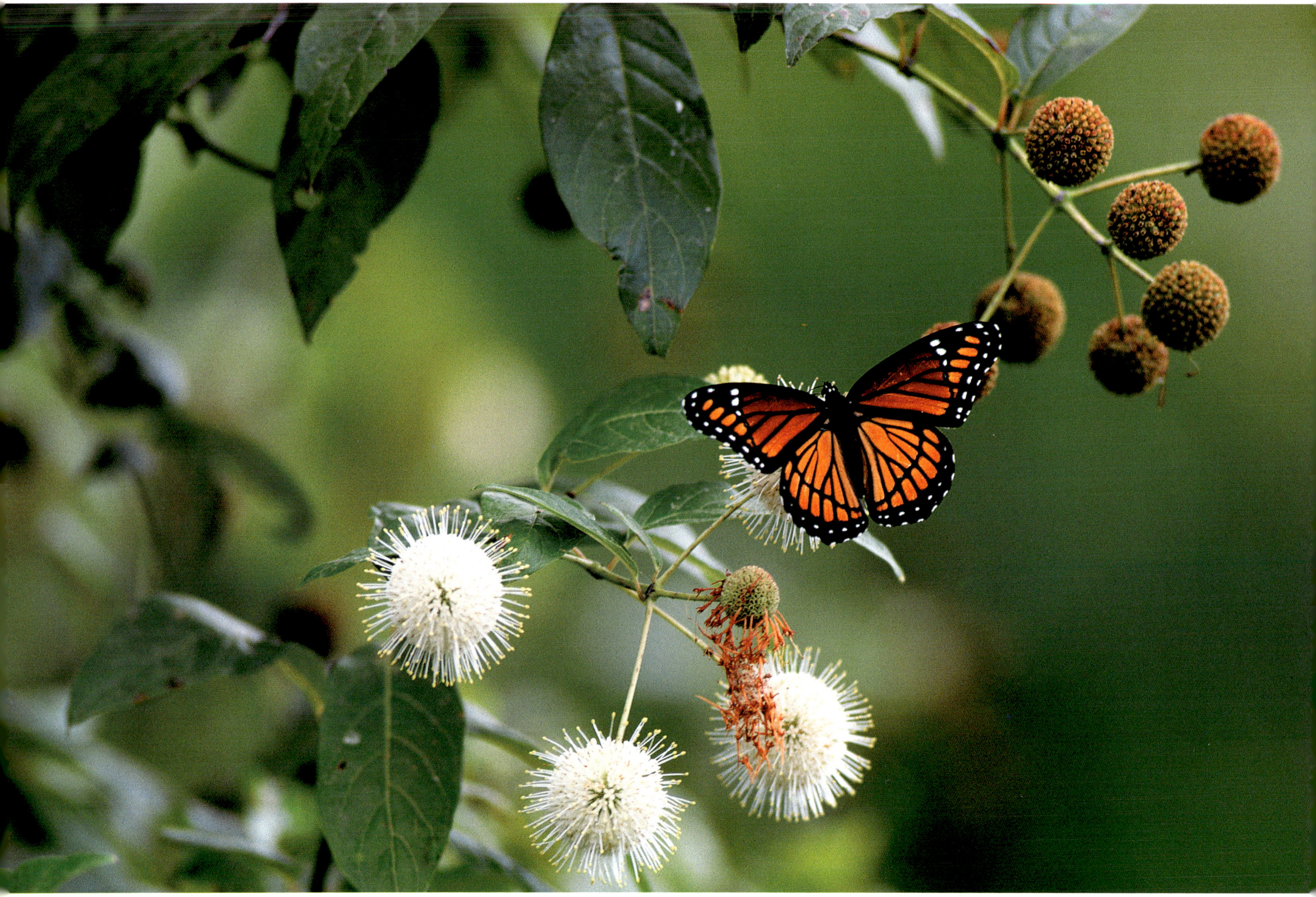

Viceroy butterfly on button bush

Least bittern

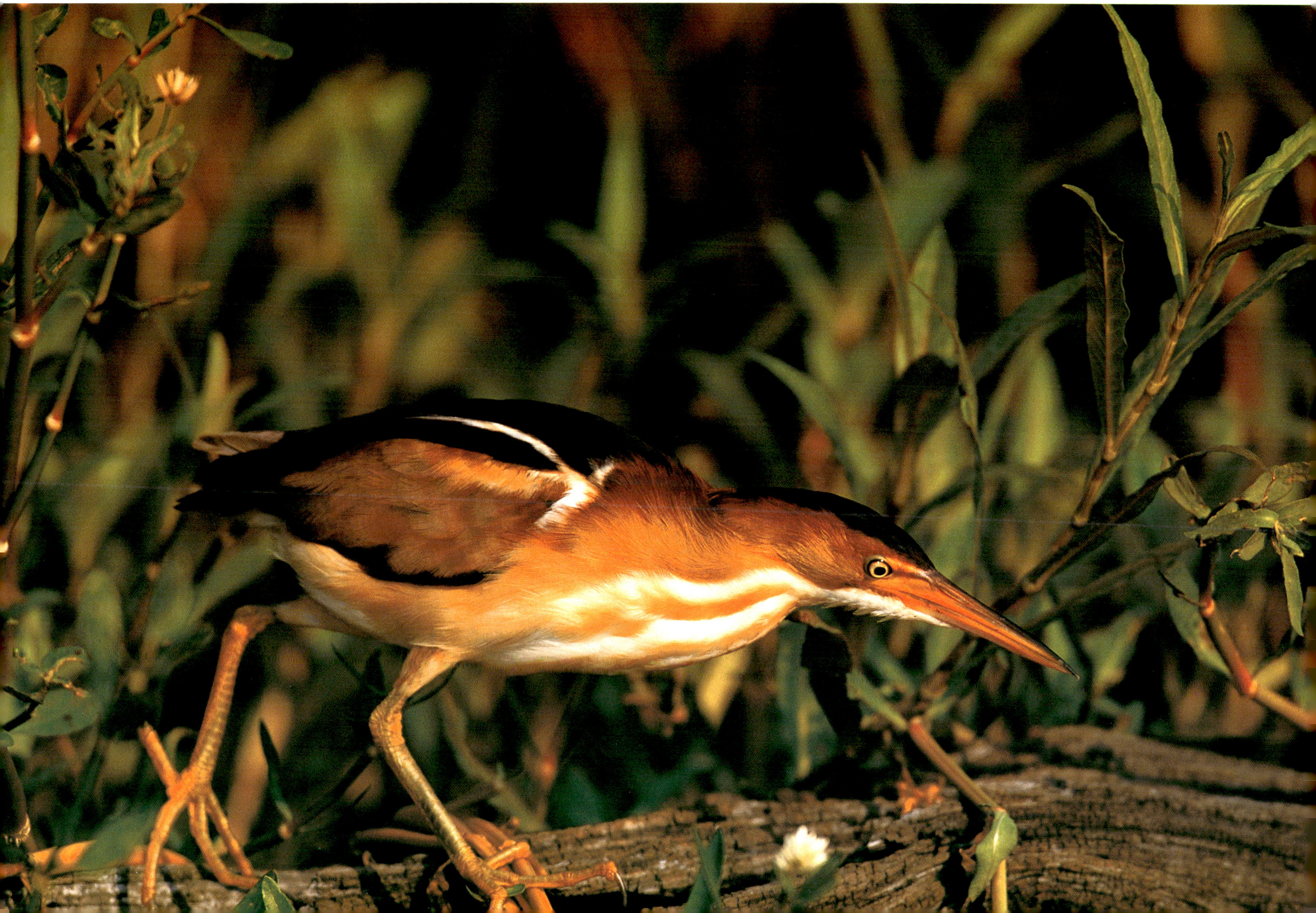

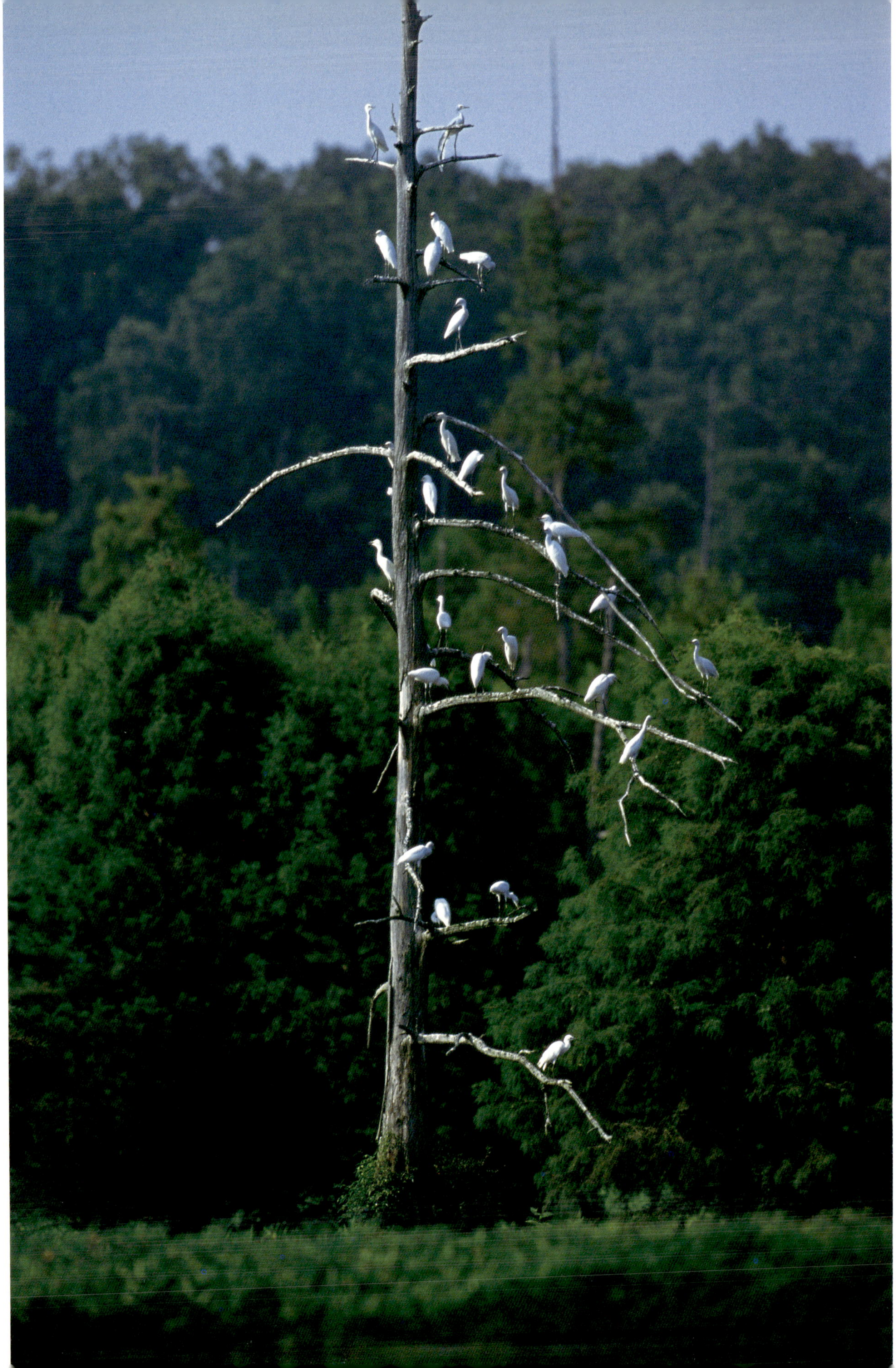

Young cattle egrets, snowy egrets, and little blue herons

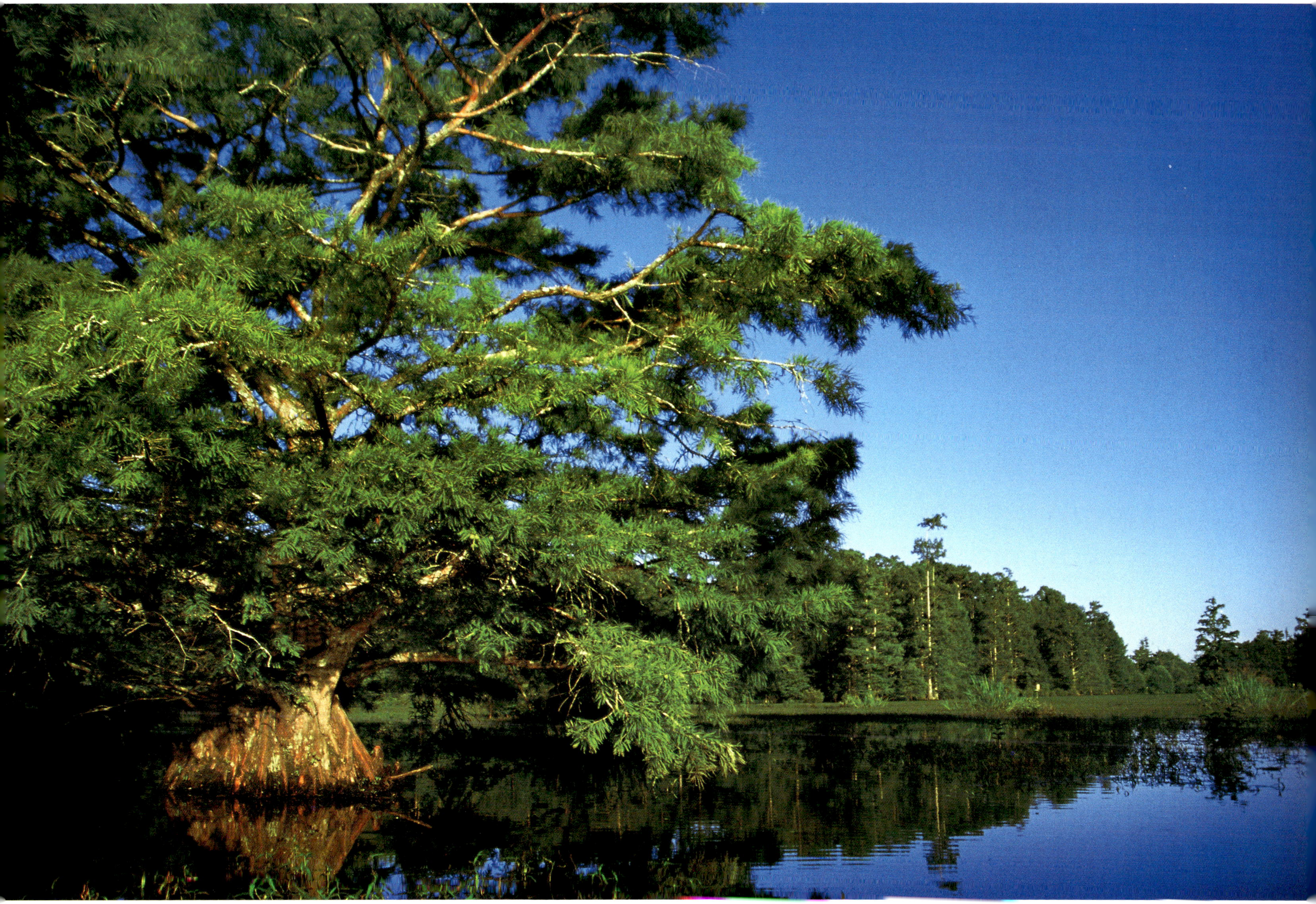

Cypress tree

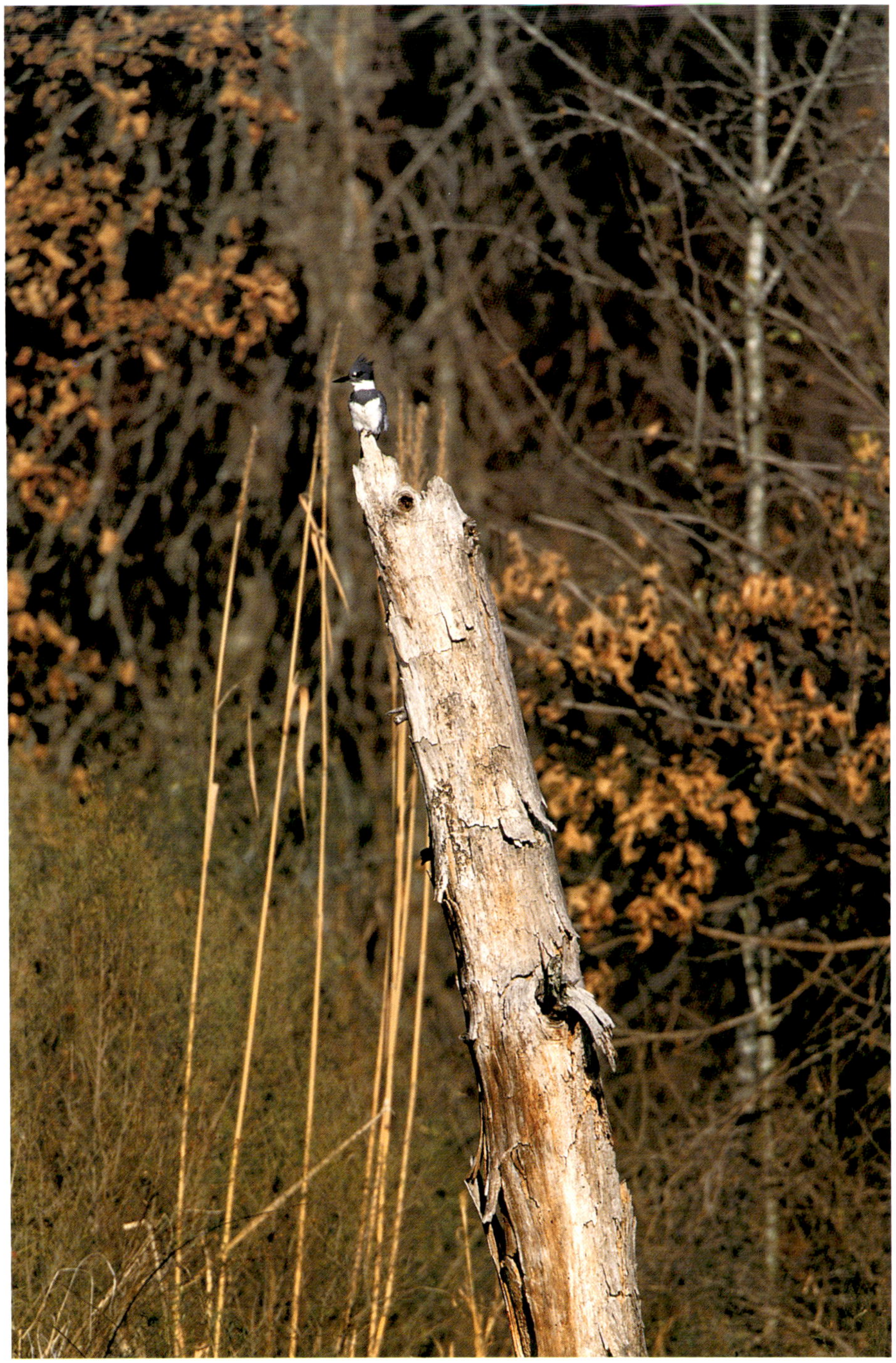

Kingfisher

Pintails

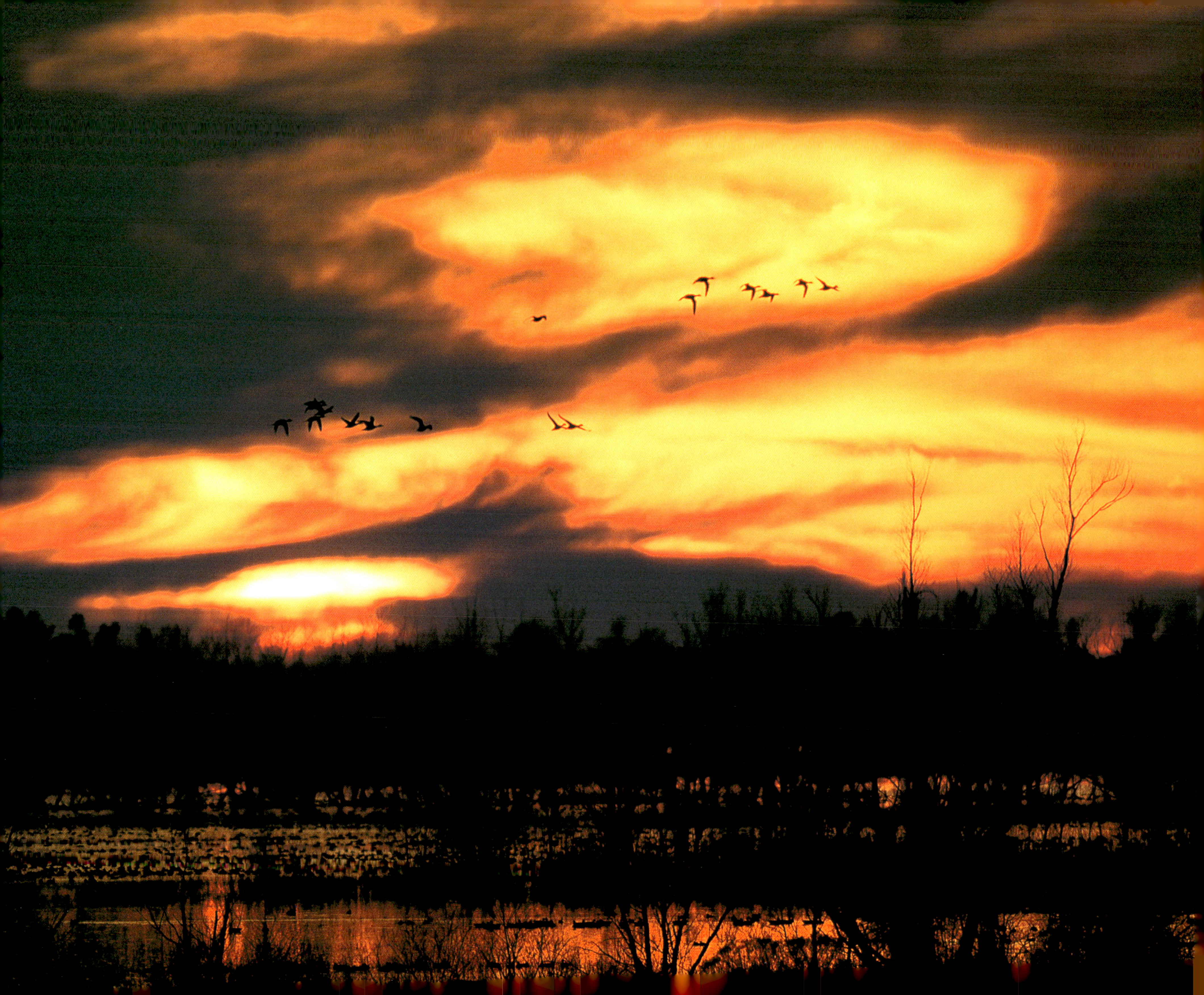

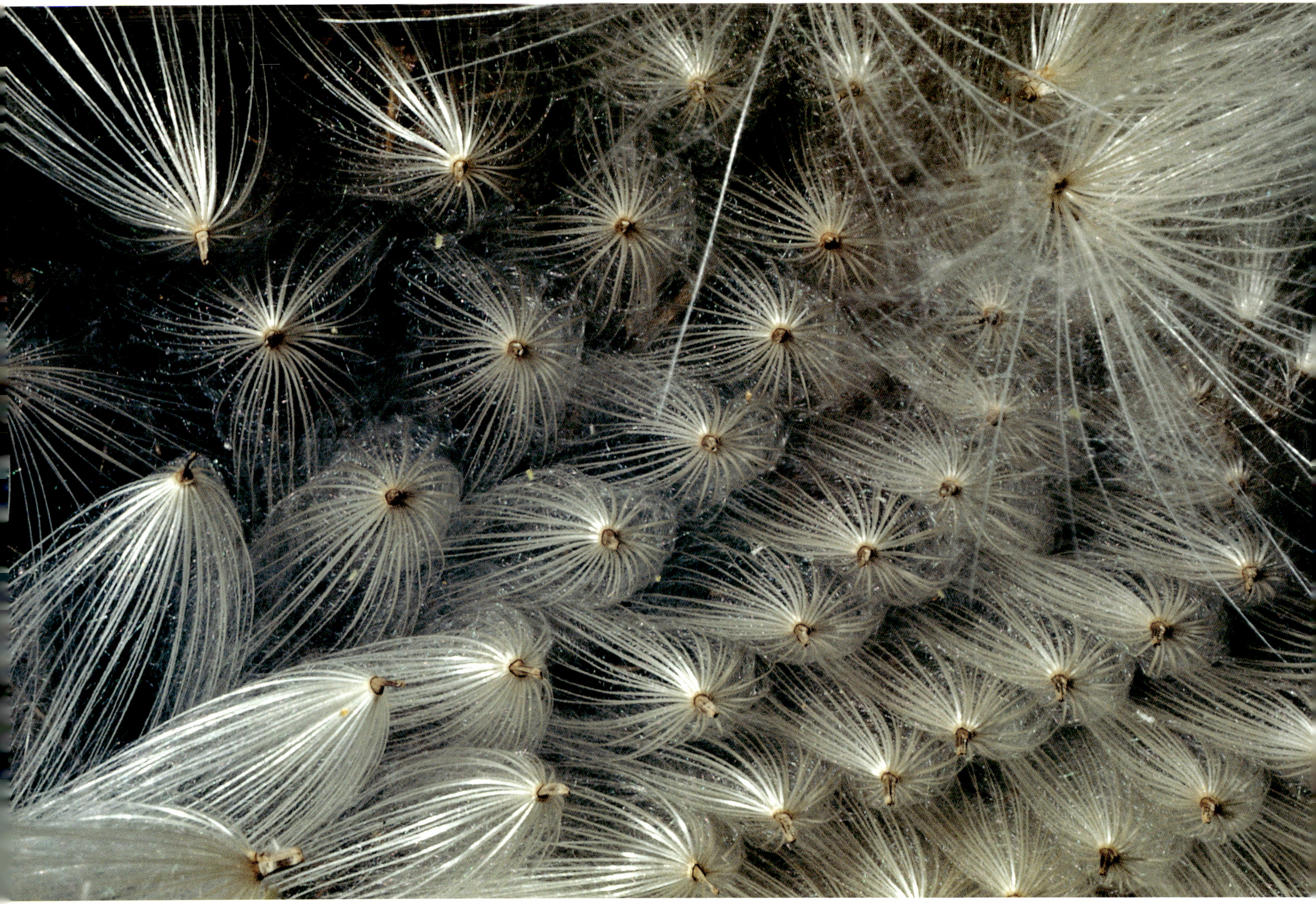

Fallen thistle

Cattle egret

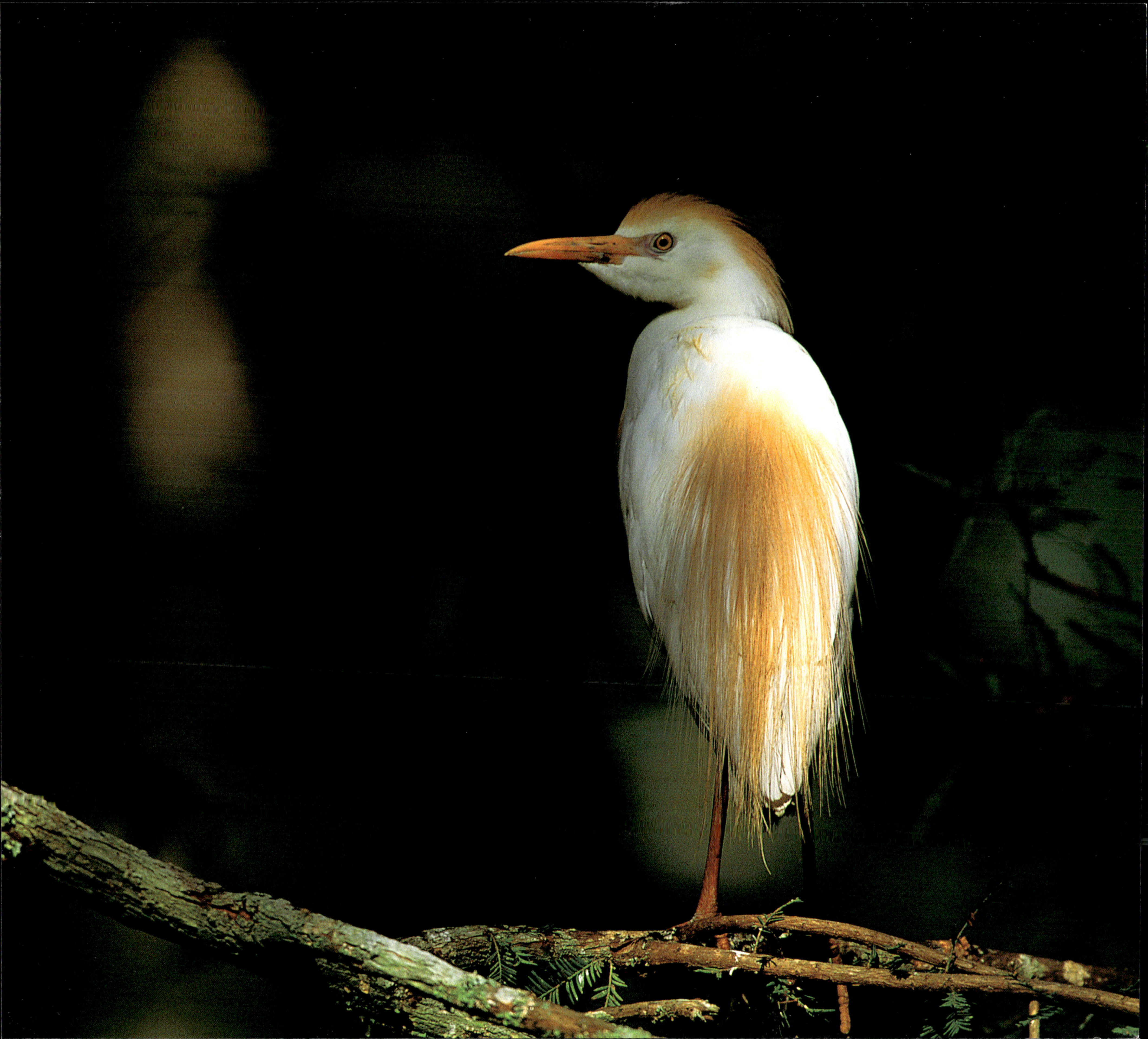

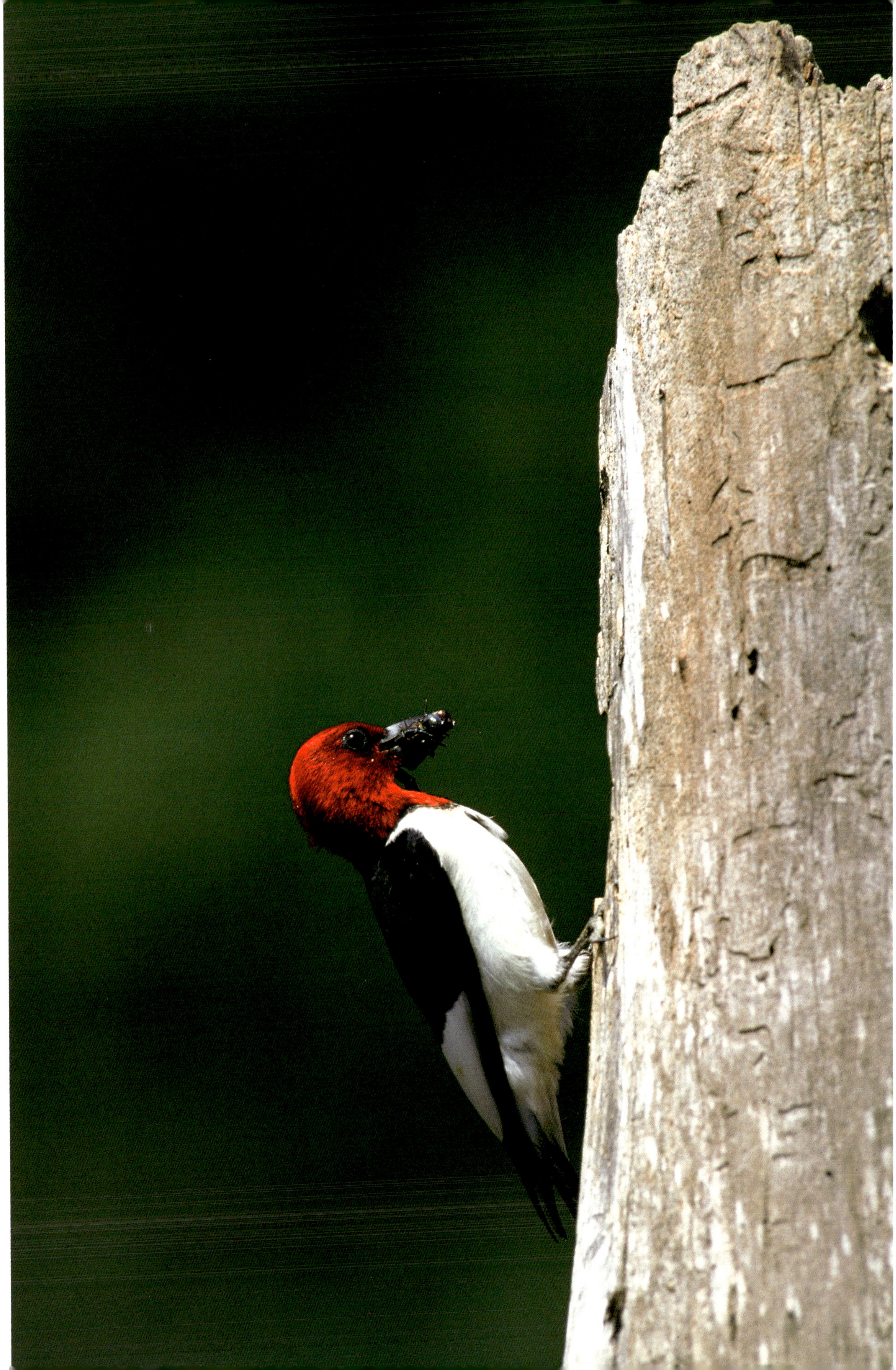

Red-headed woodpecker

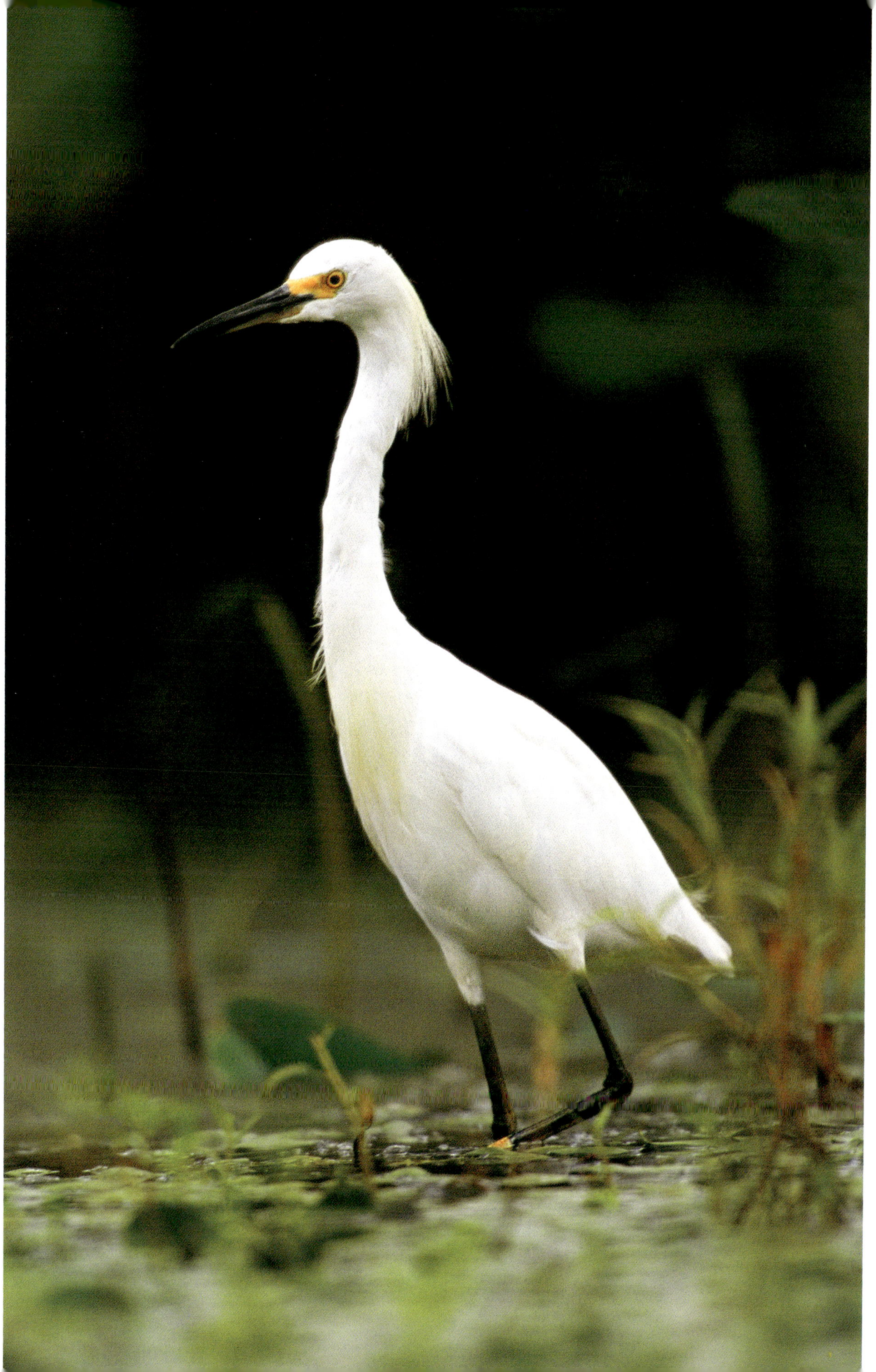

Snowy egret

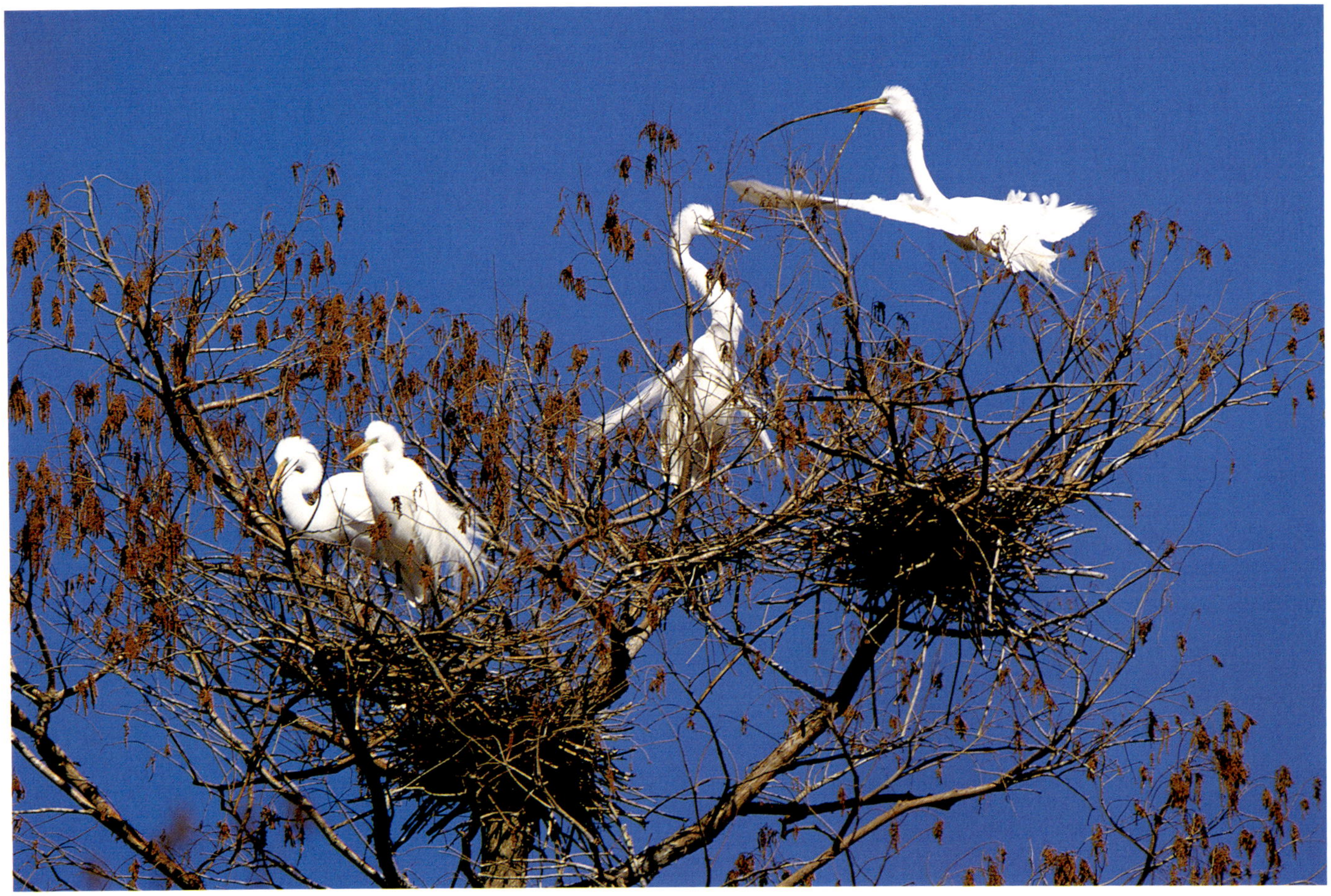
Great white egrets nesting

Great white egret

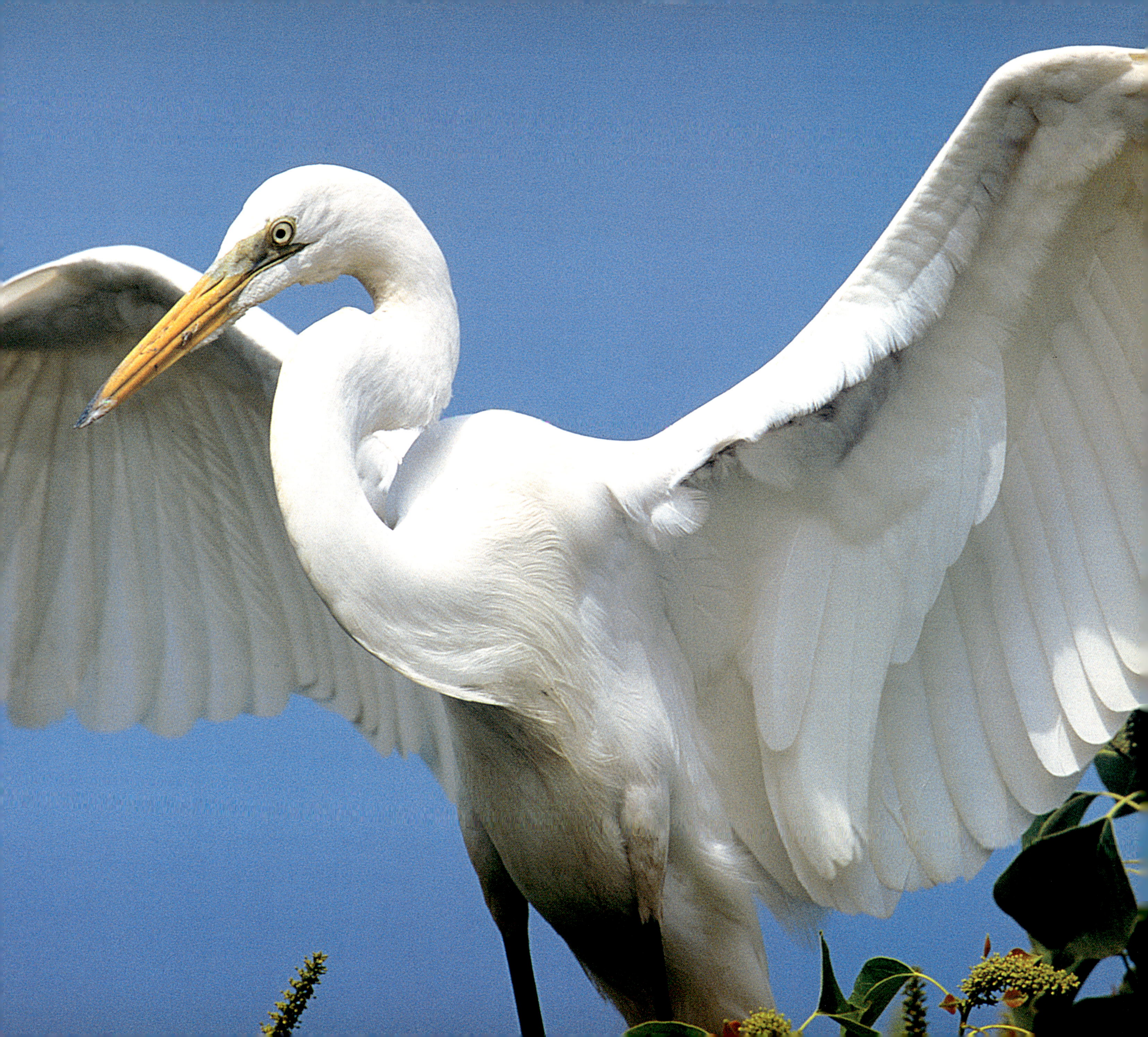

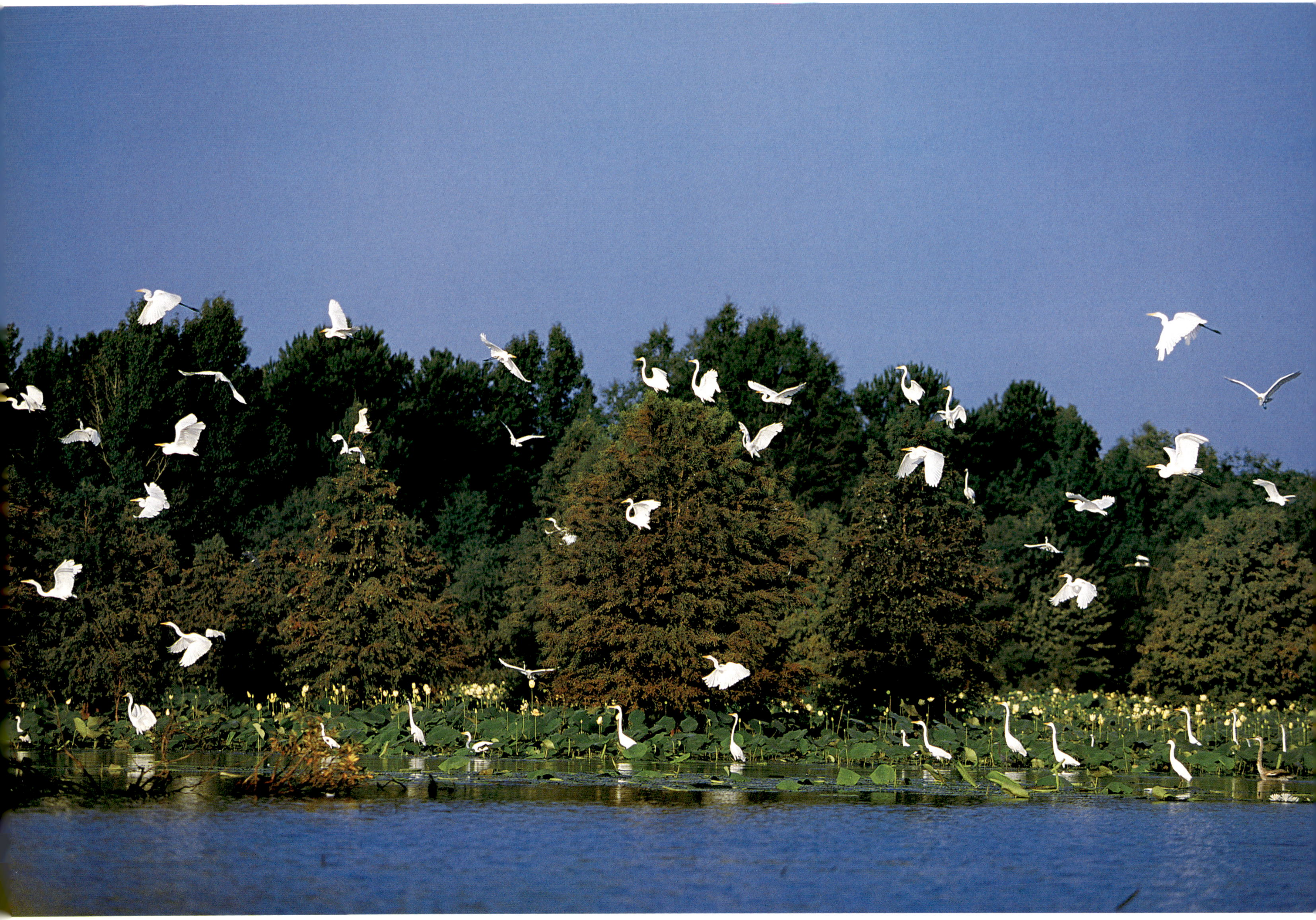

Great white egrets

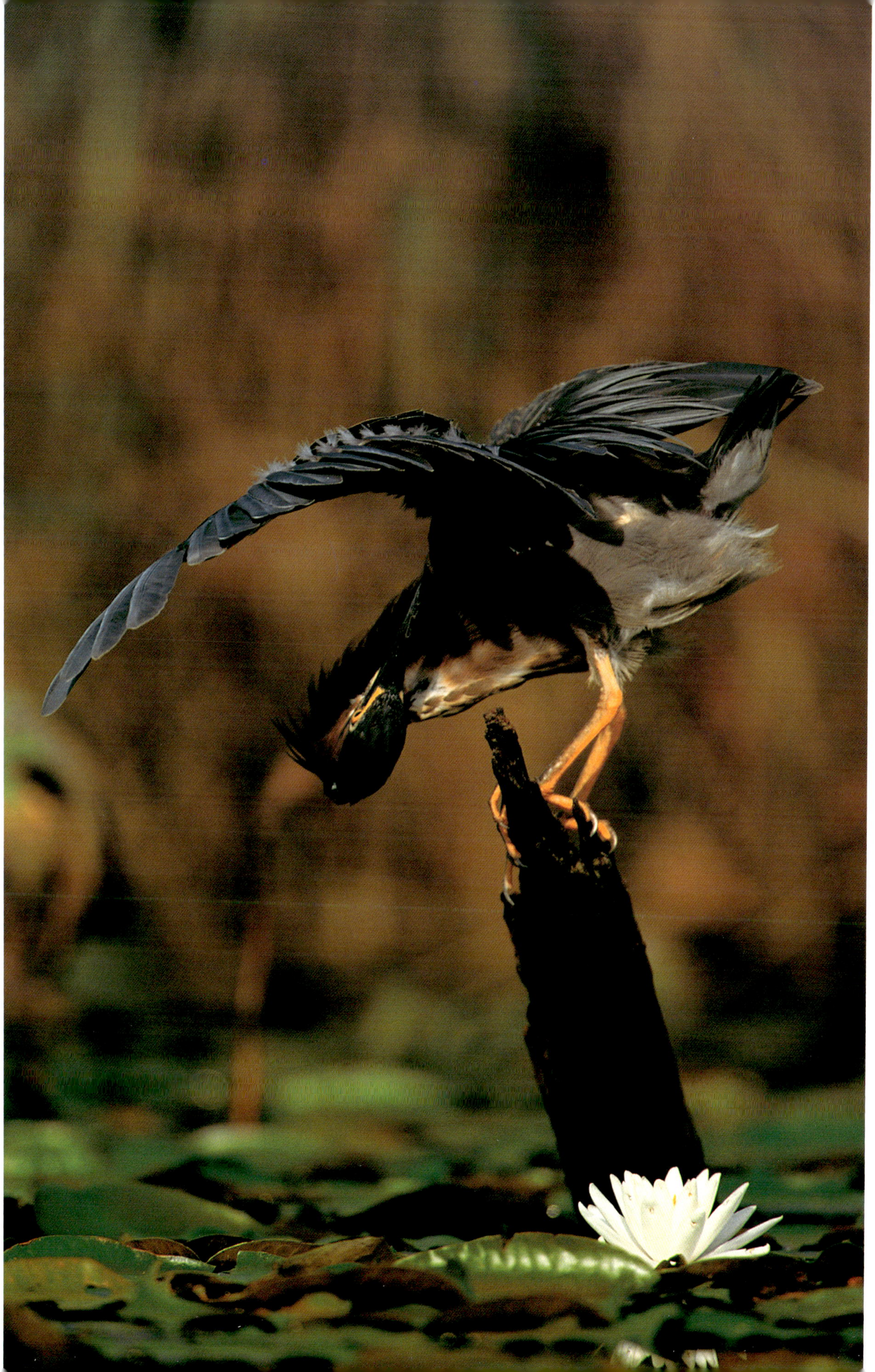

Green heron

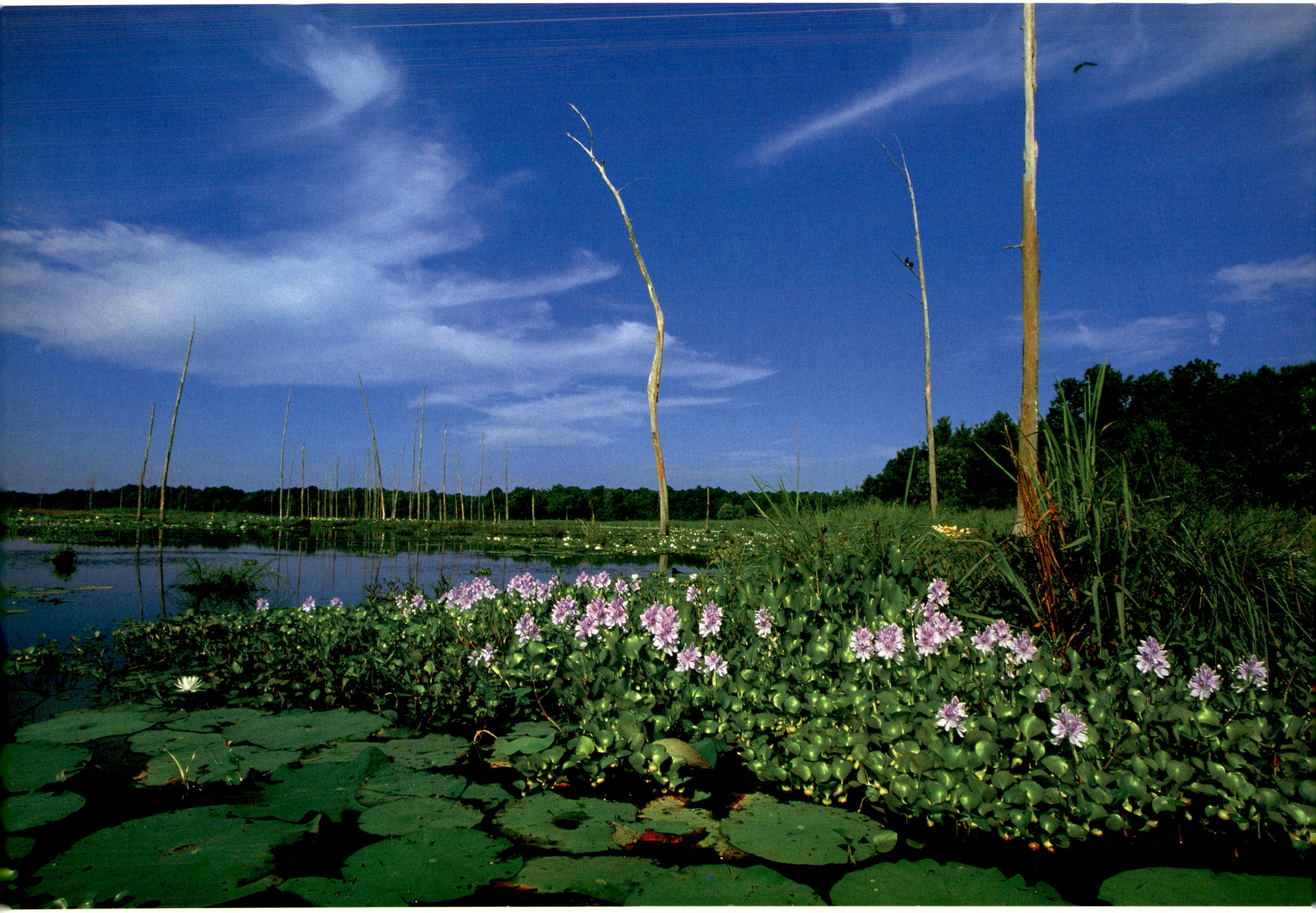

Water hyacinth and lotus

Common moorhen on lily pads

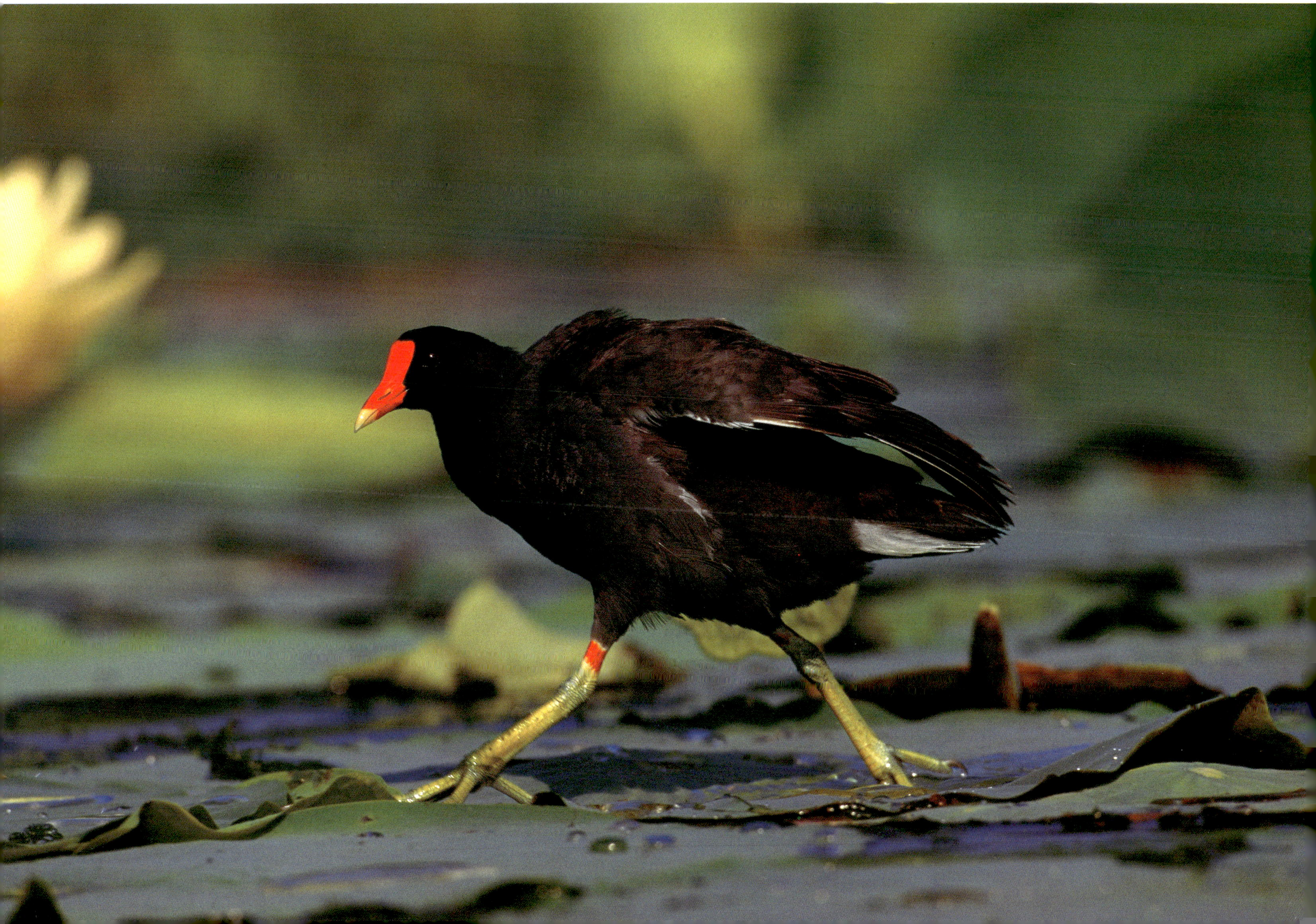

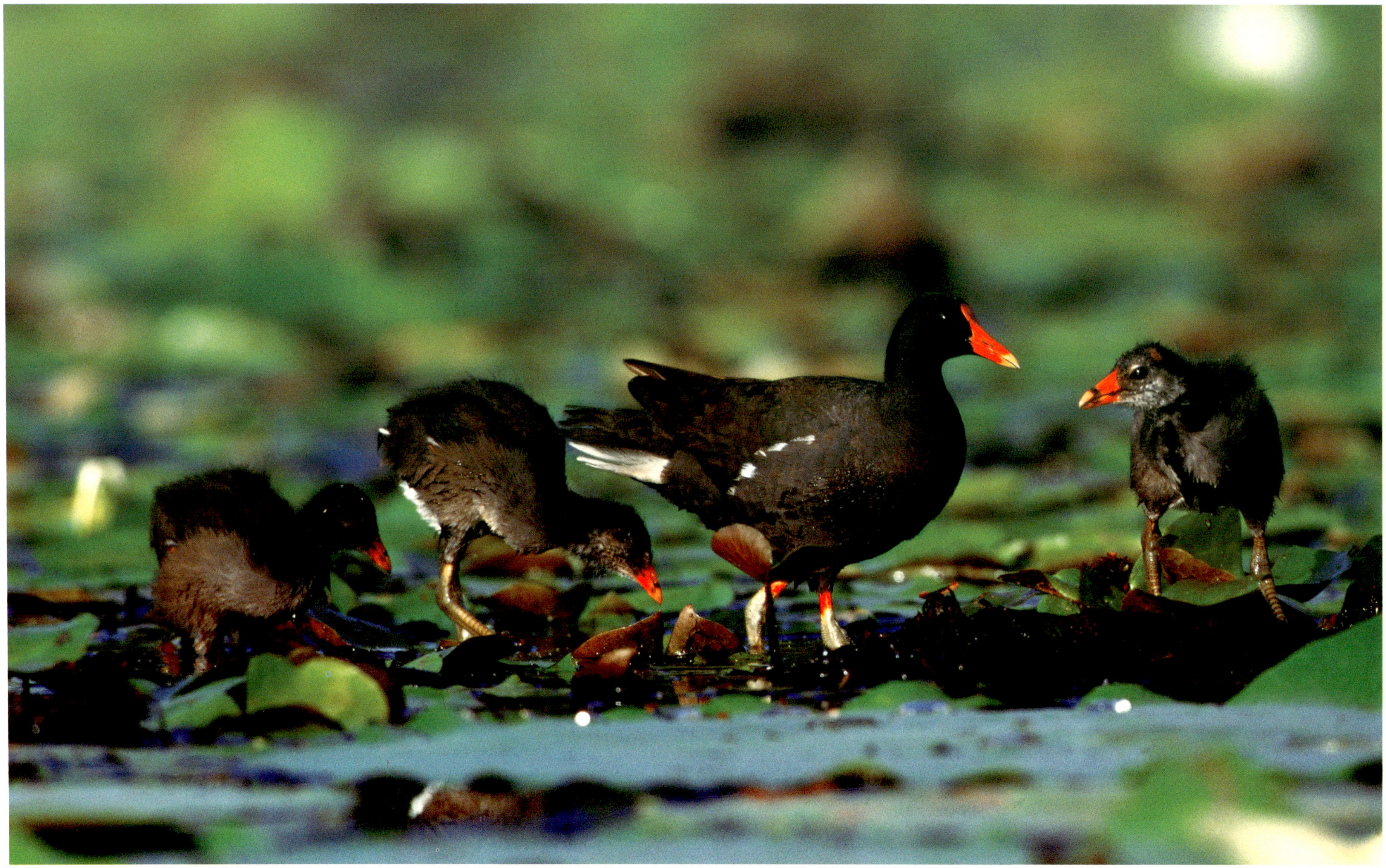

Common moorhen with young

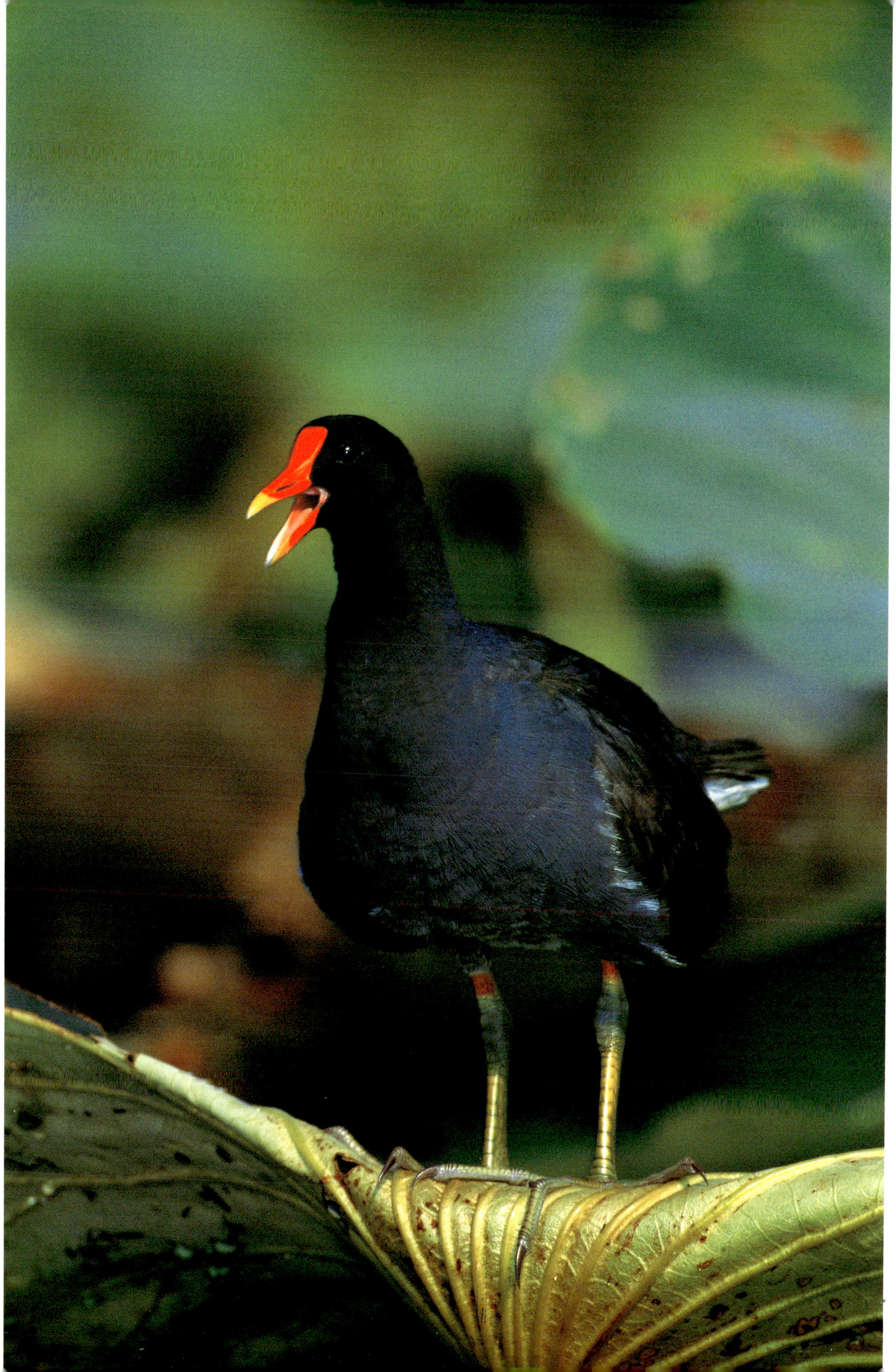

Common moorhen on American lotus leaf

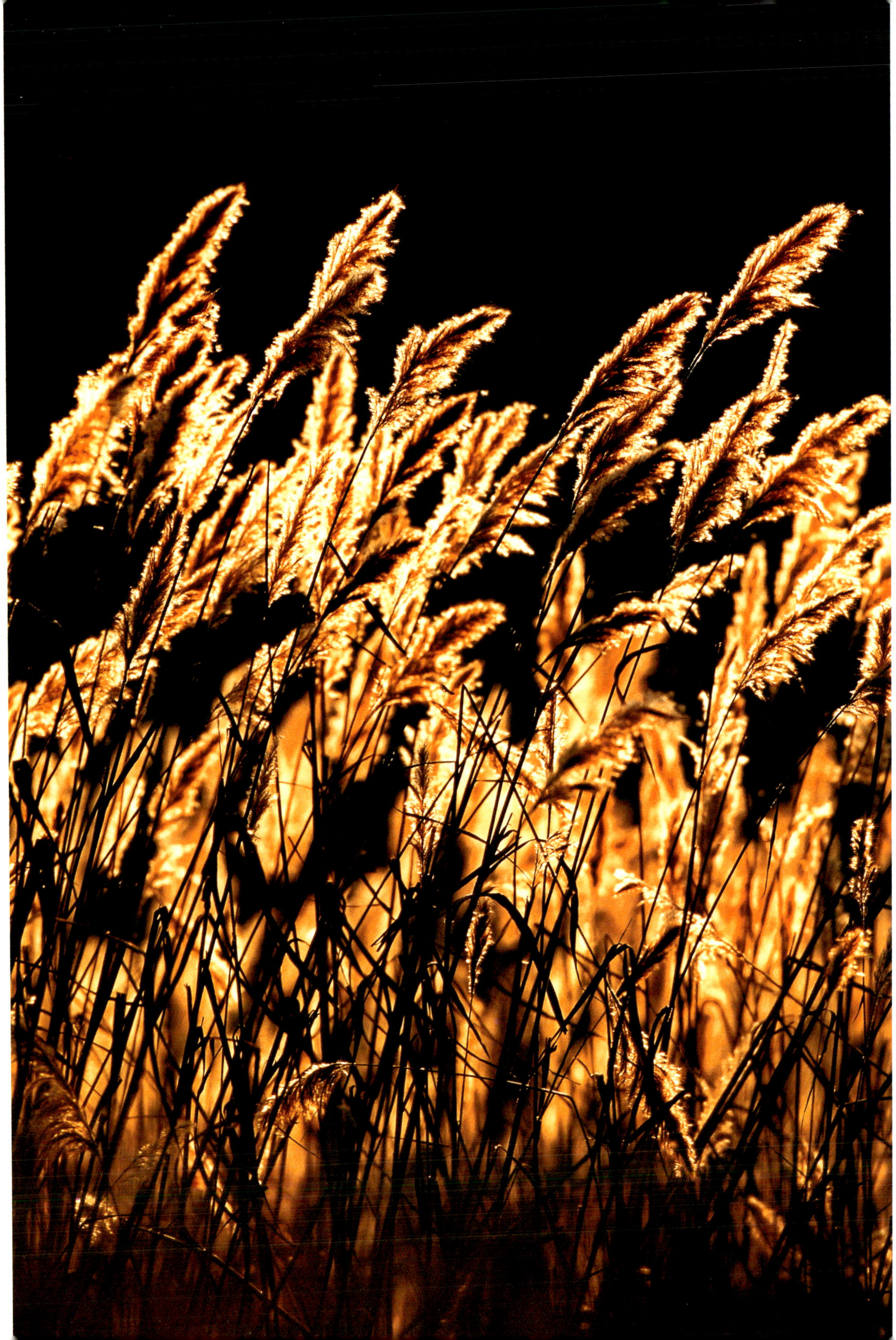

Sugarcane plumegrass

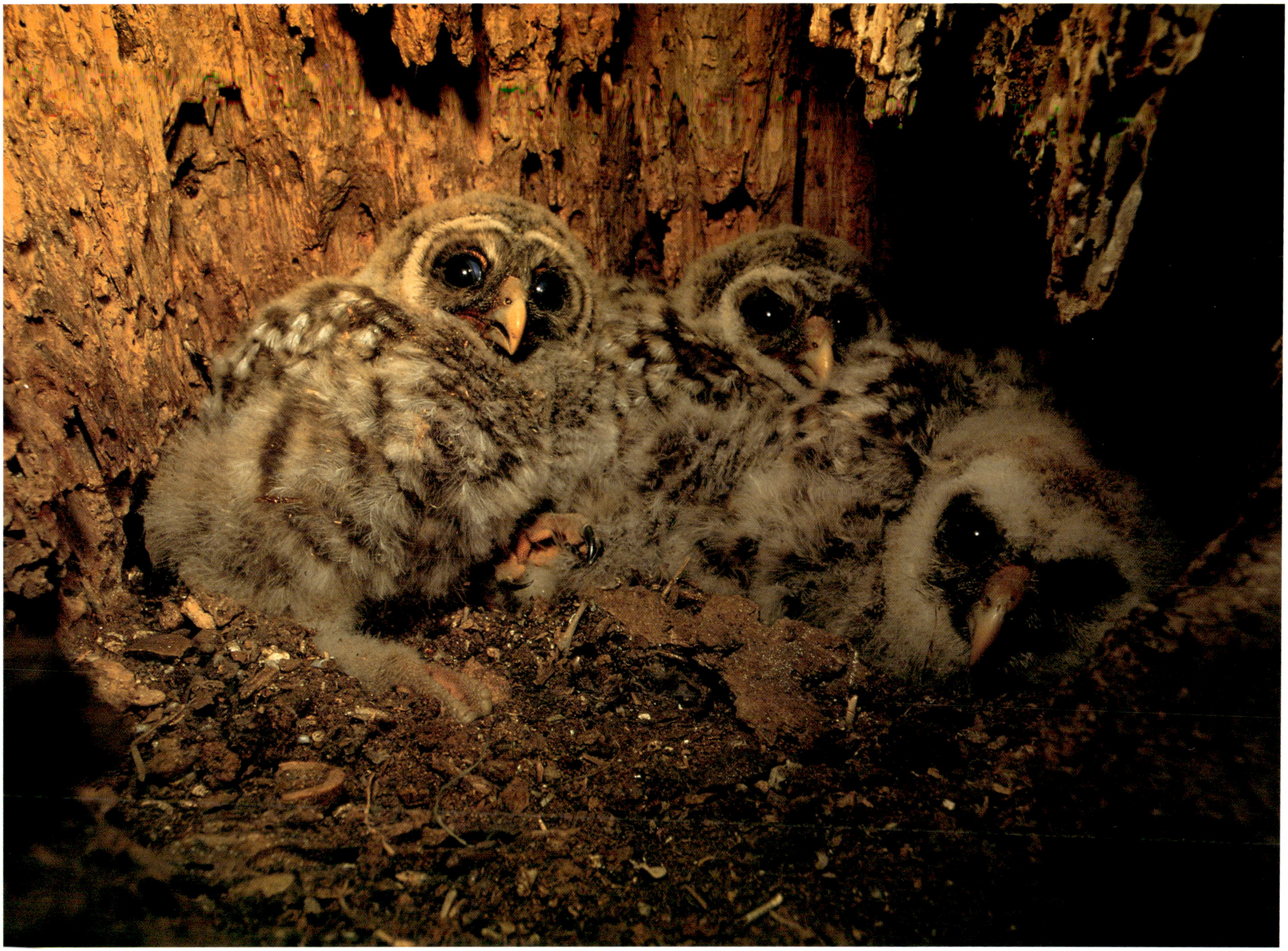

Young barred owls

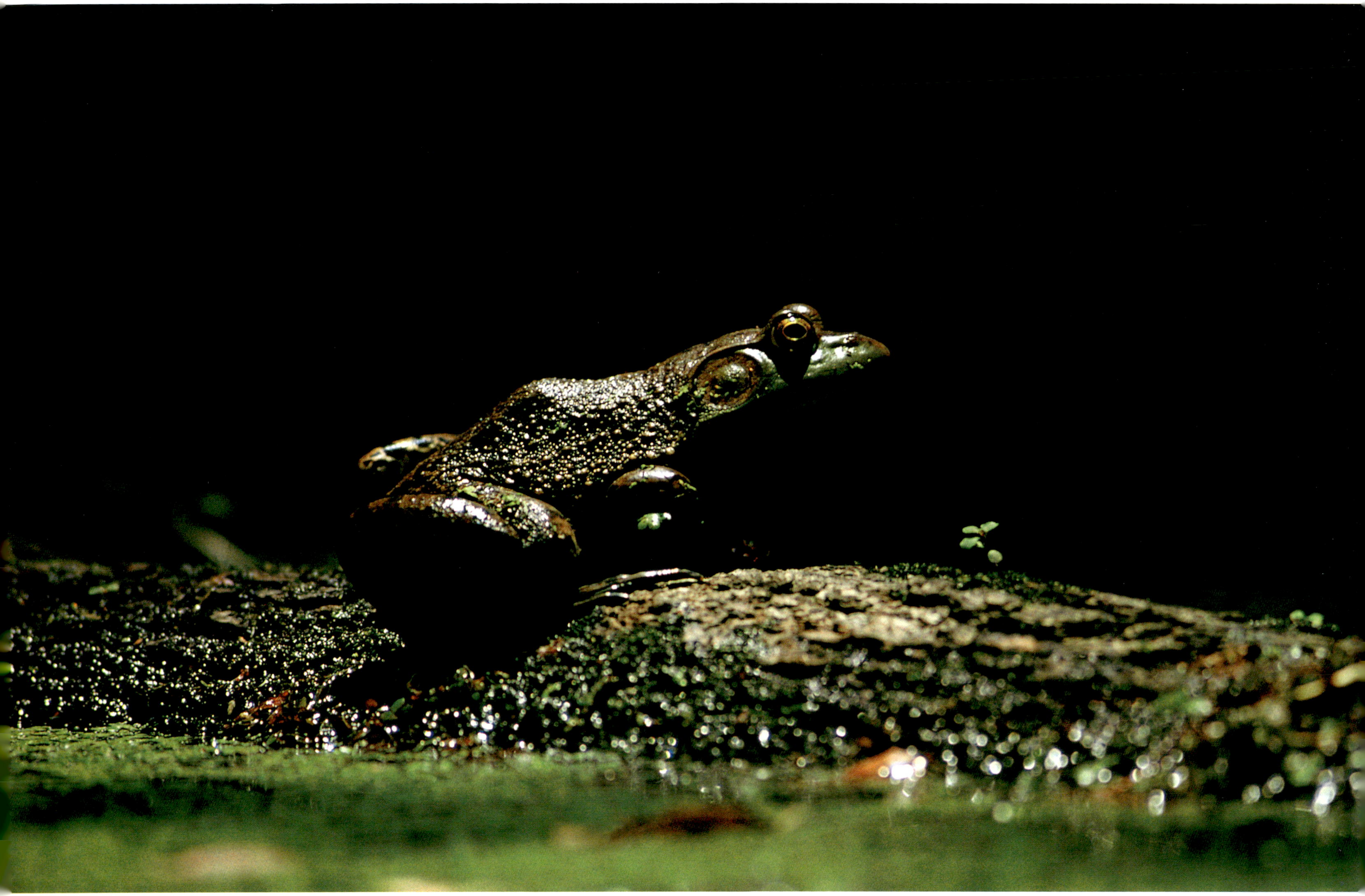

Bullfrog

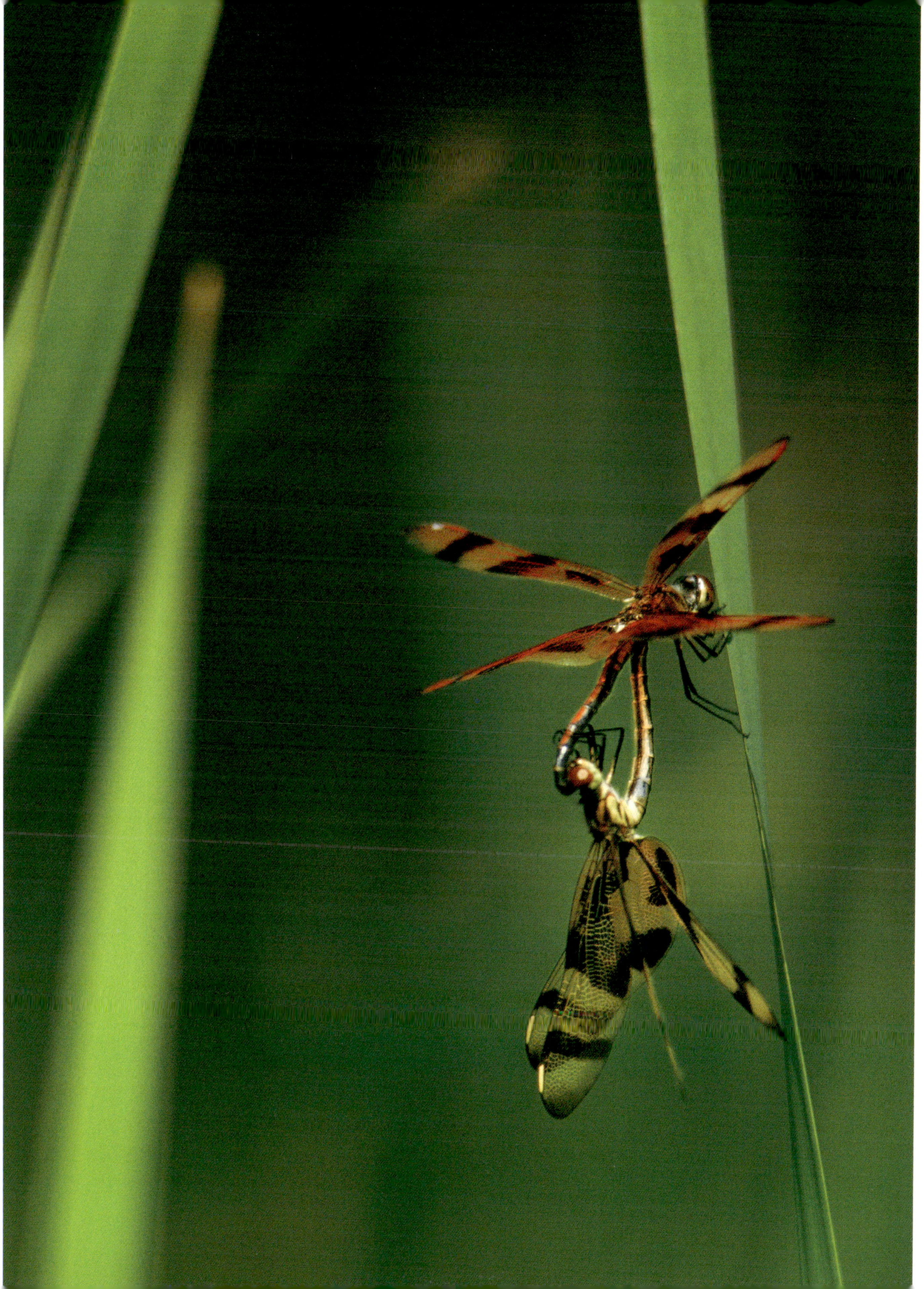

Halloween pennant dragonfly

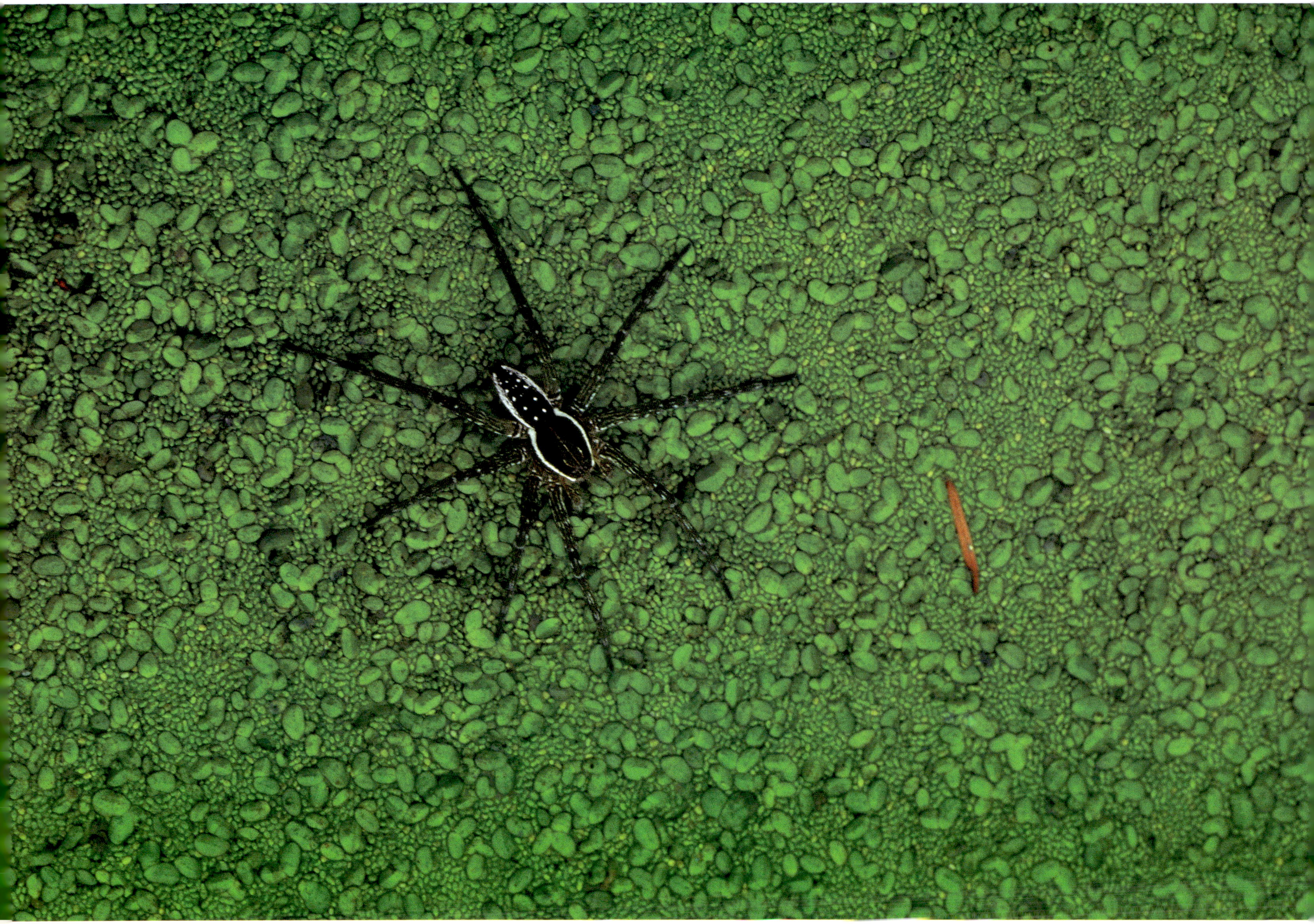

Six-spotted fishing spider on duck weed

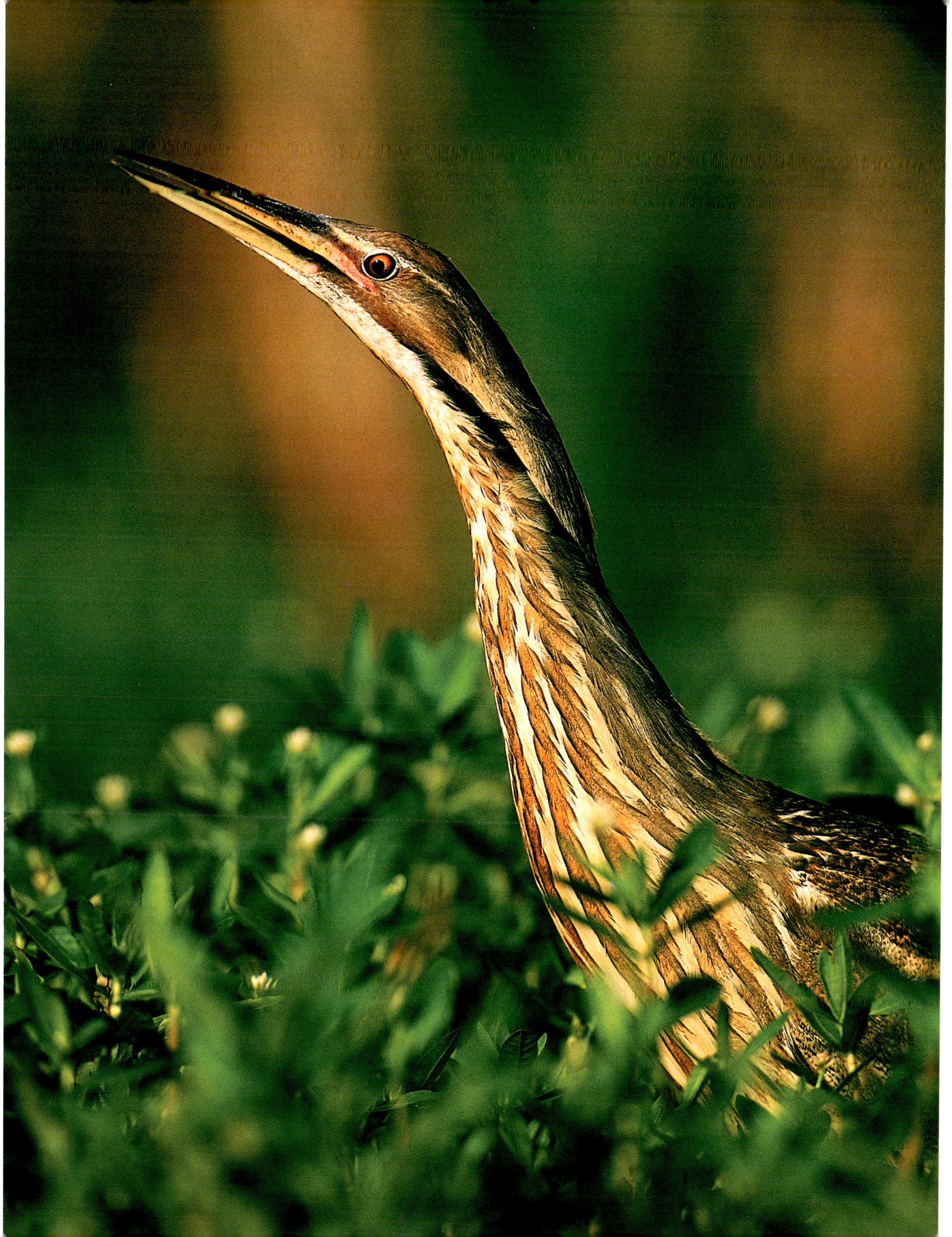

American Bittern

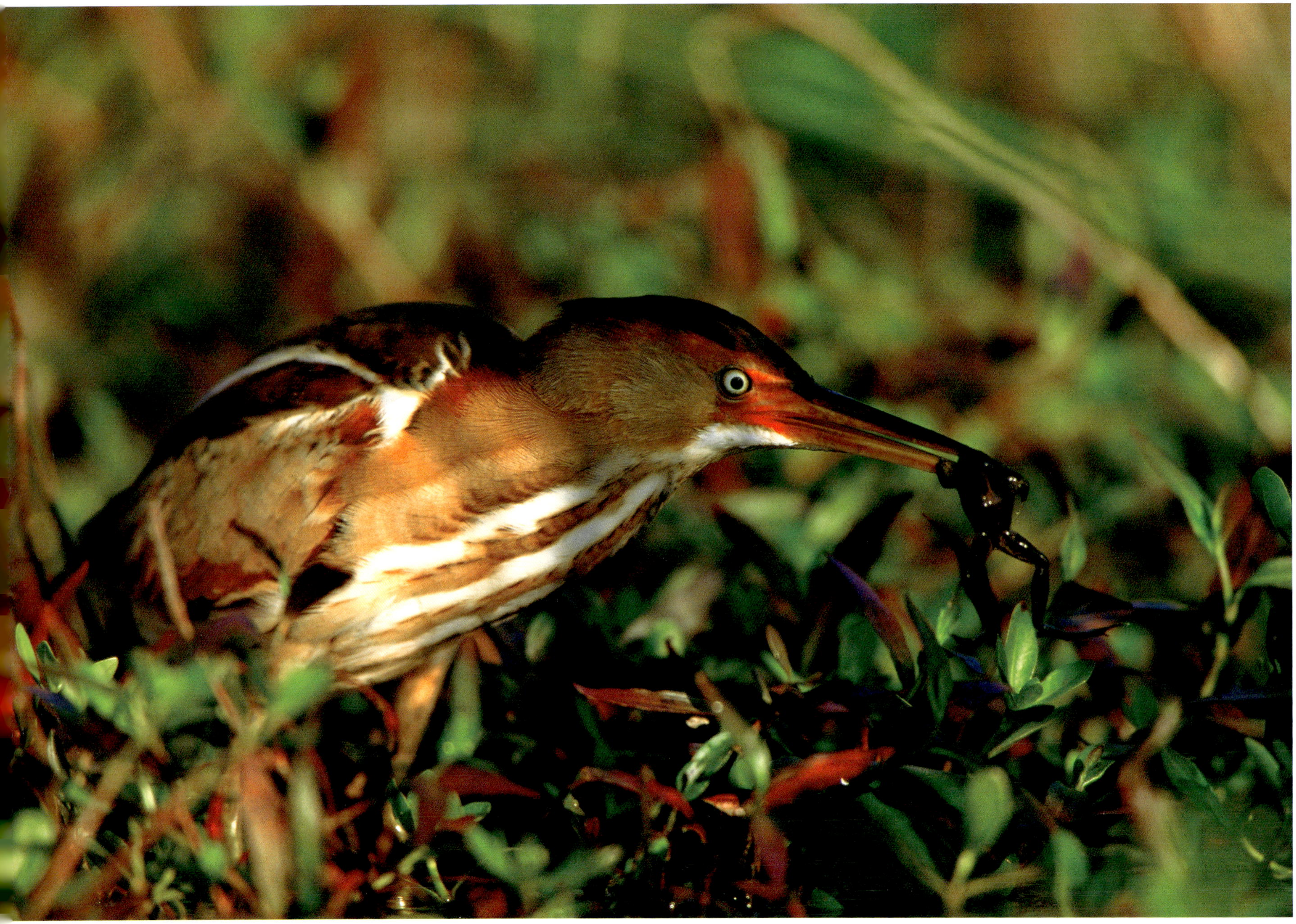

Least bittern

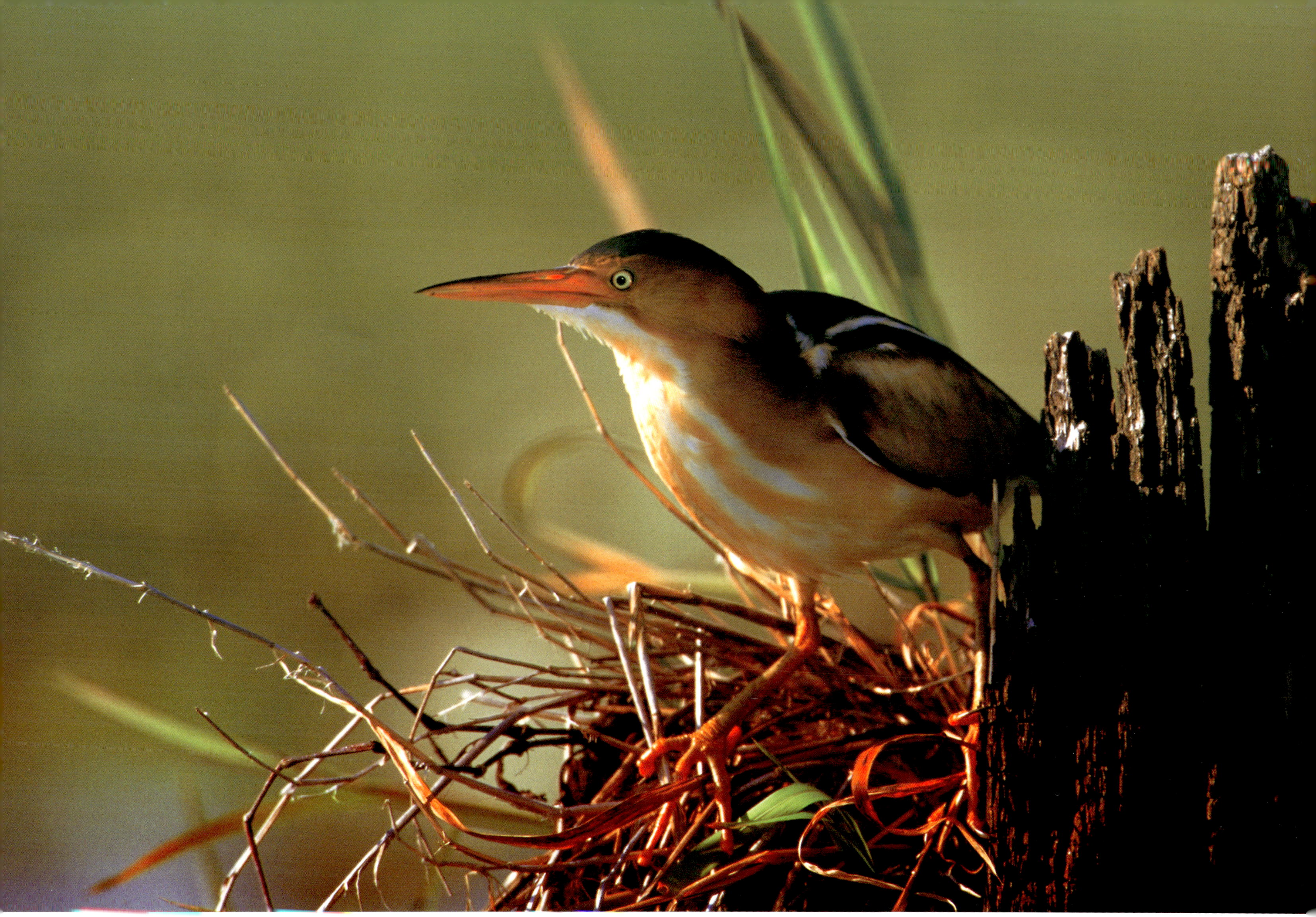

Least bittern

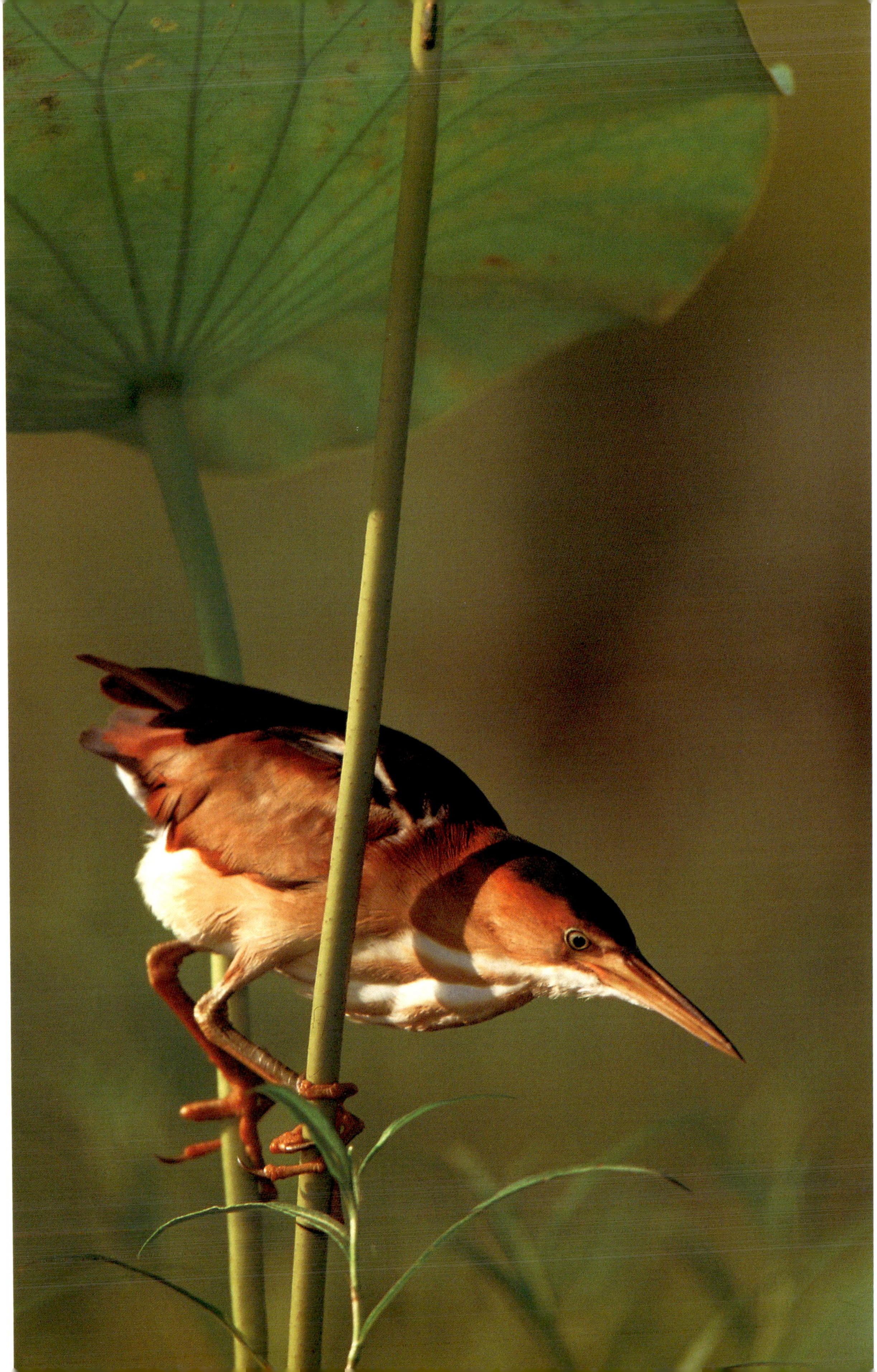

Least bittern

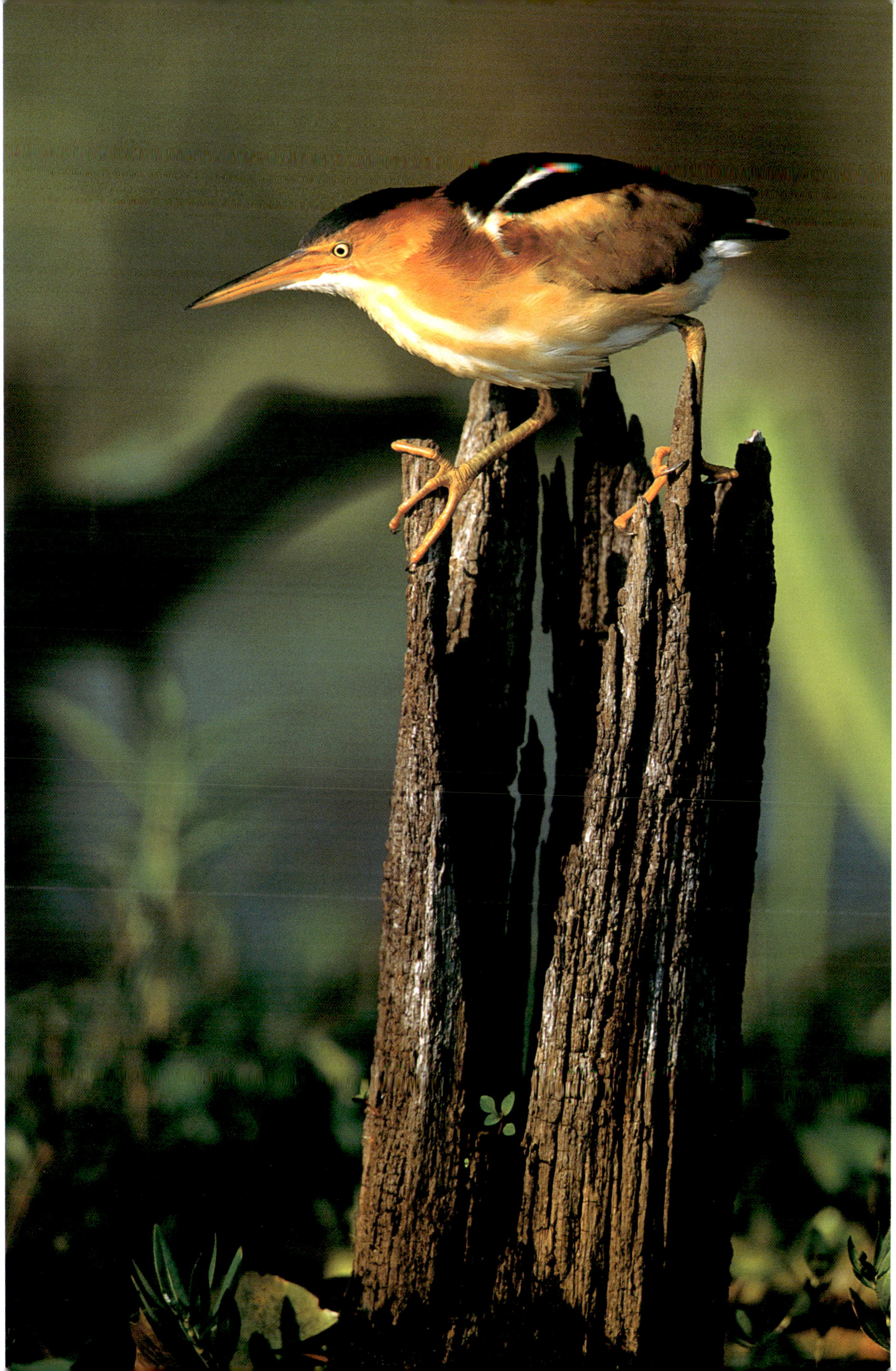

Least bittern

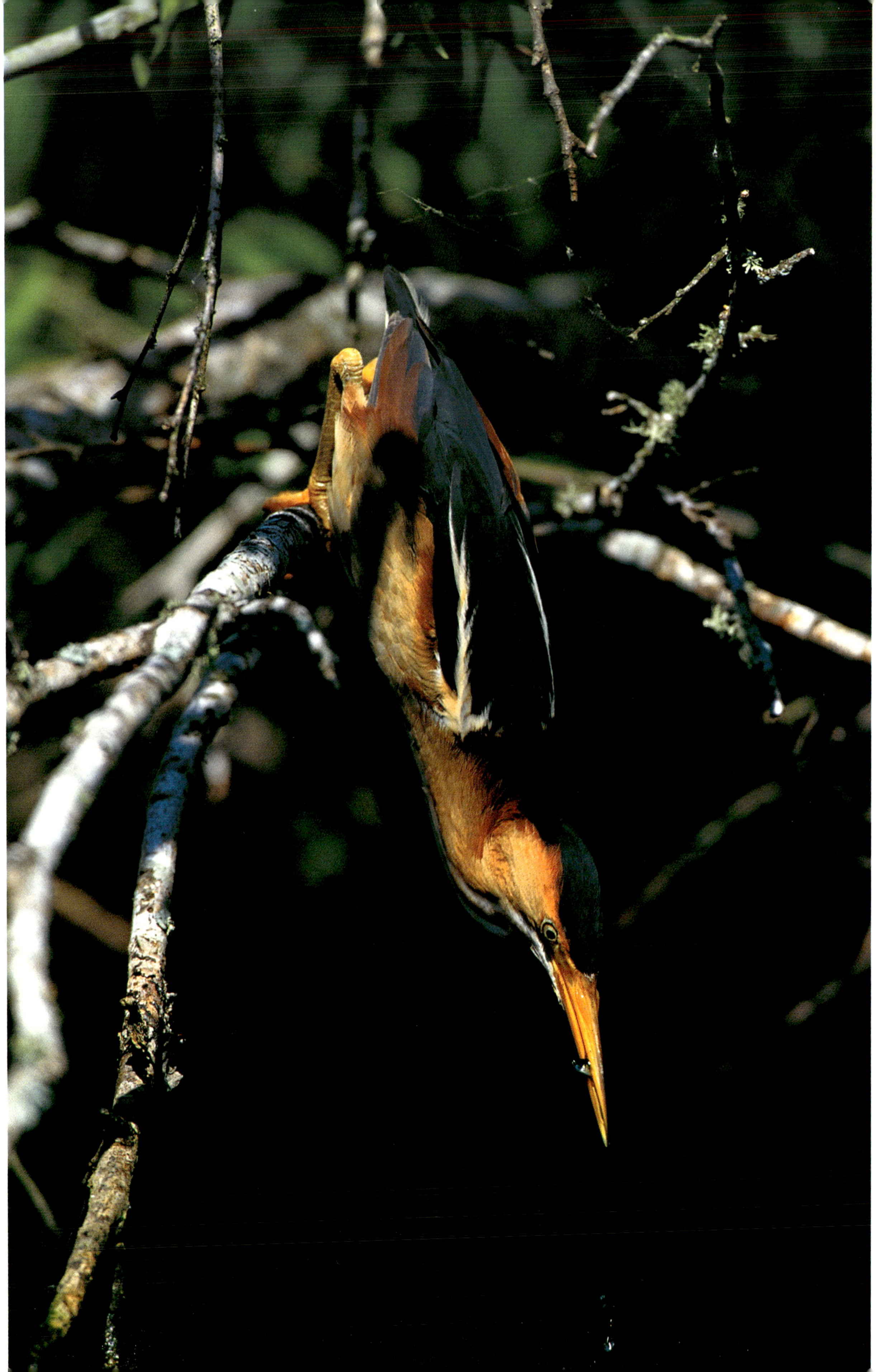

Least bittern

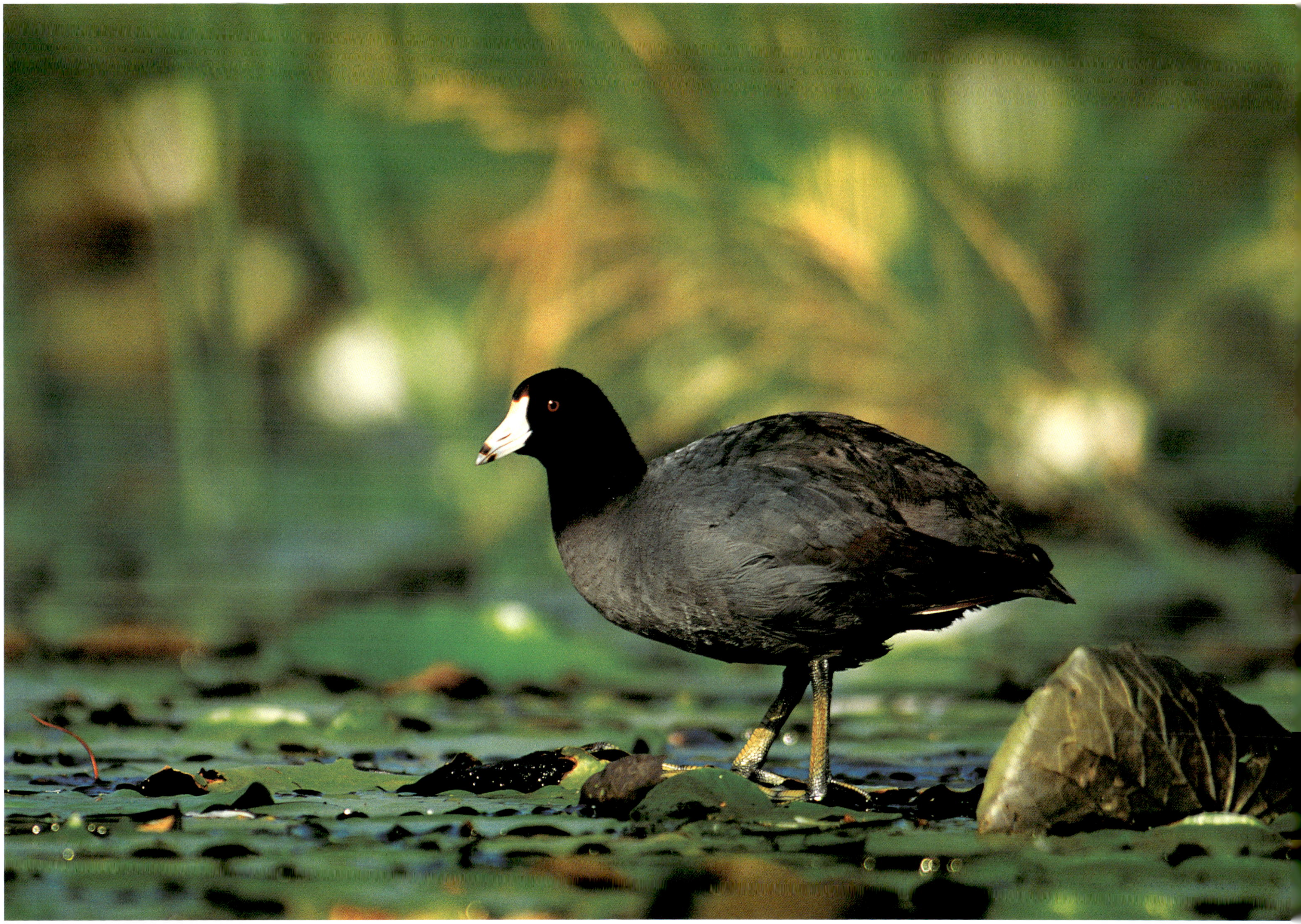

American coot

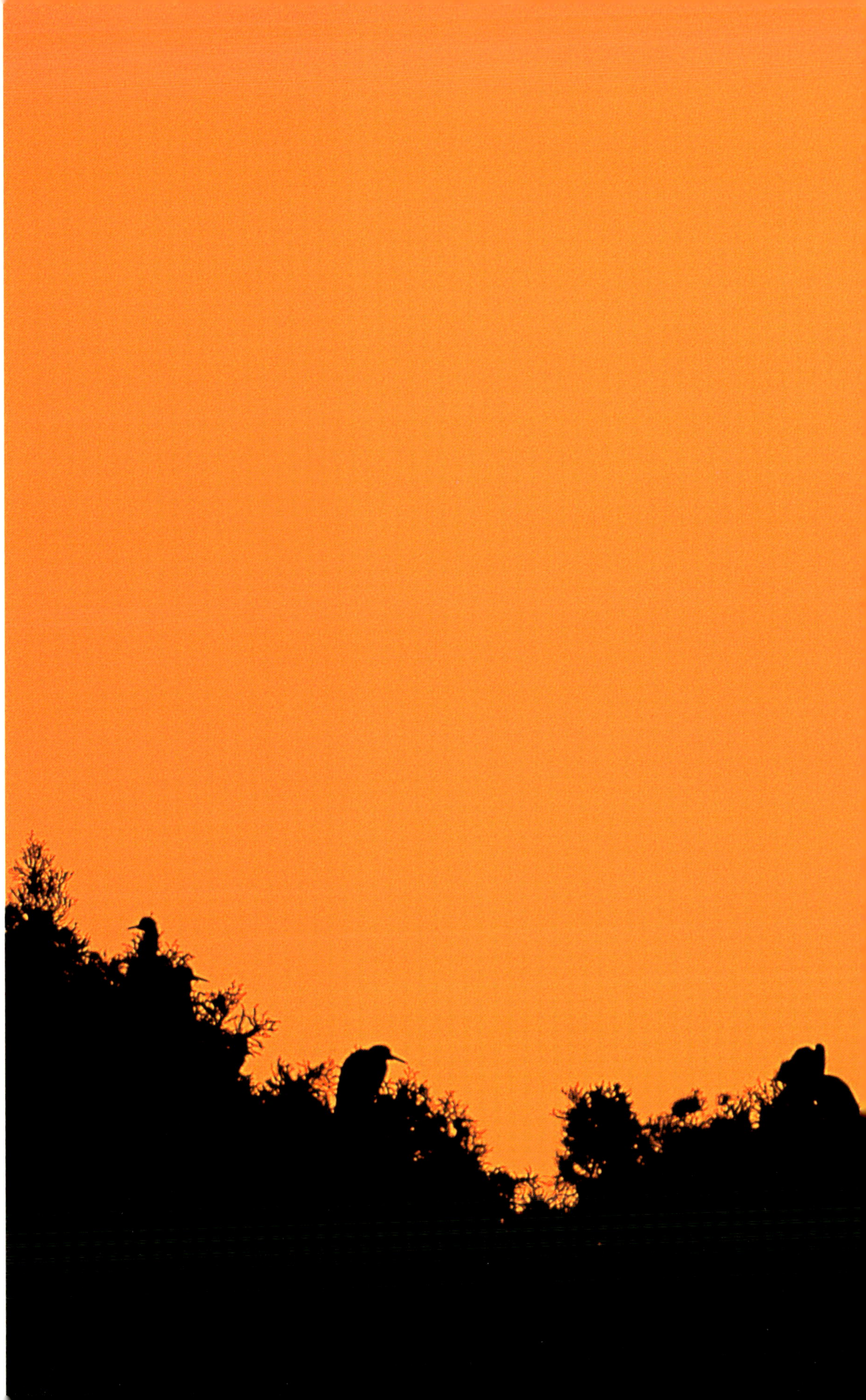

Sunset on heron rookery

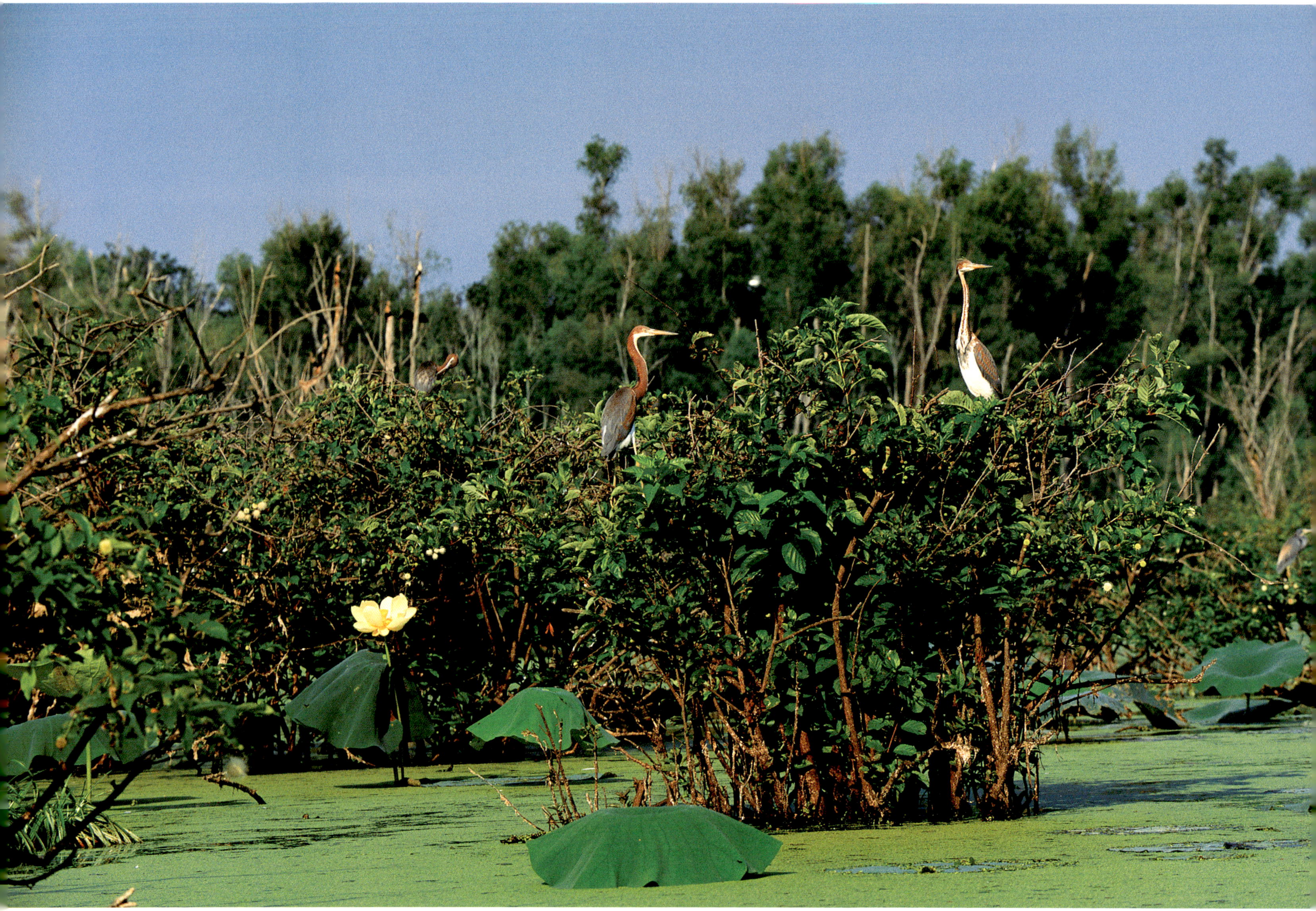

Immature tricolored herons at nest

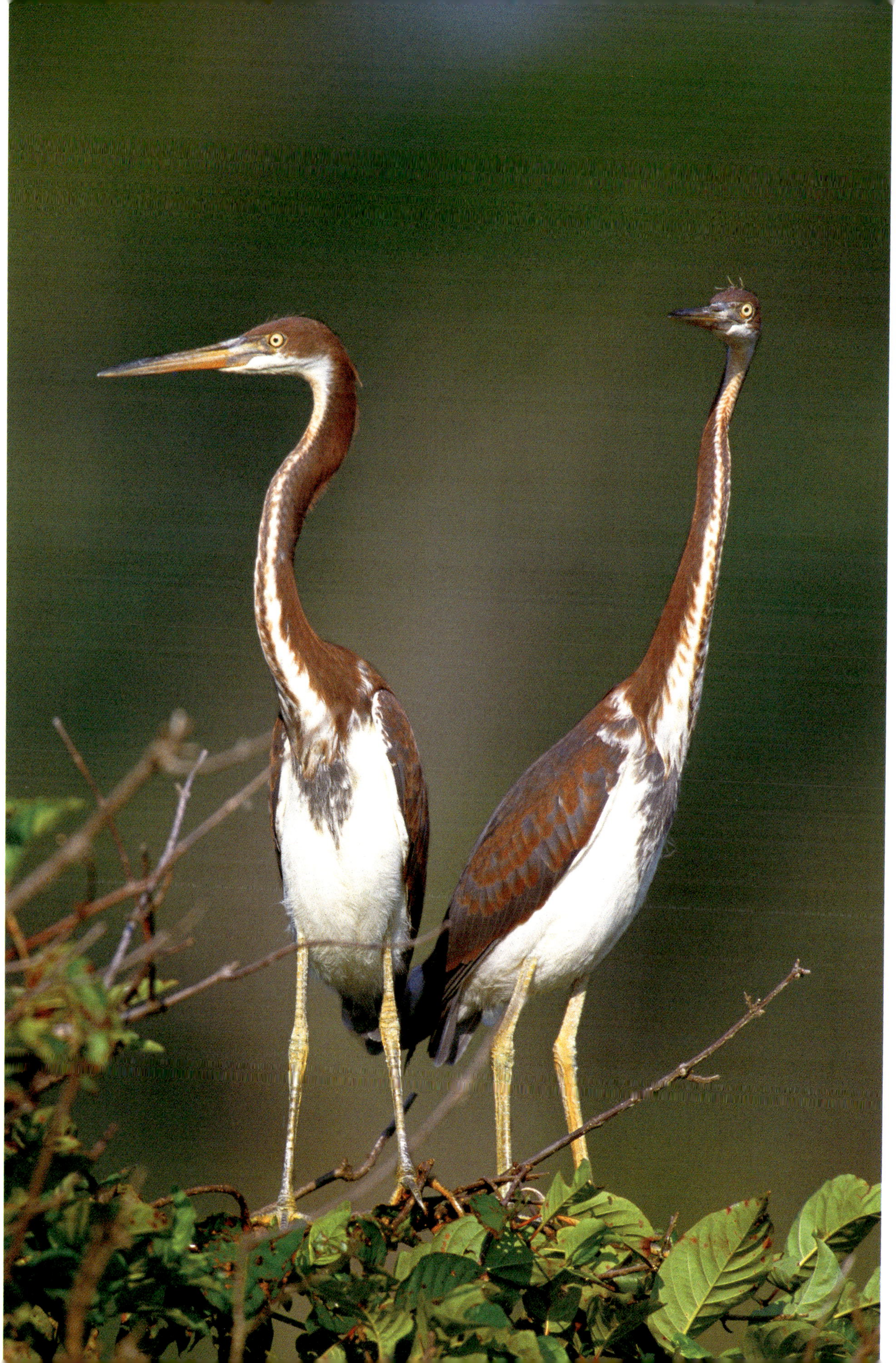

Immature tricolored herons

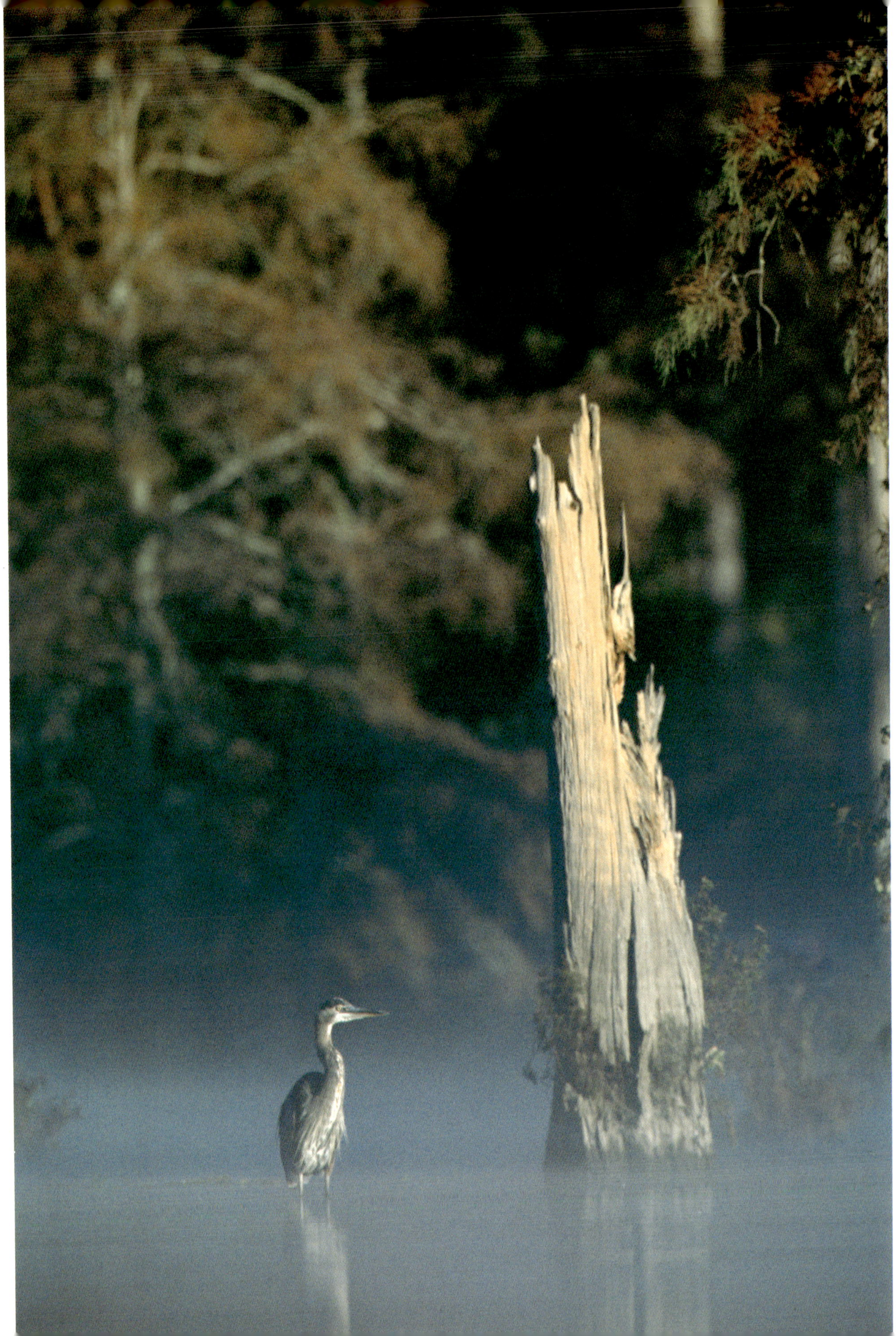

Great blue heron in fog

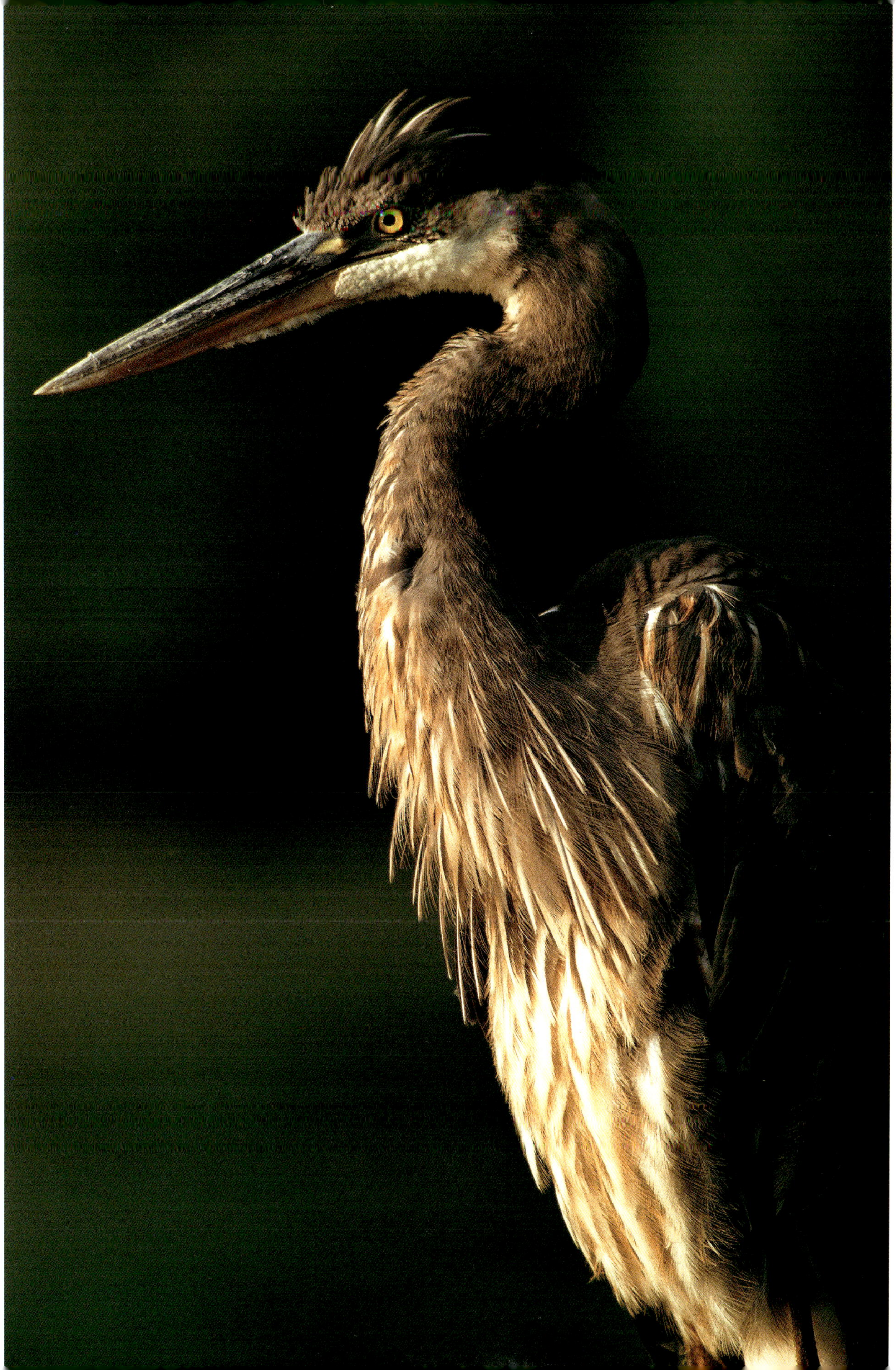

Great blue heron

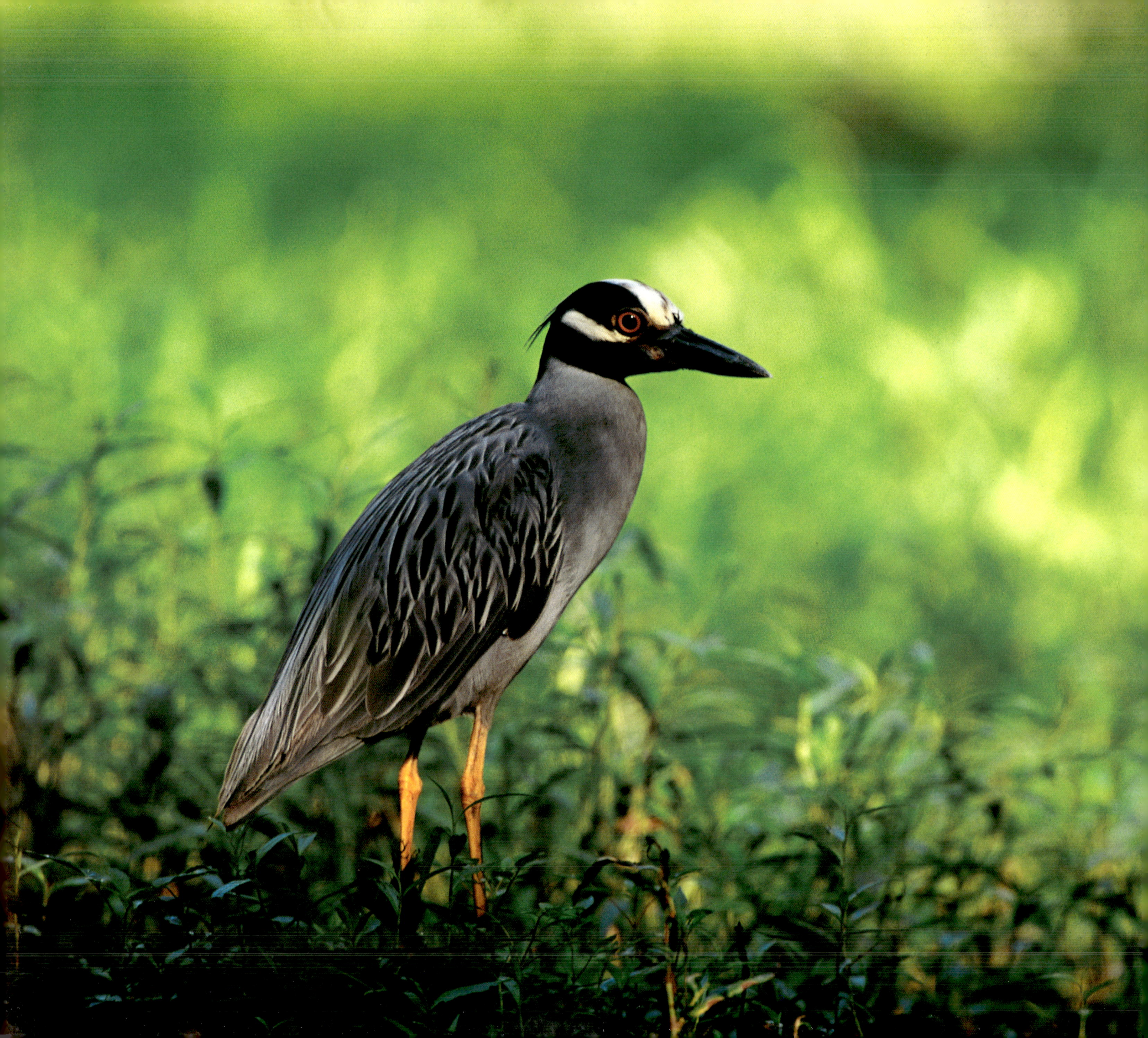

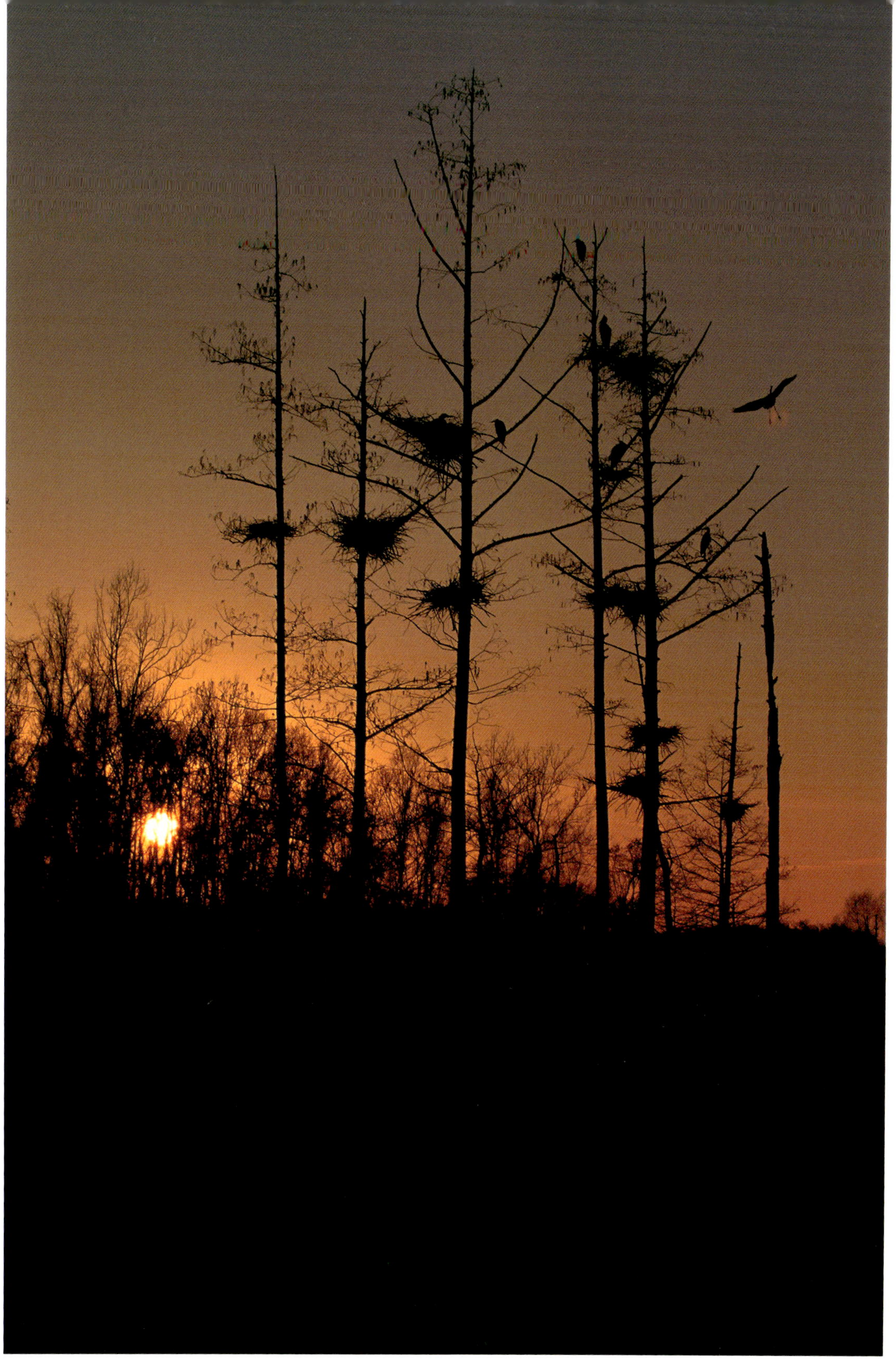

Great blue heron rookery at sunset

Yellow-crowned night heron

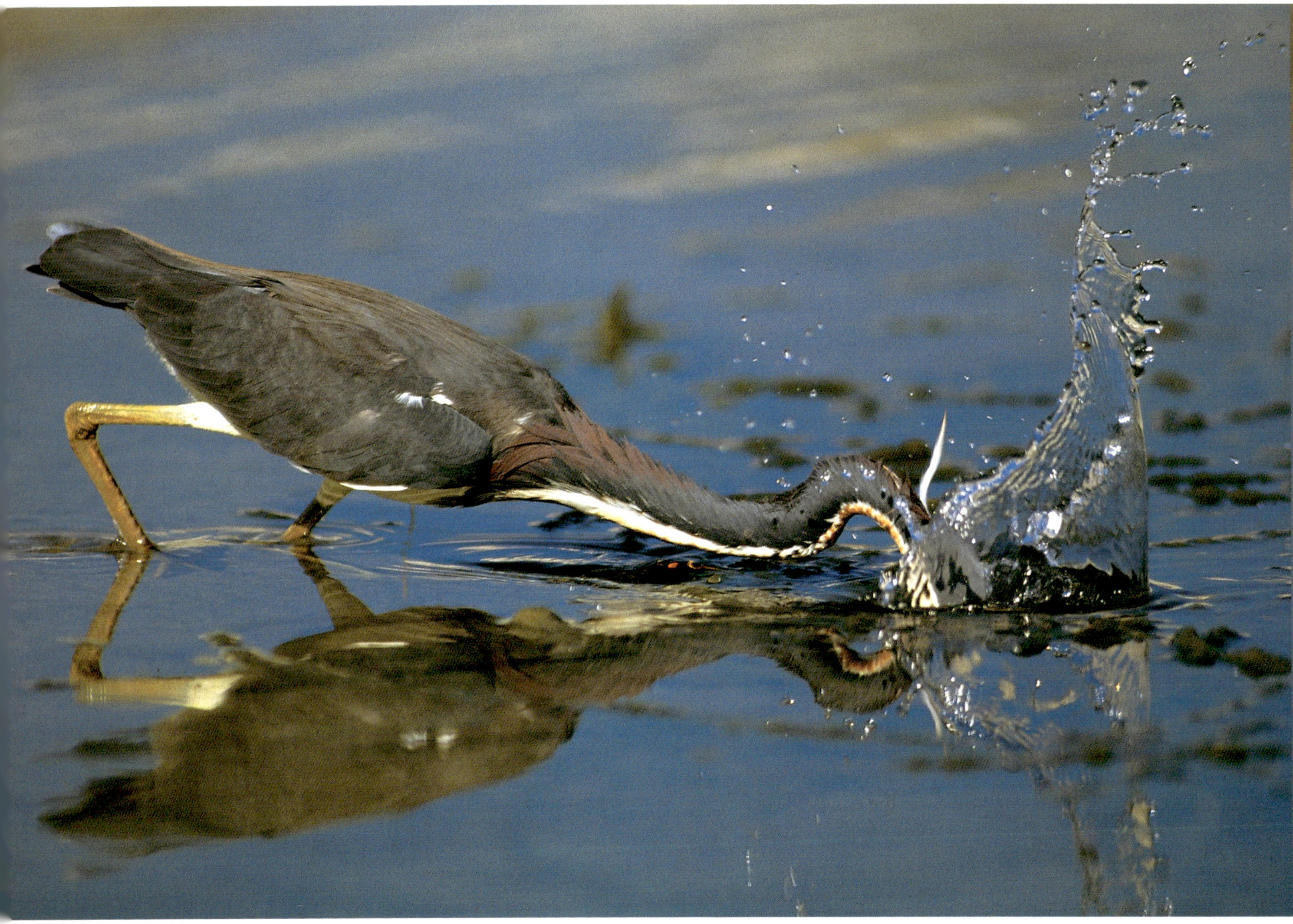

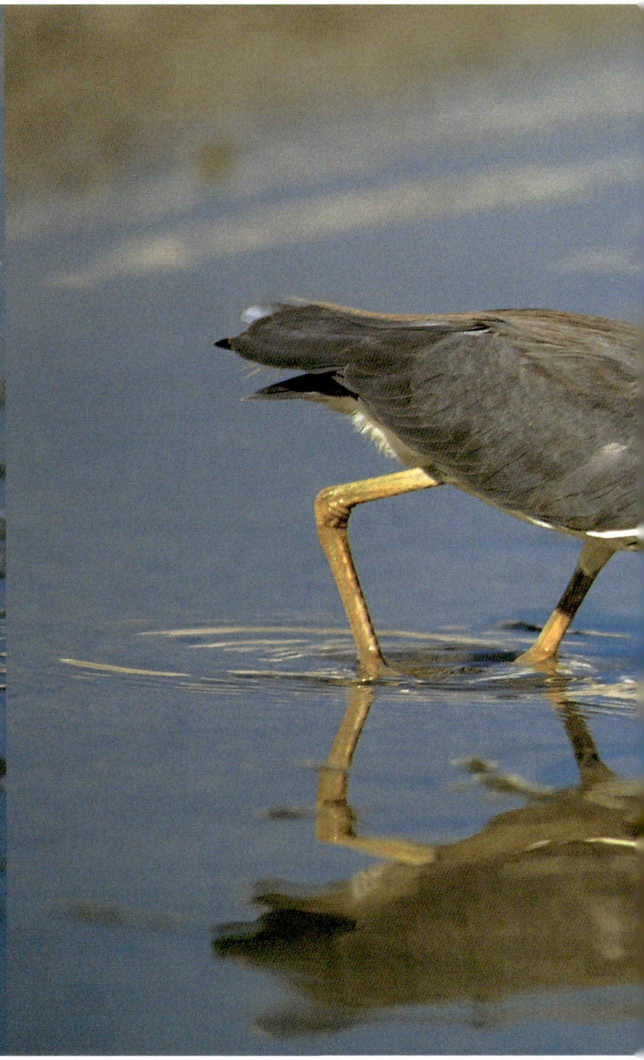

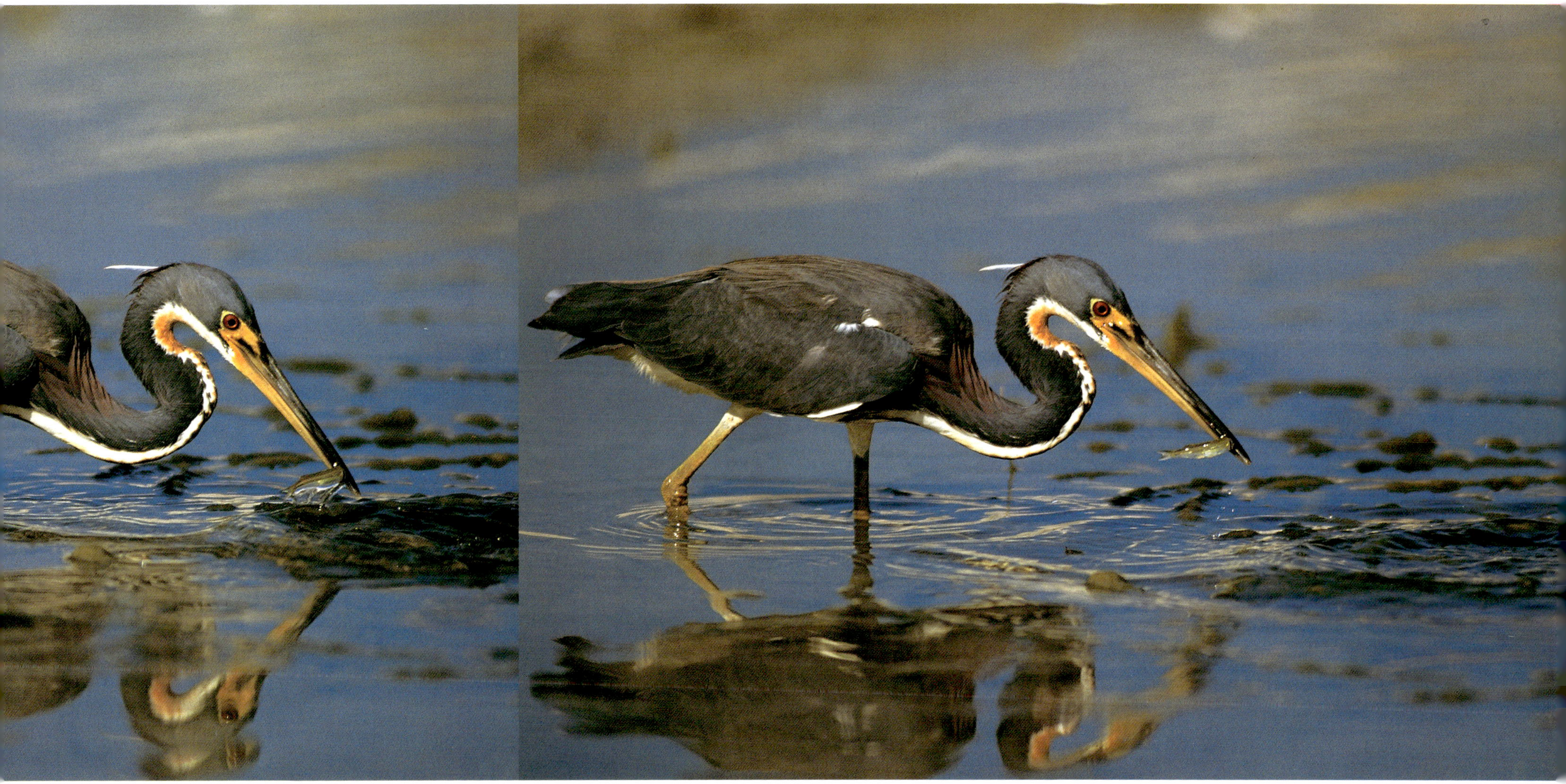

Tricolored heron catching a minnow

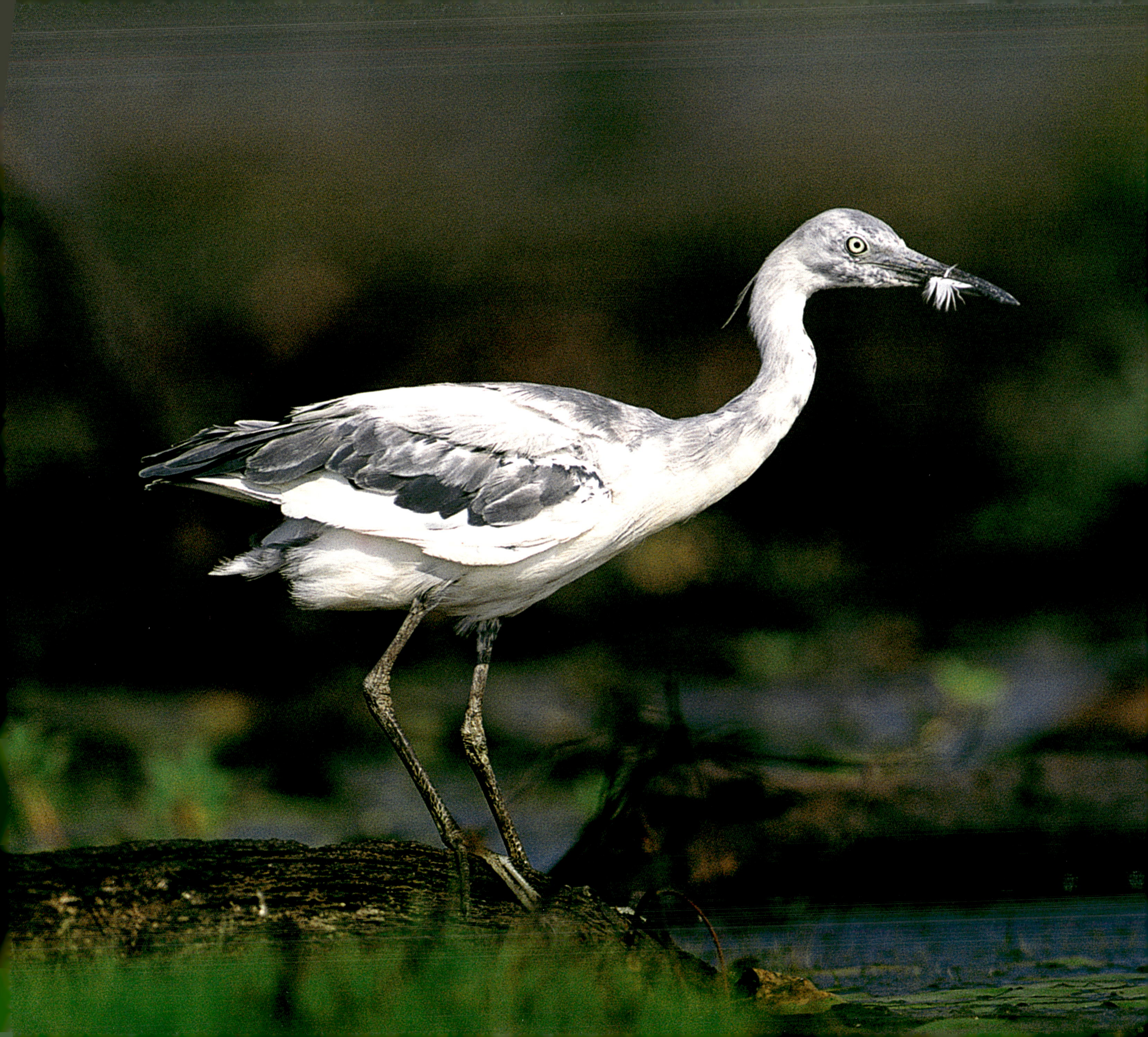

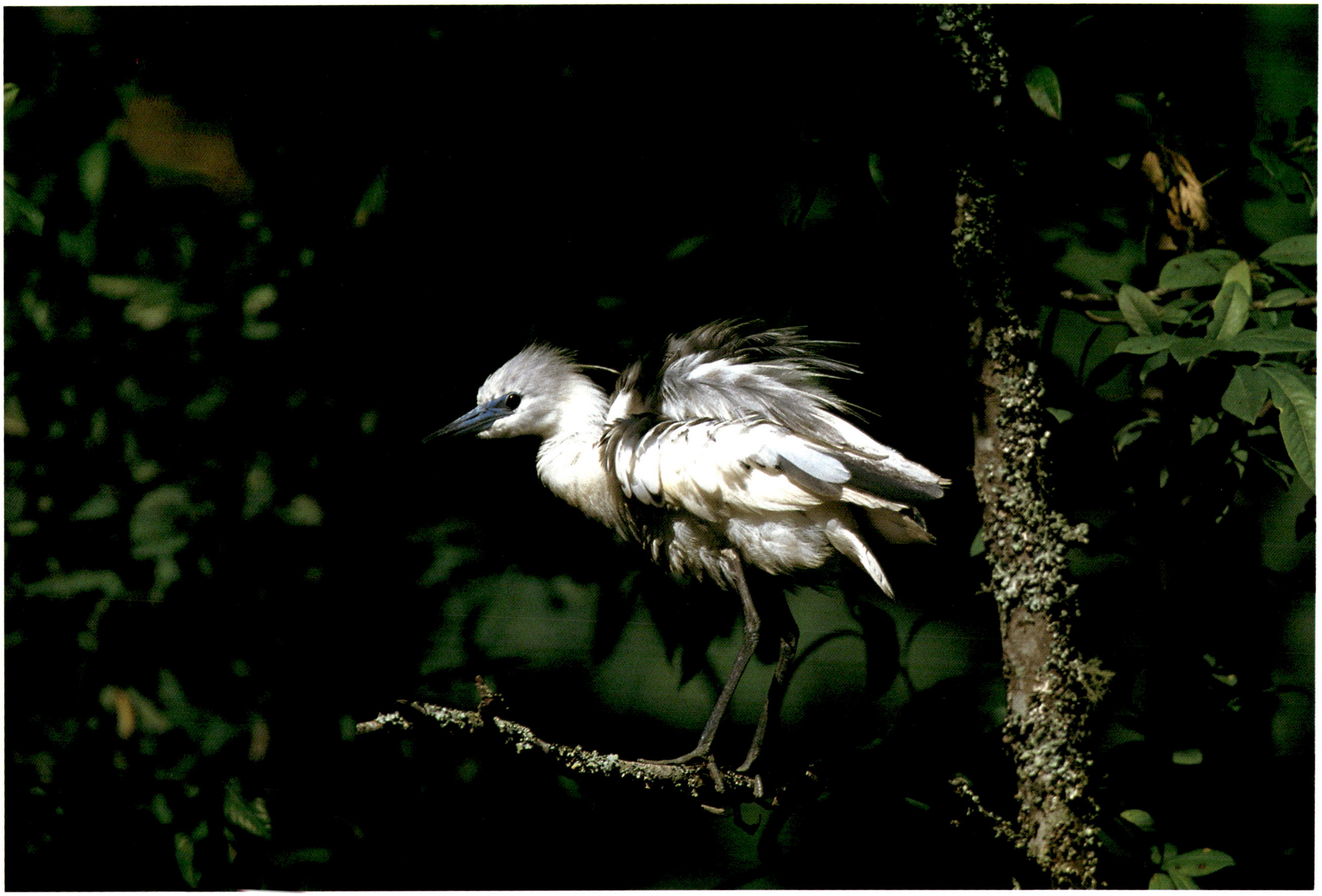

Little blue heron, immature

Little blue heron, immature

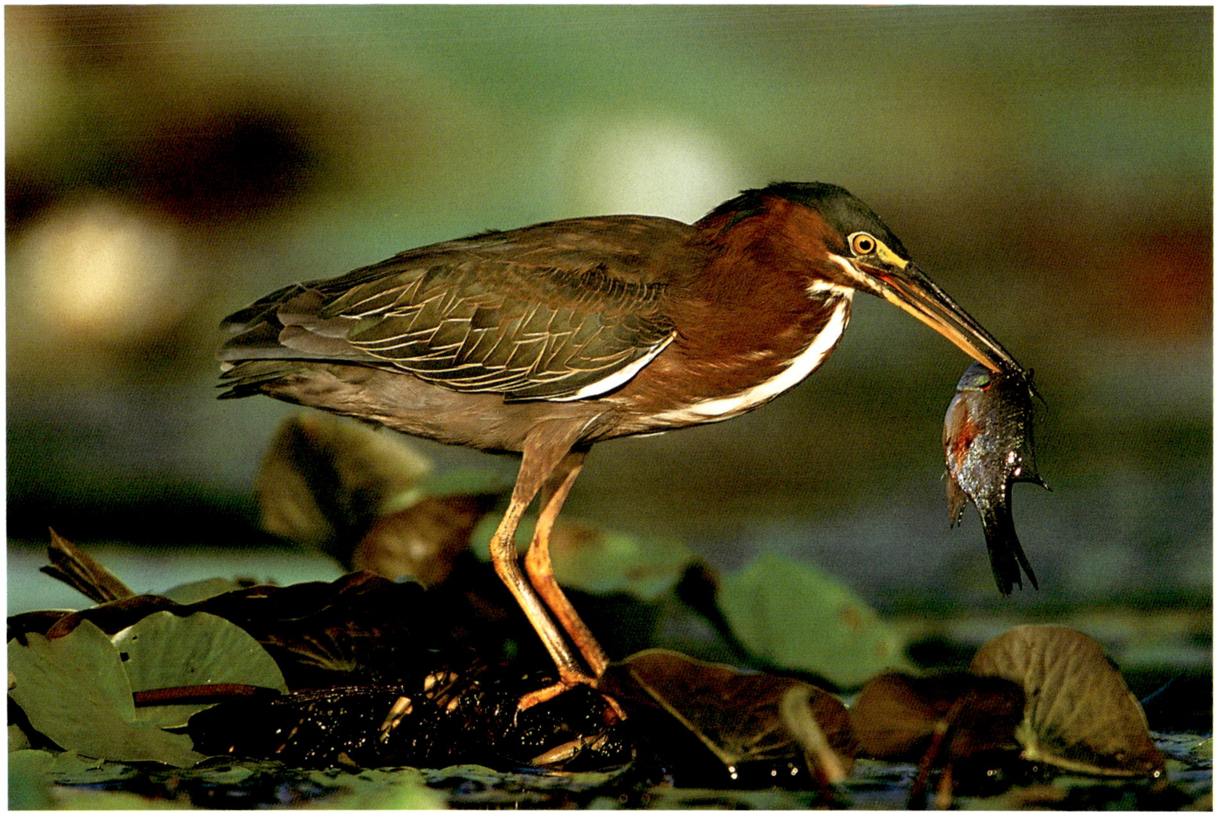

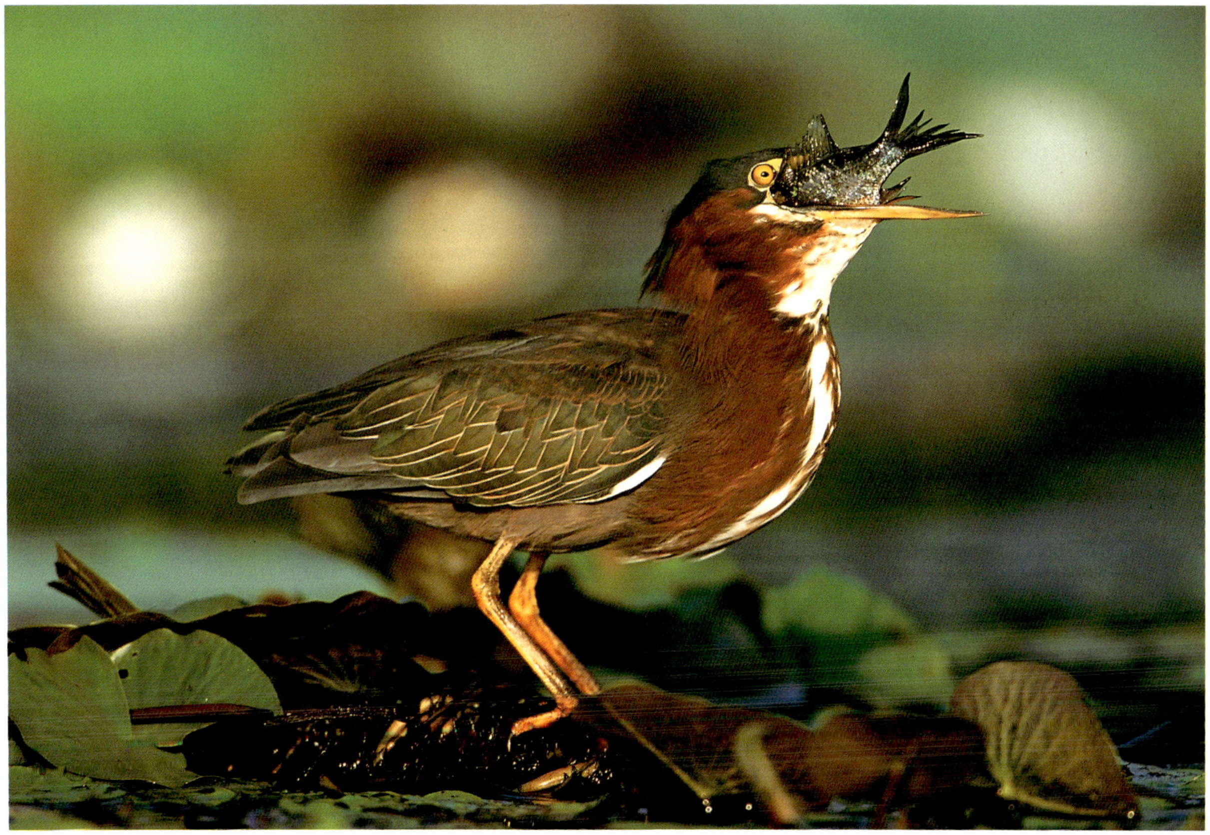

Green heron feeding on bream

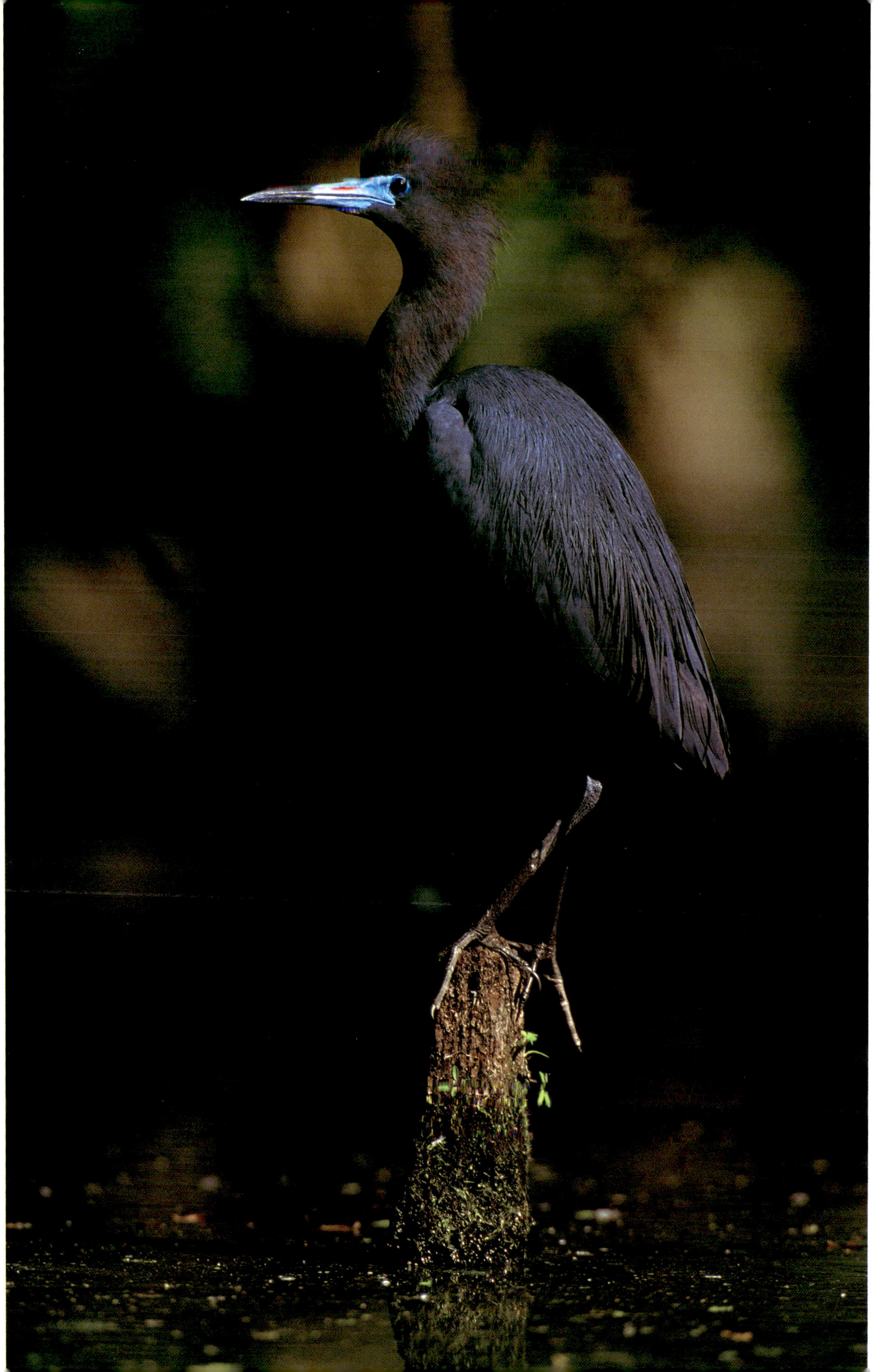

Little blue heron

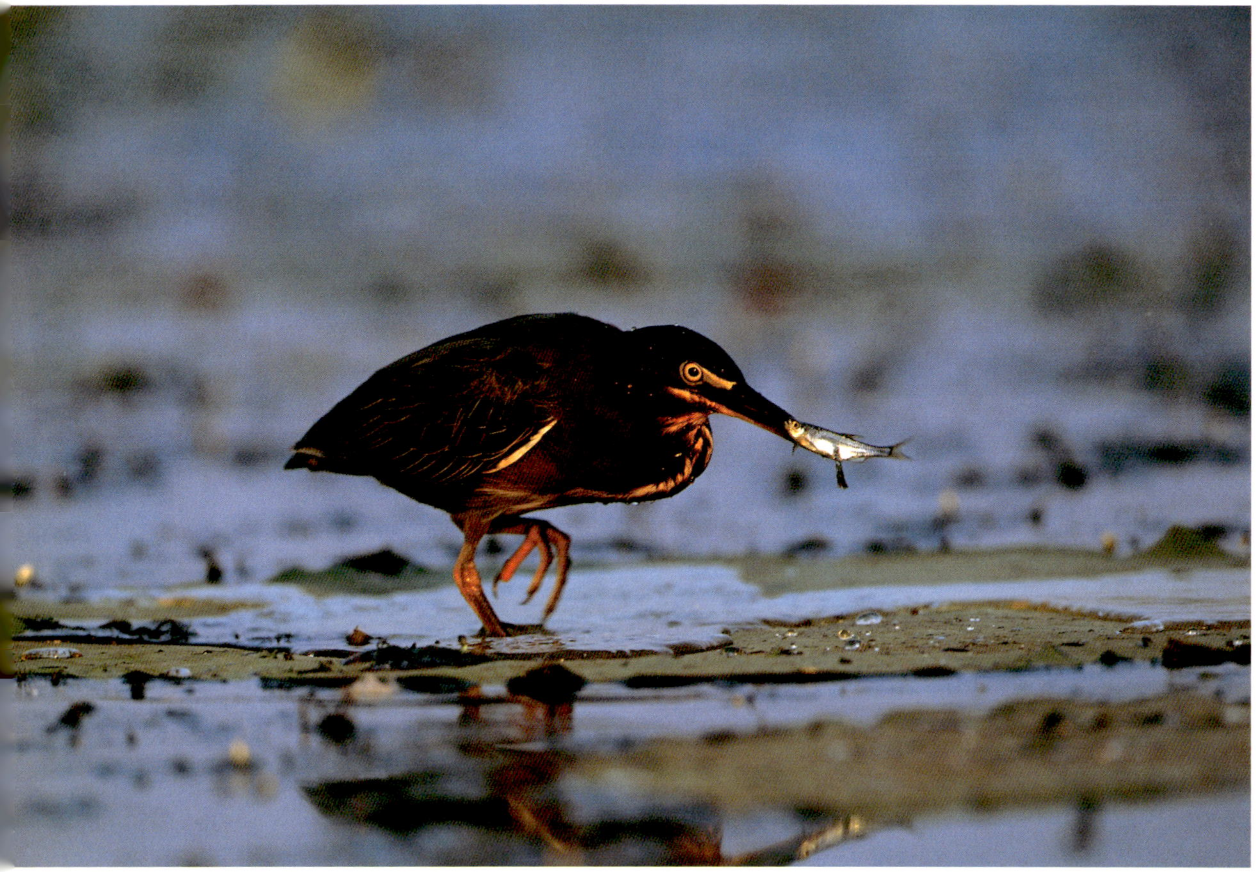

Green heron with minnow

Green heron on American lotus

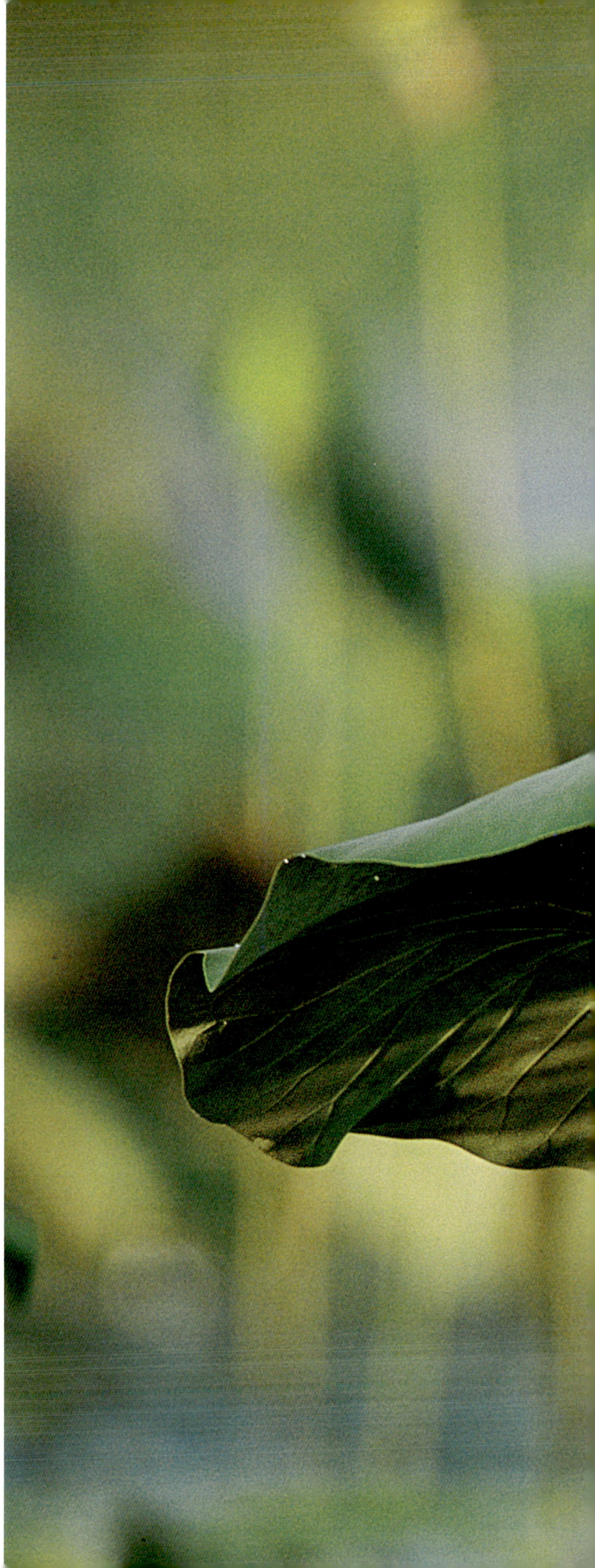

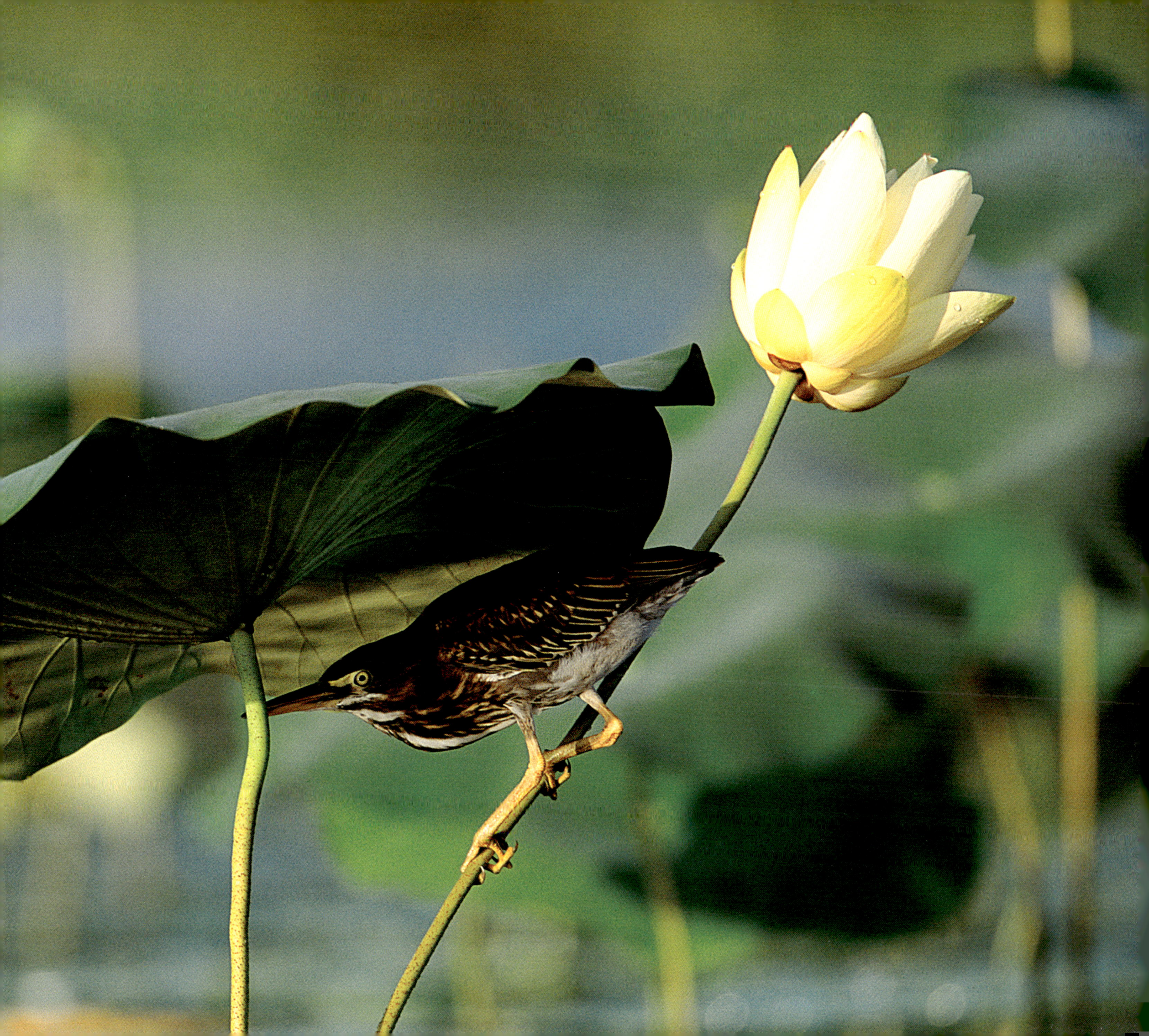

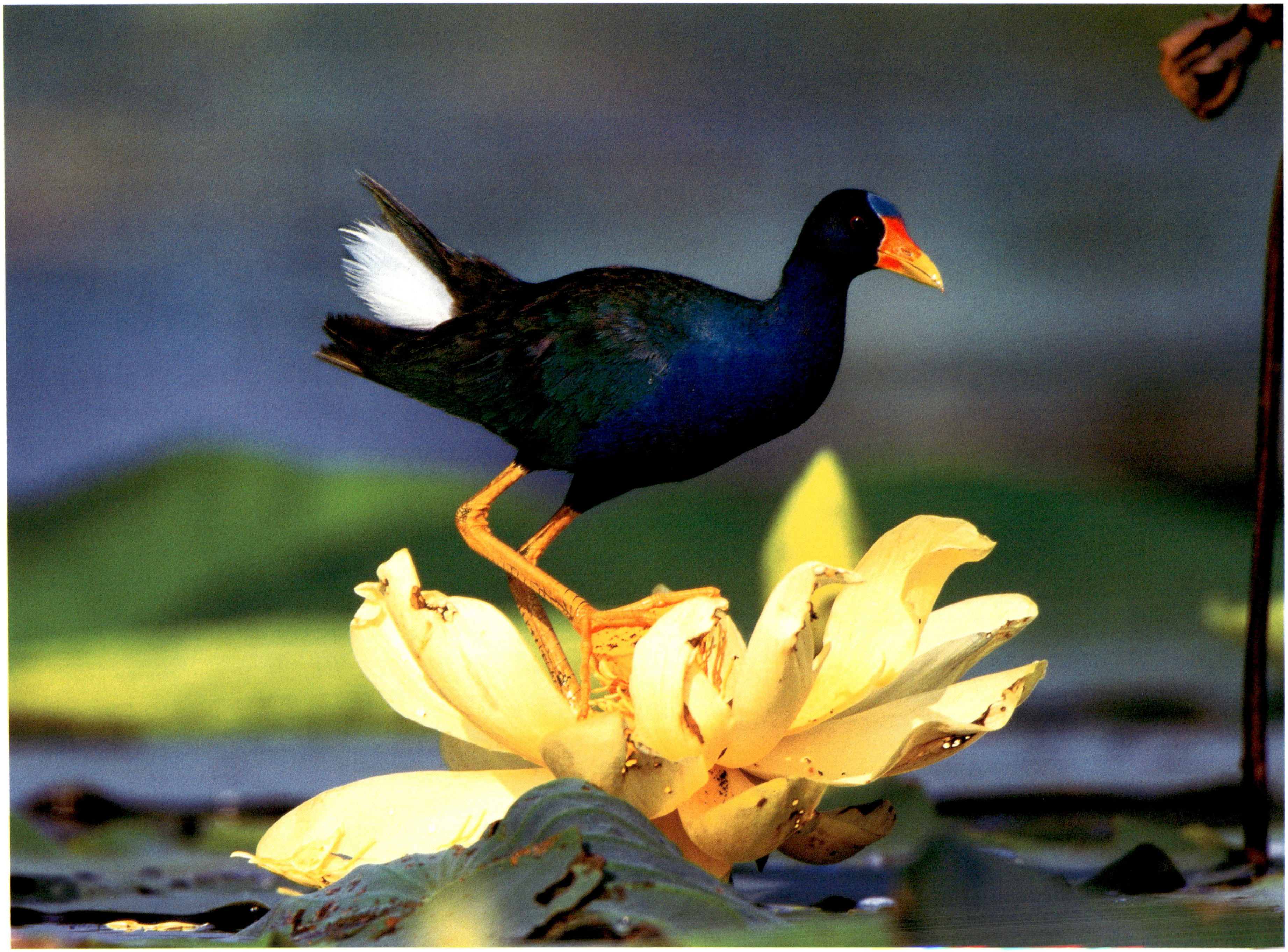

Purple gallinule on American lotus

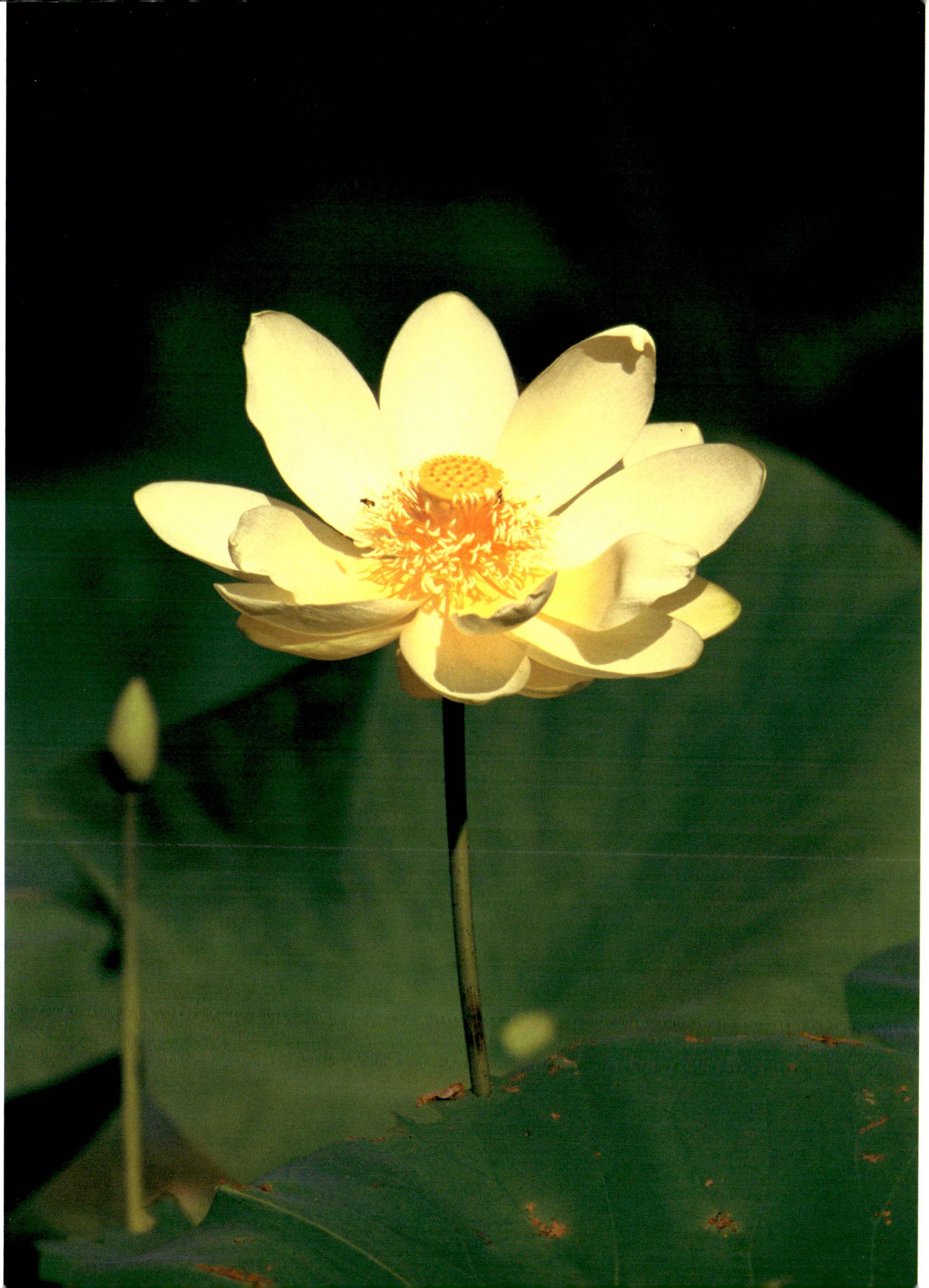

American lotus

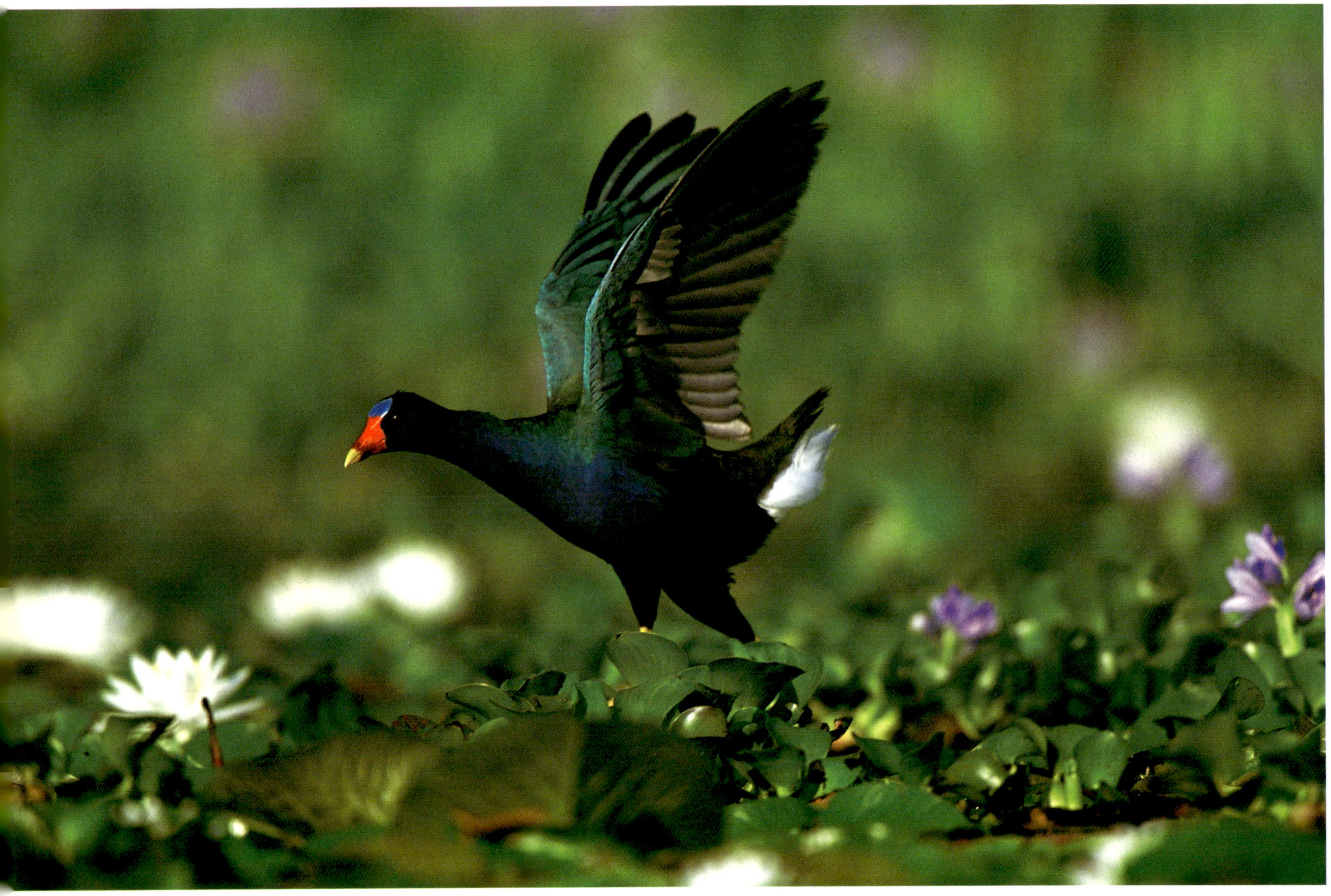
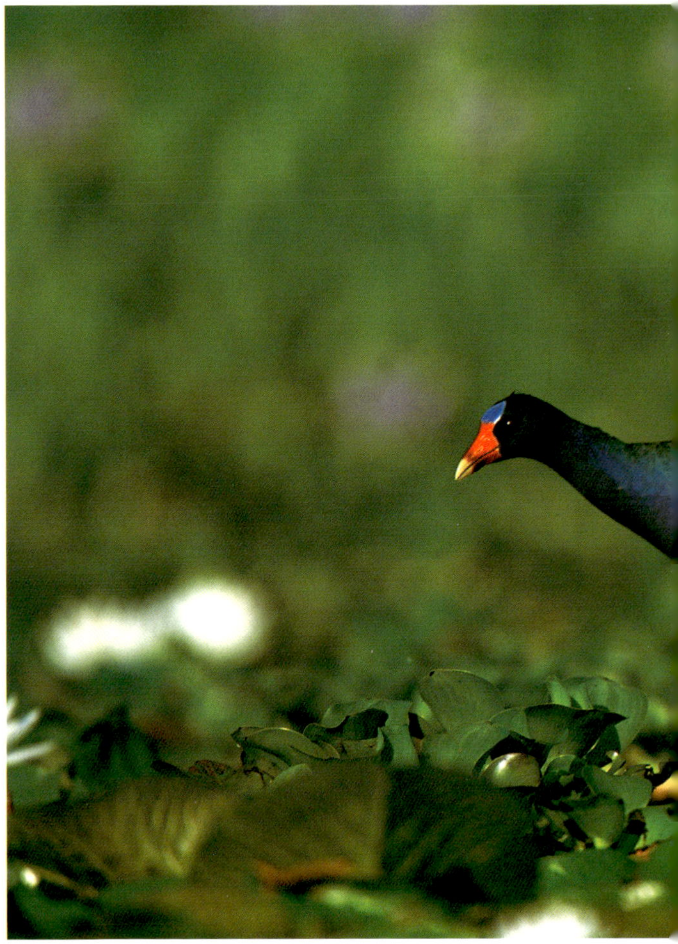

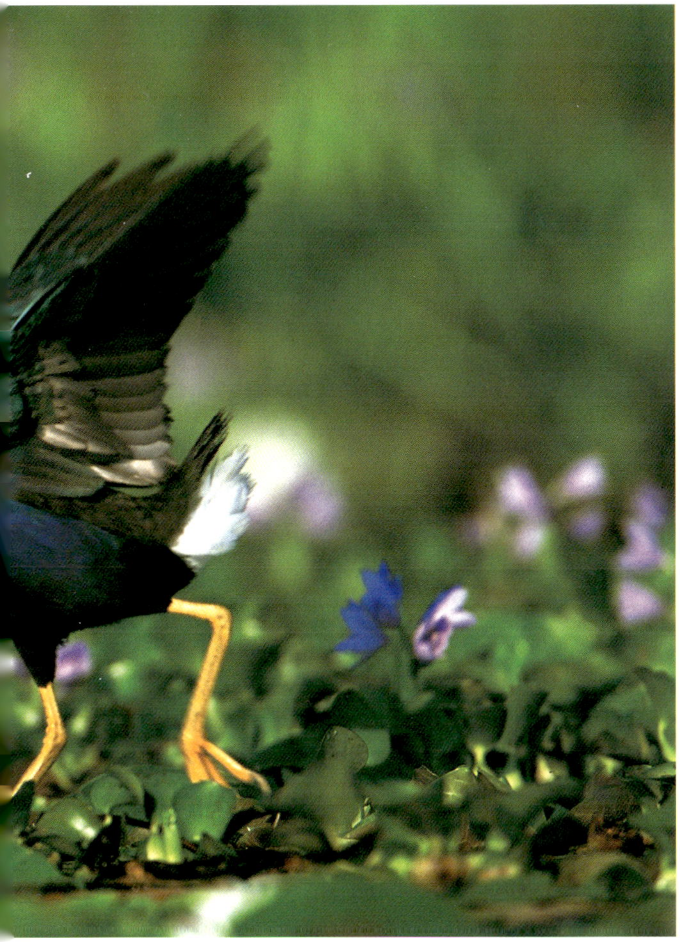

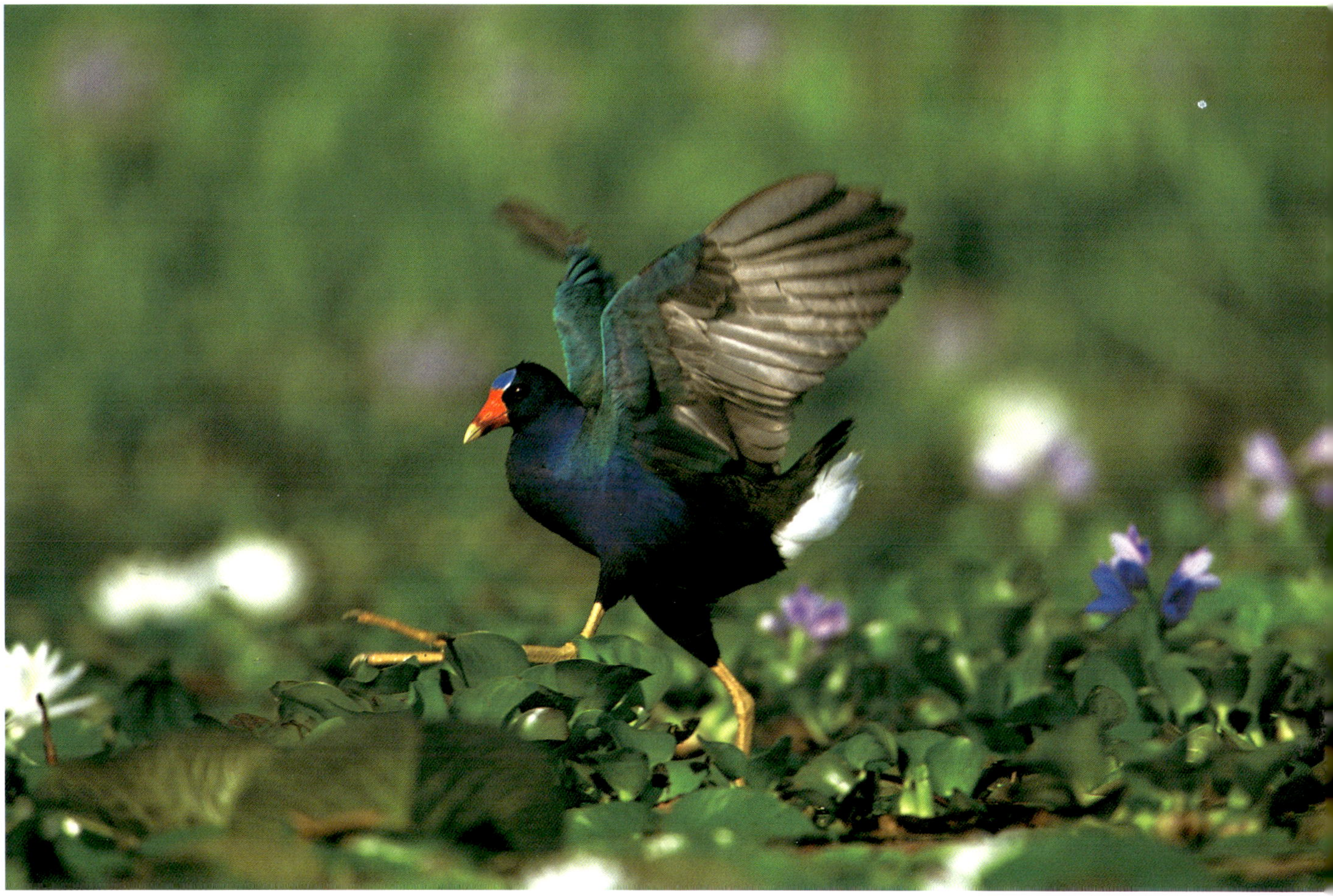

Running purple gallinule

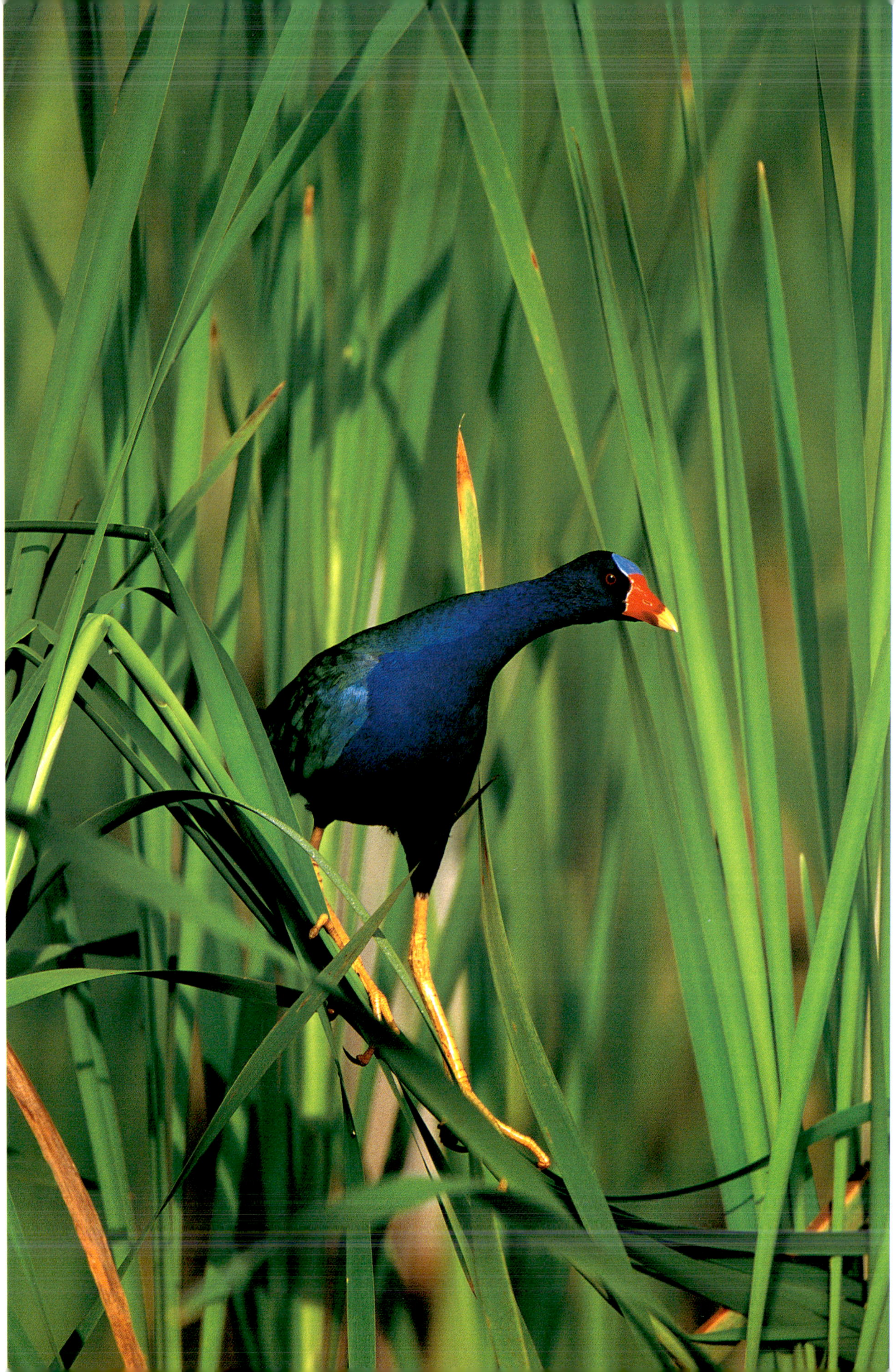

Purple gallinule on cattails

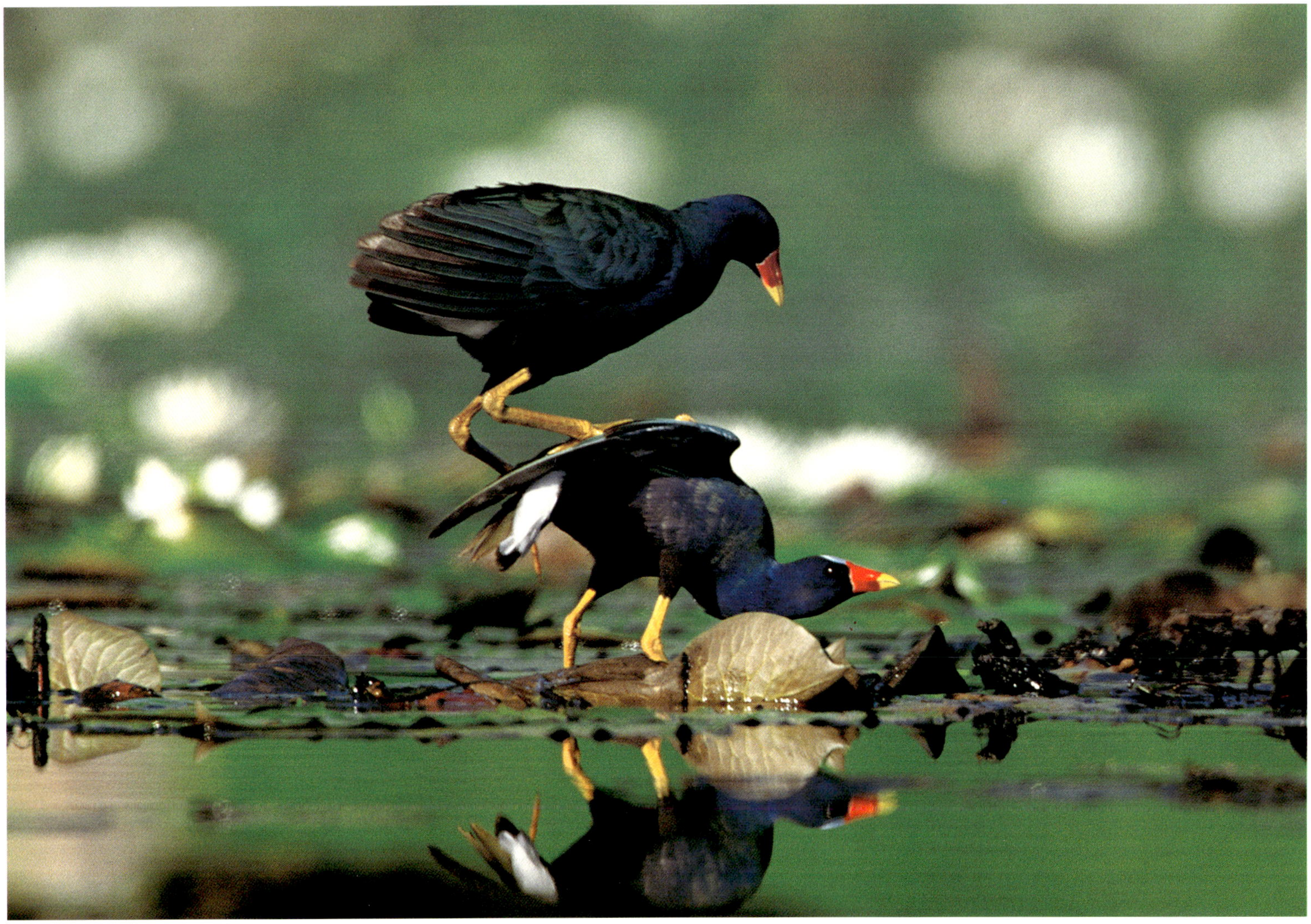

Purple gallinules in courtship

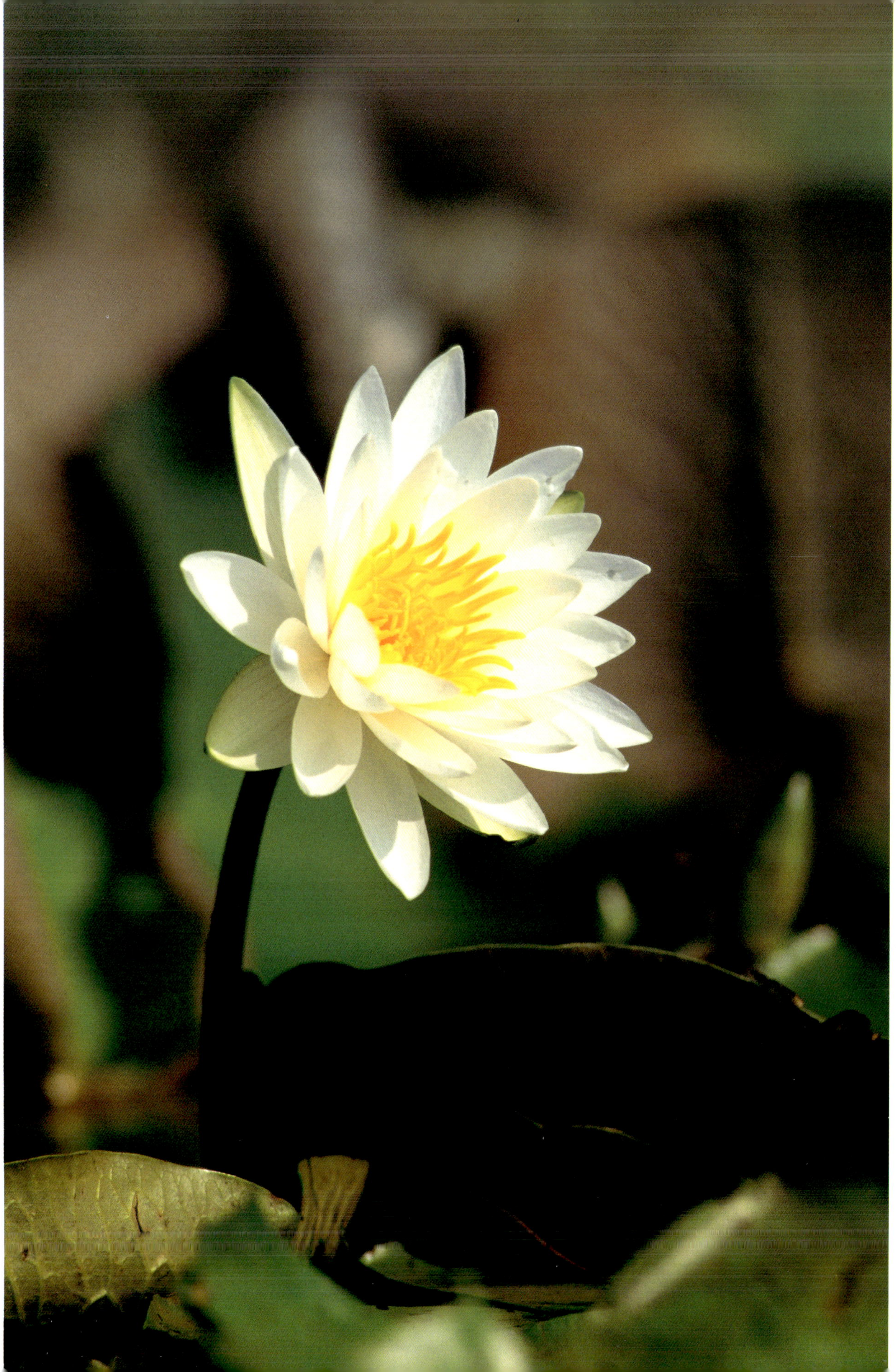

Fragrant water lily

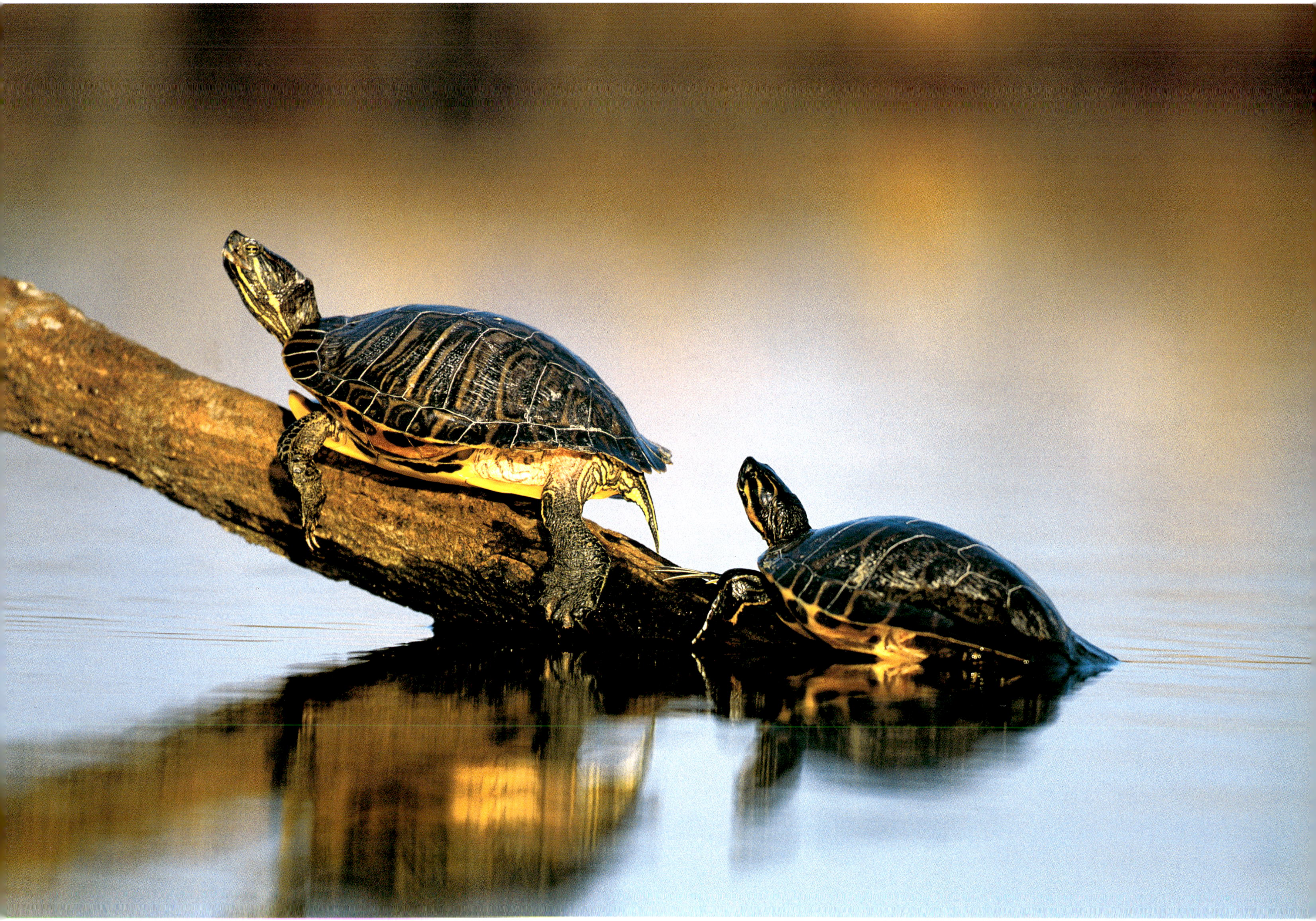

Red-eared sliders

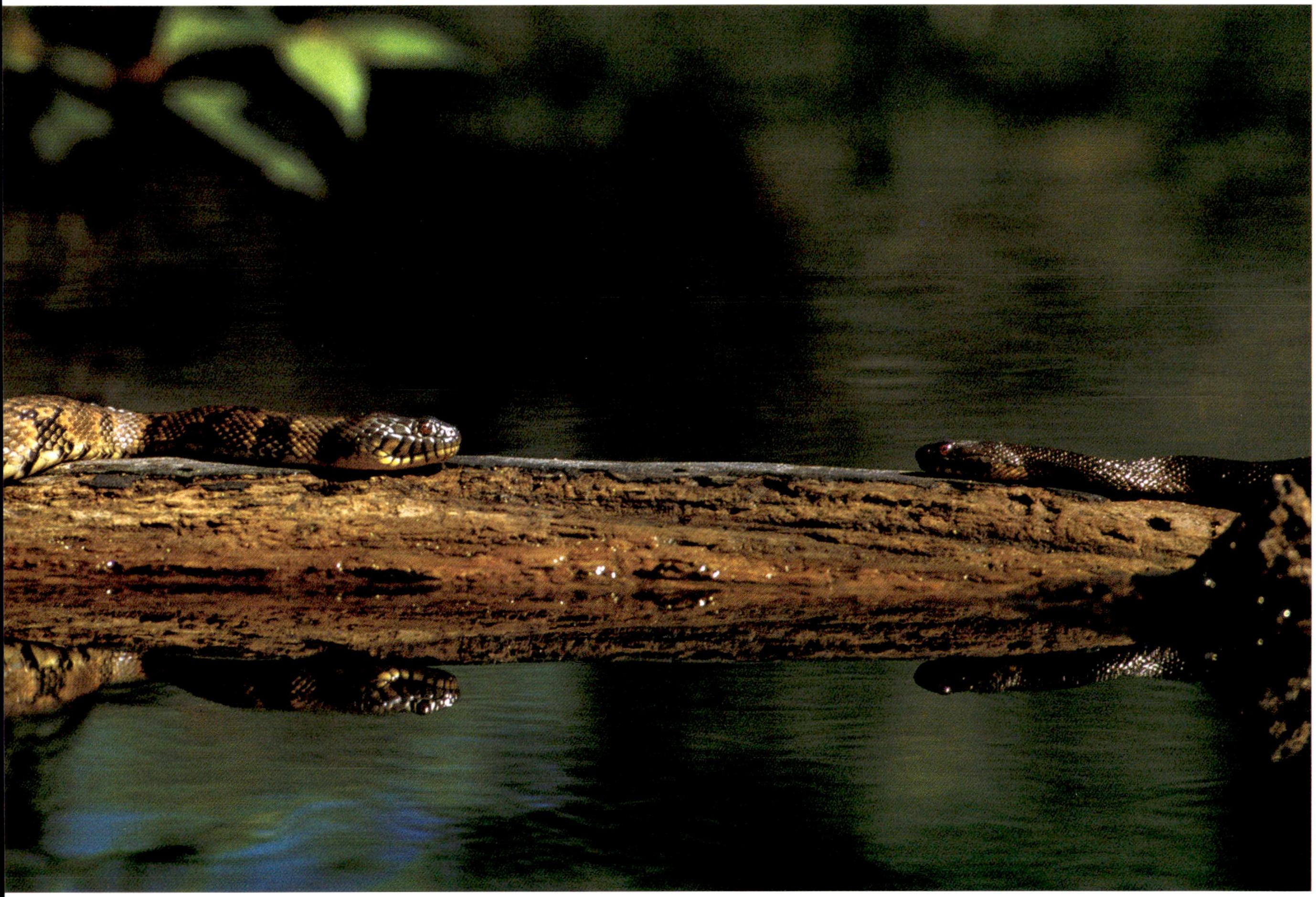

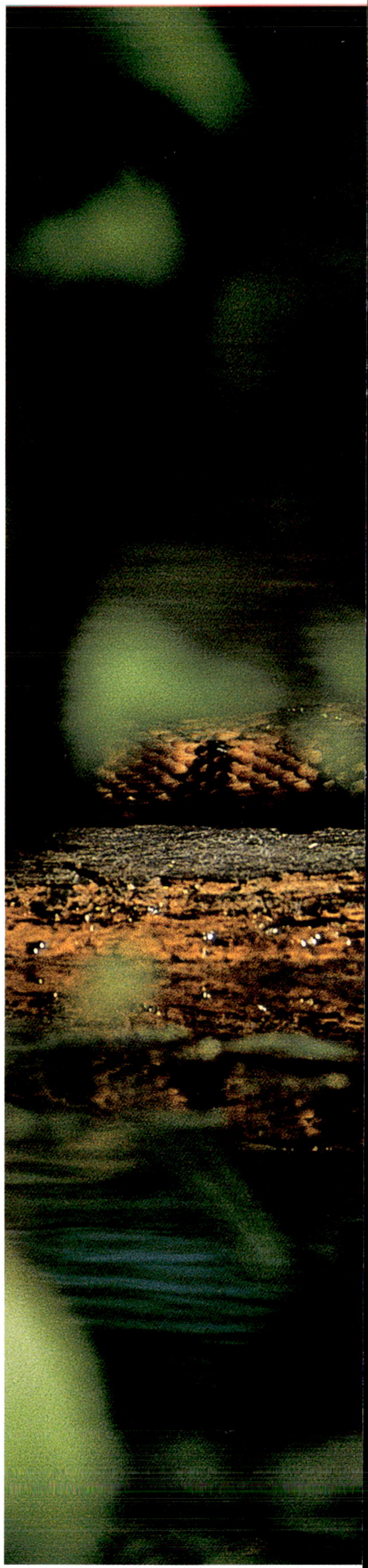

Diamondback water snakes

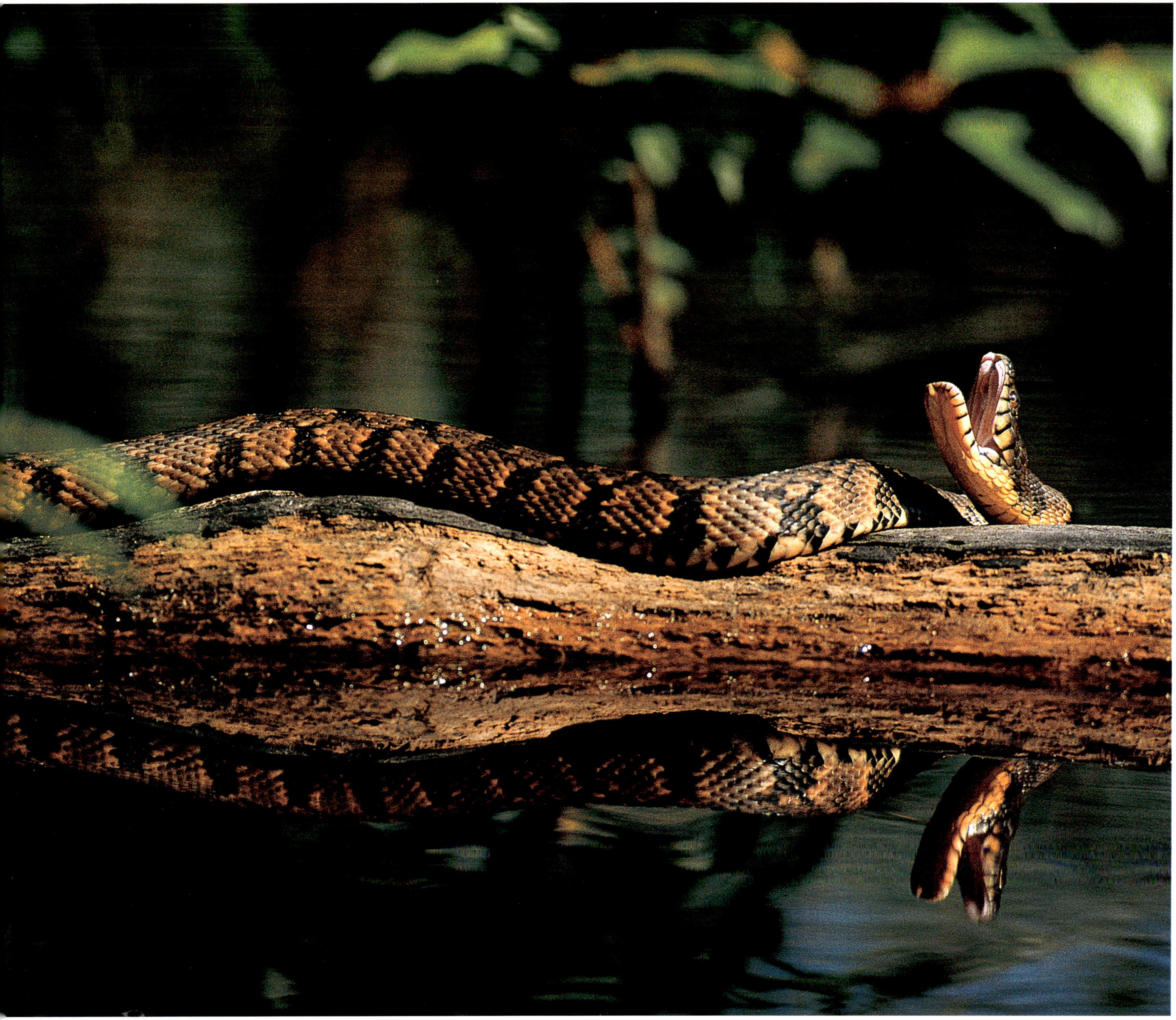

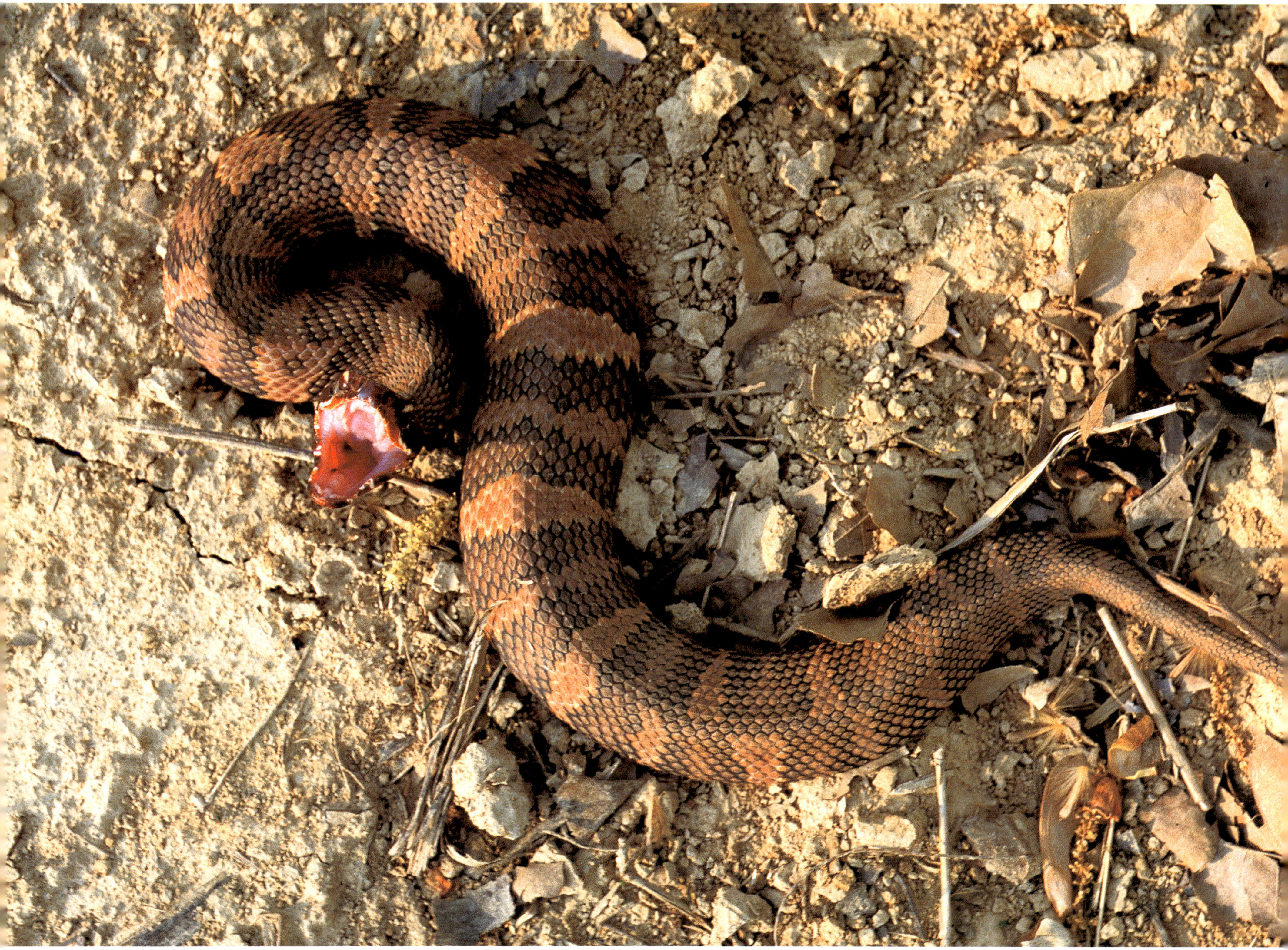

Water moccasin

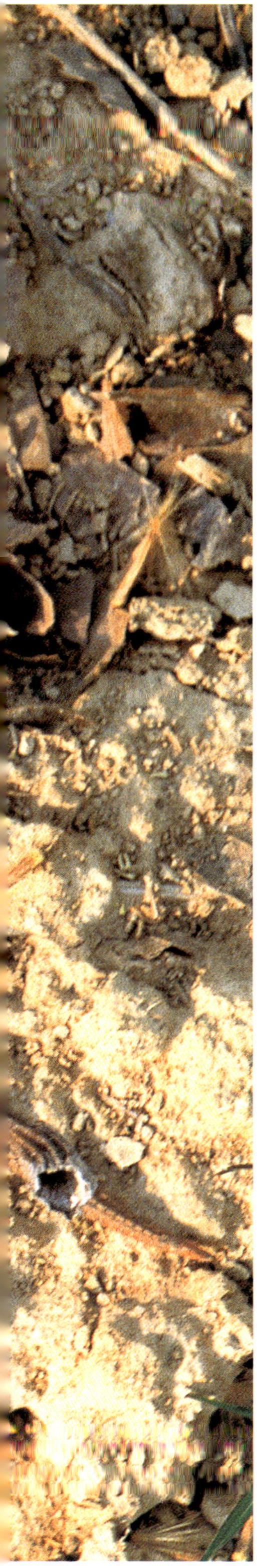

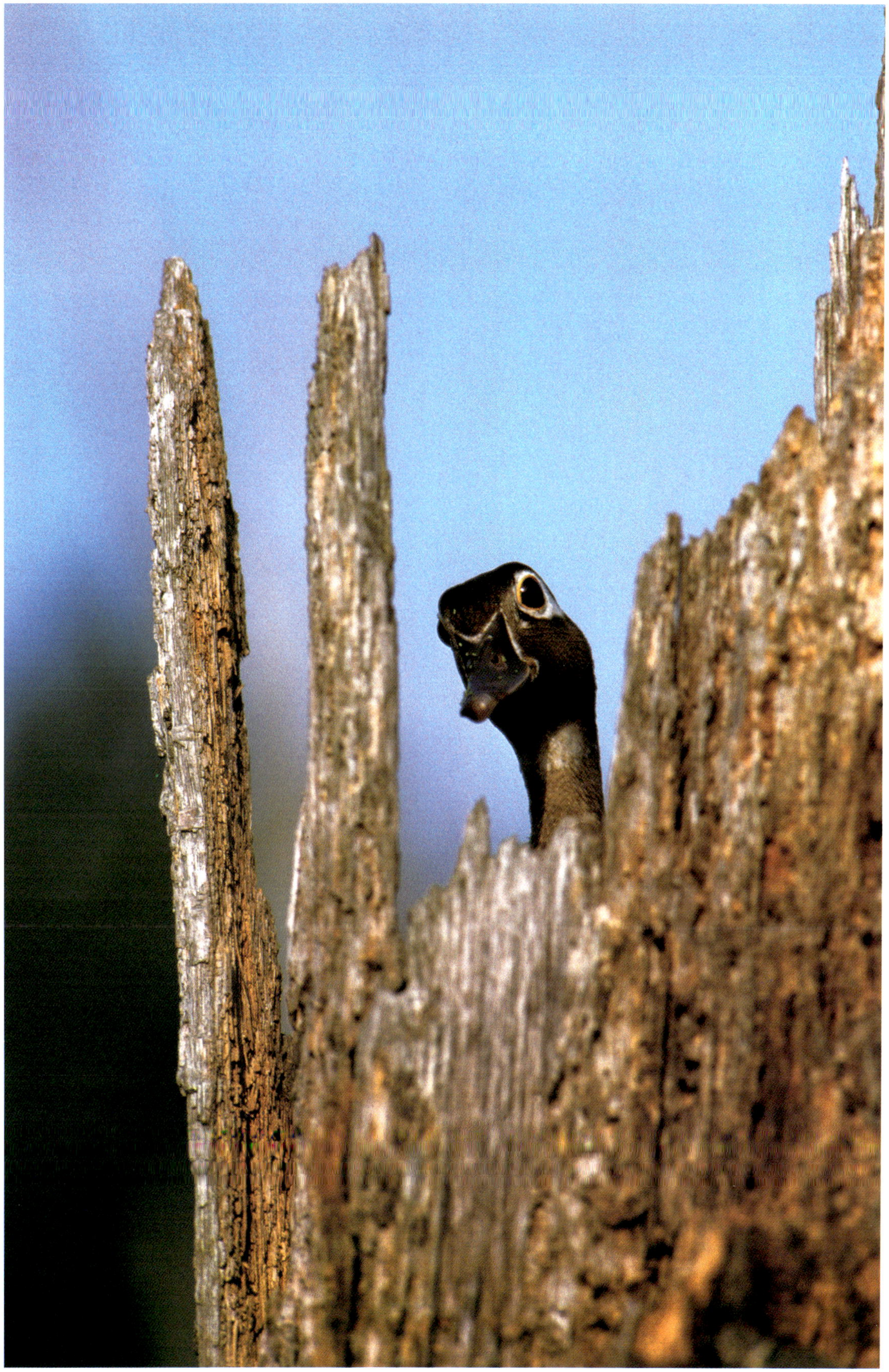

Wood duck on nest in tree cavity

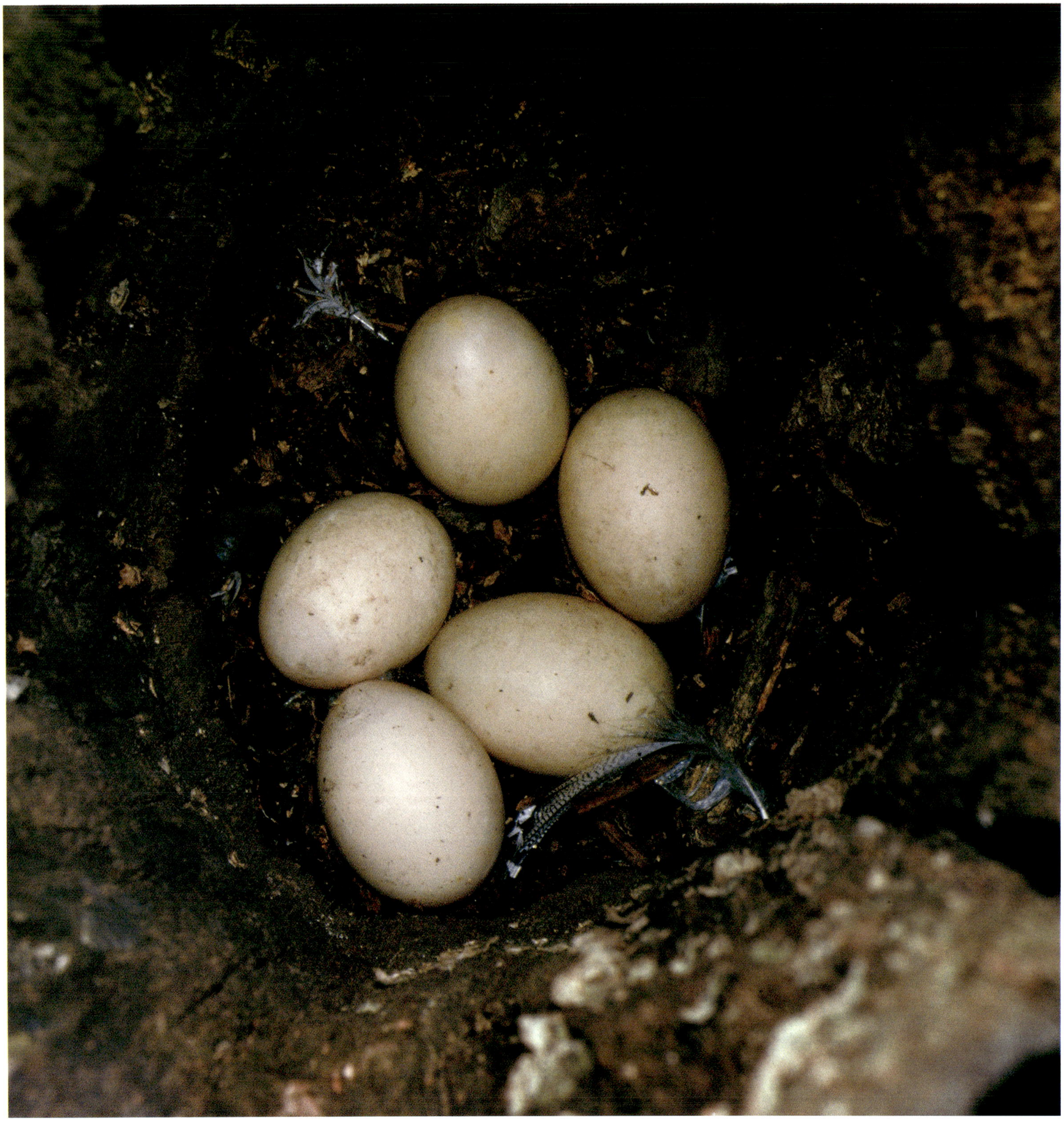

Wood duck eggs in nesting tree cavity

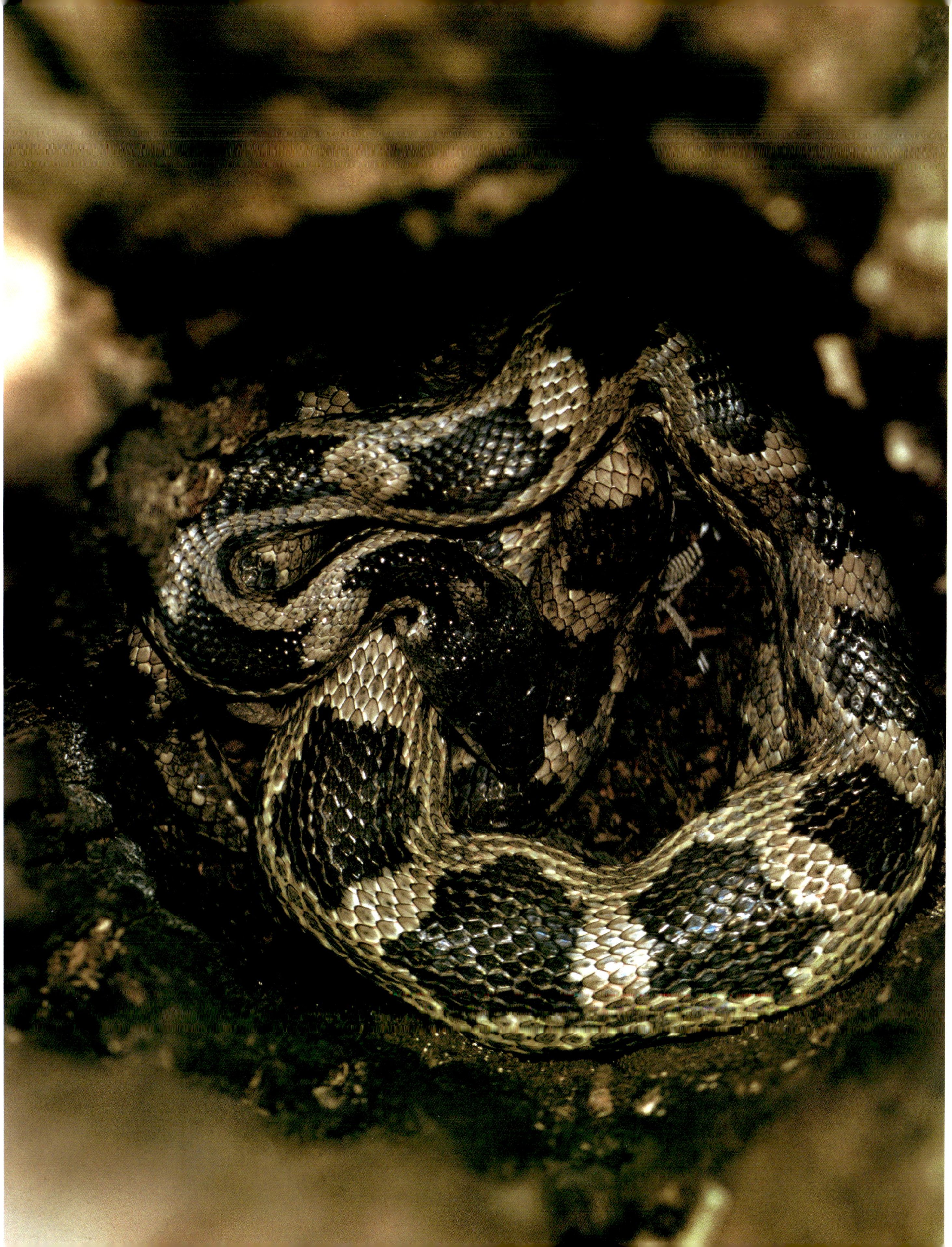

Gray rat snake with
wood duck eggs in stomach
in nesting tree cavity

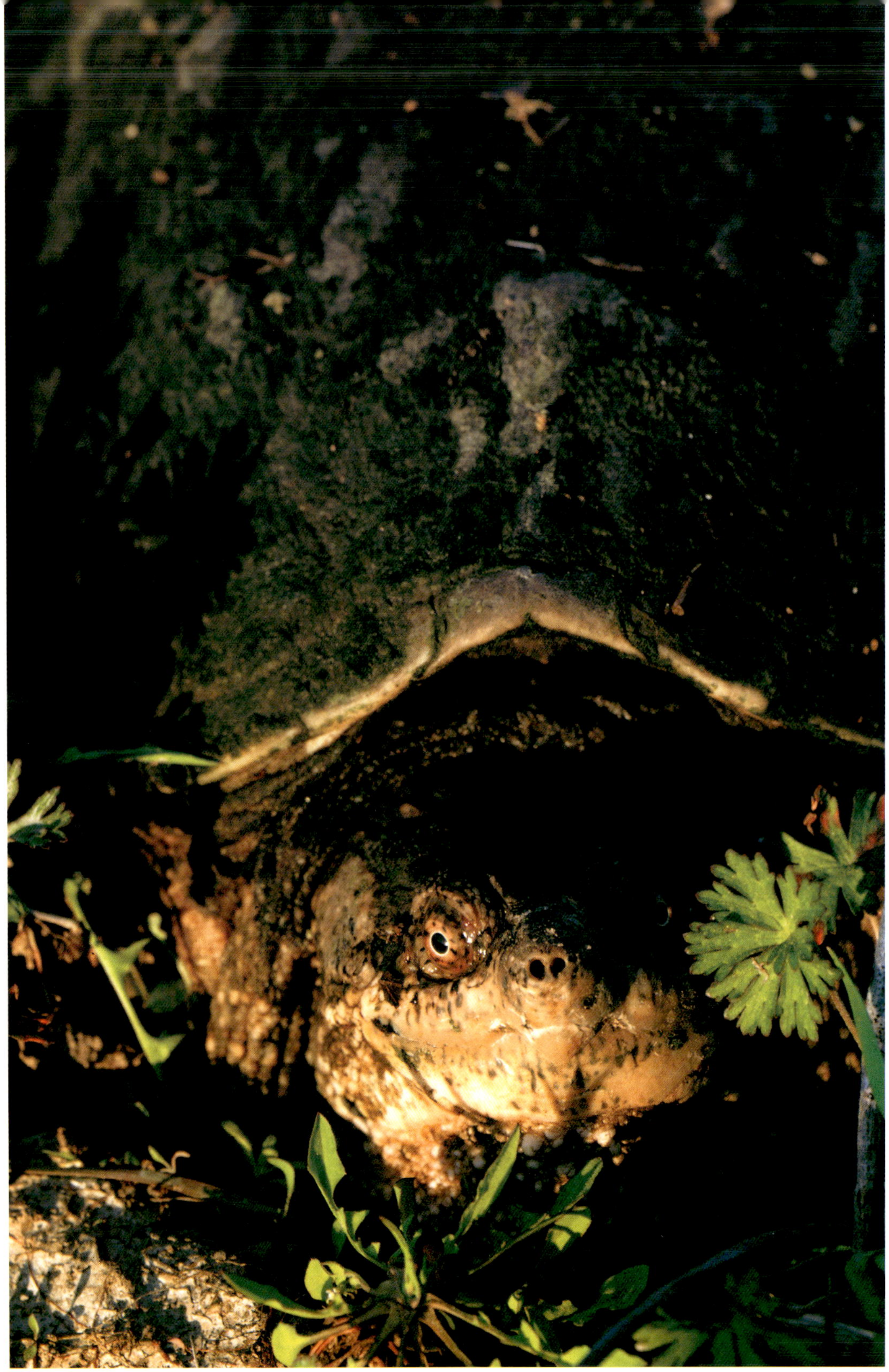

Snapping turtle

American alligator

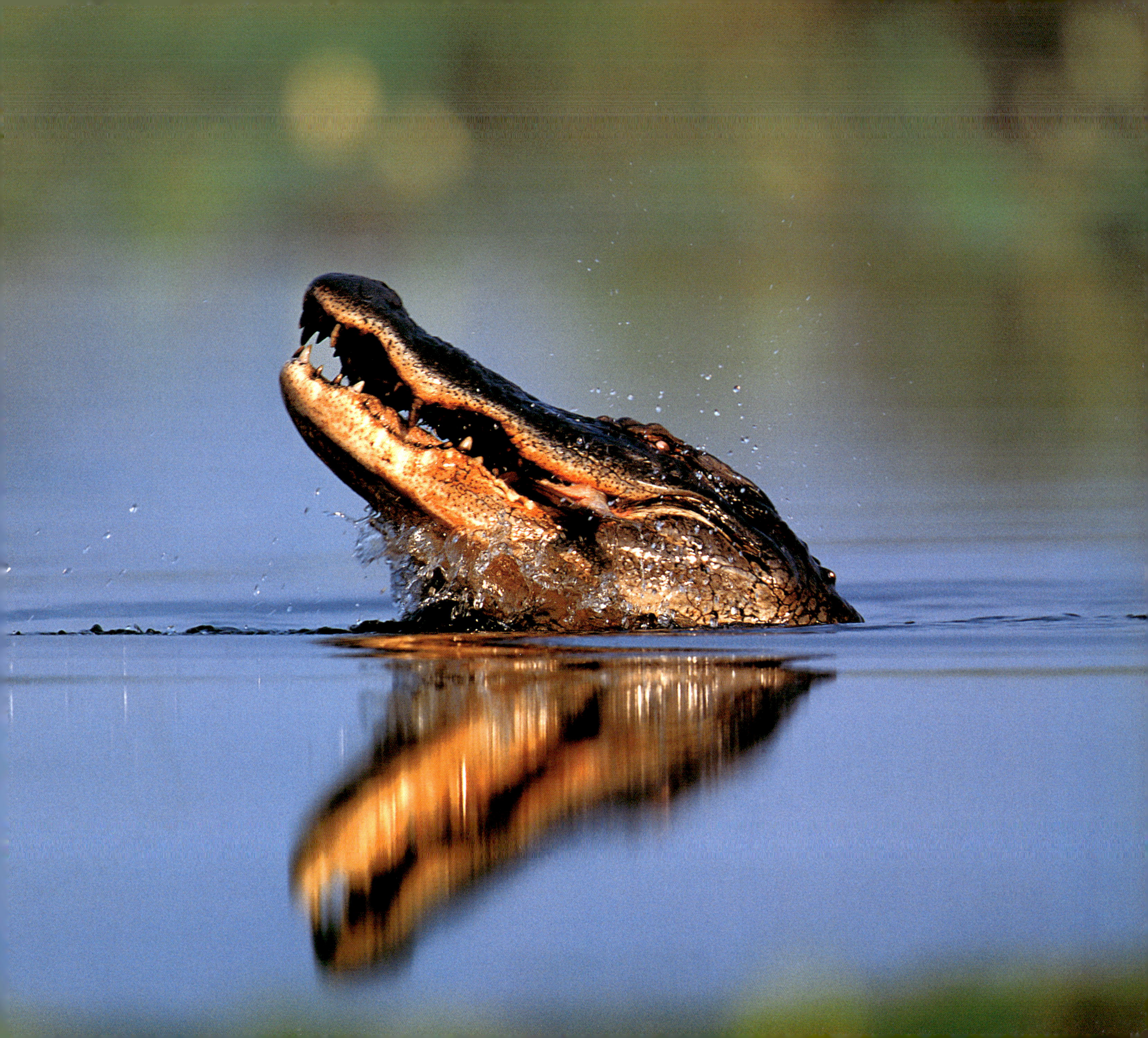

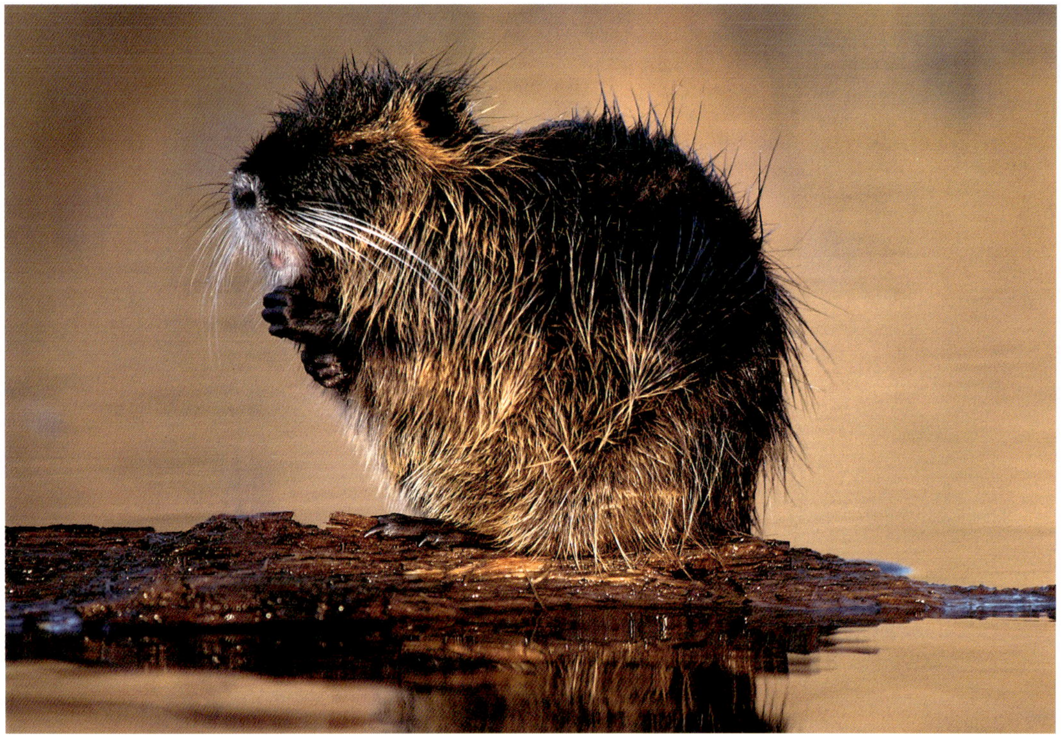

Nutria

Hooded merganser

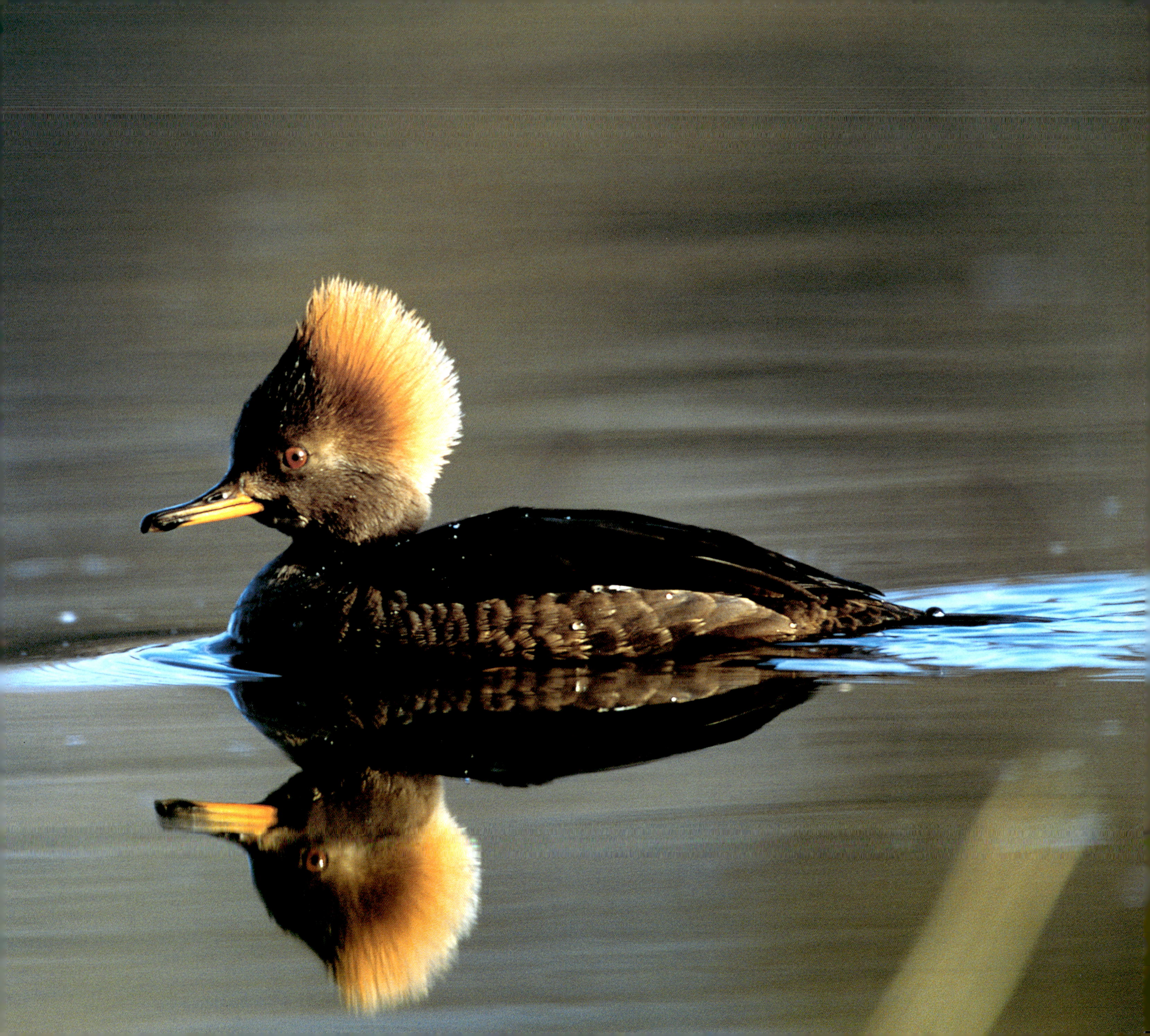

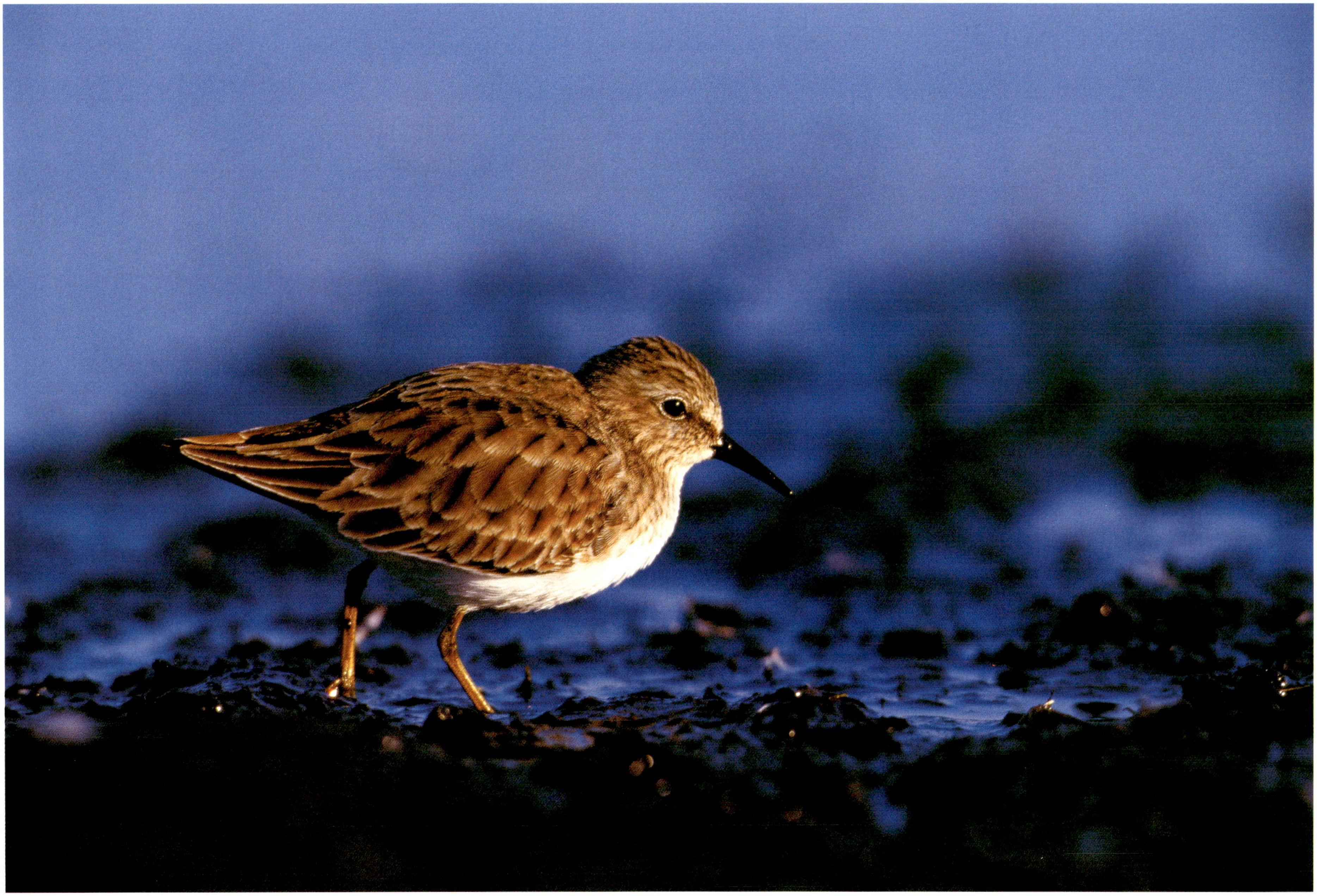

Least sandpiper

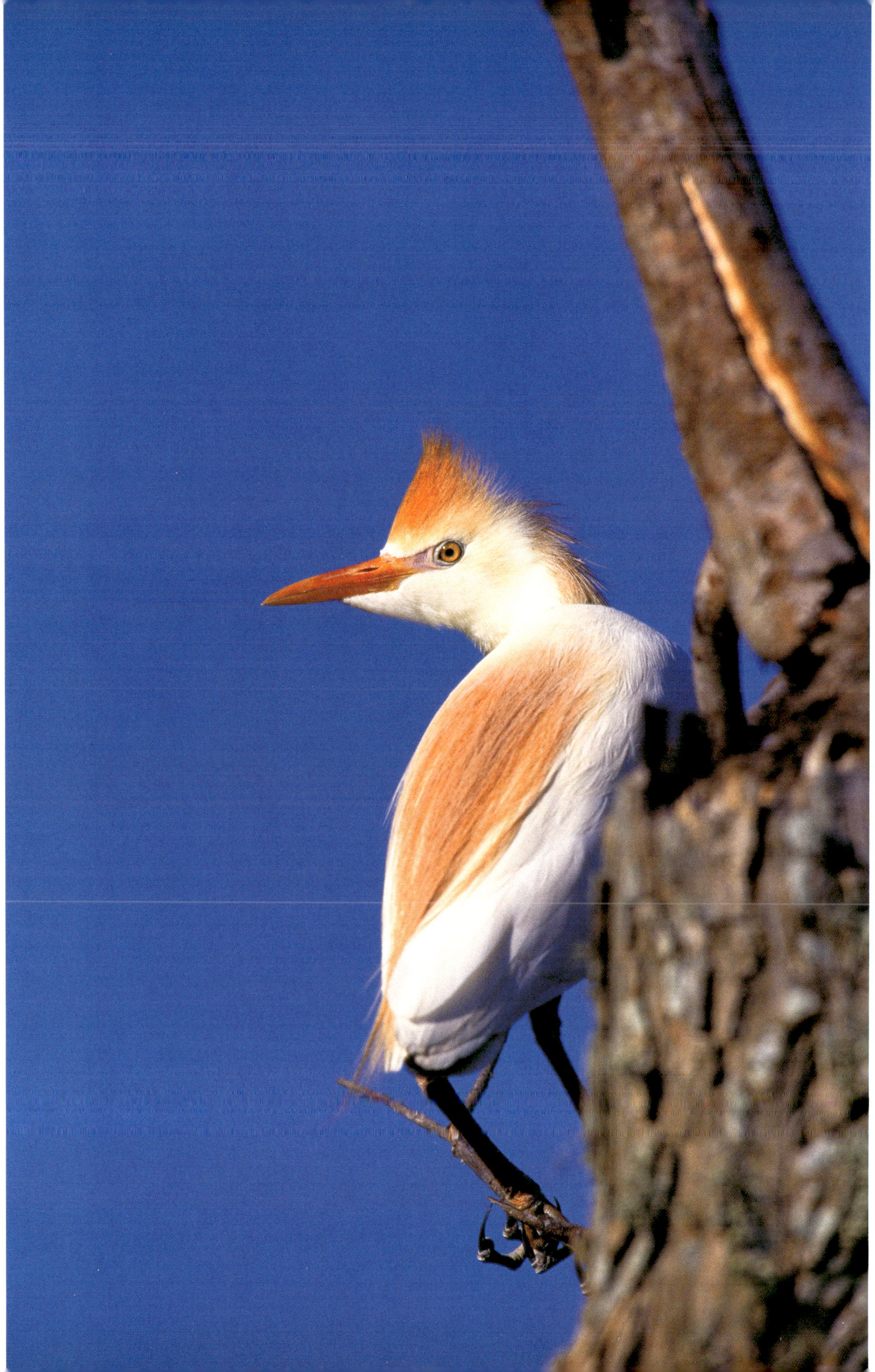

Cattle egret

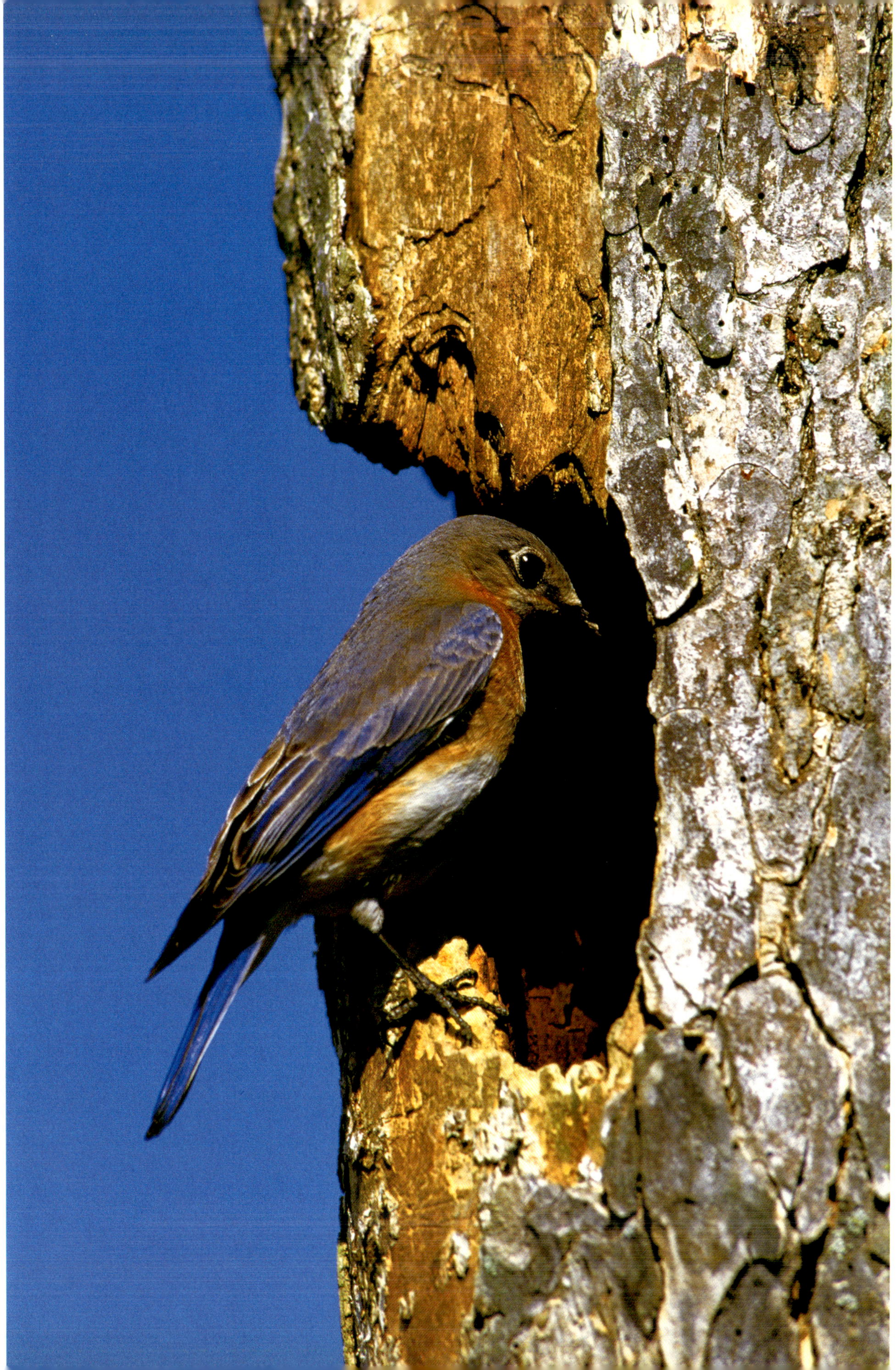

Eastern bluebird

Hooded merganser

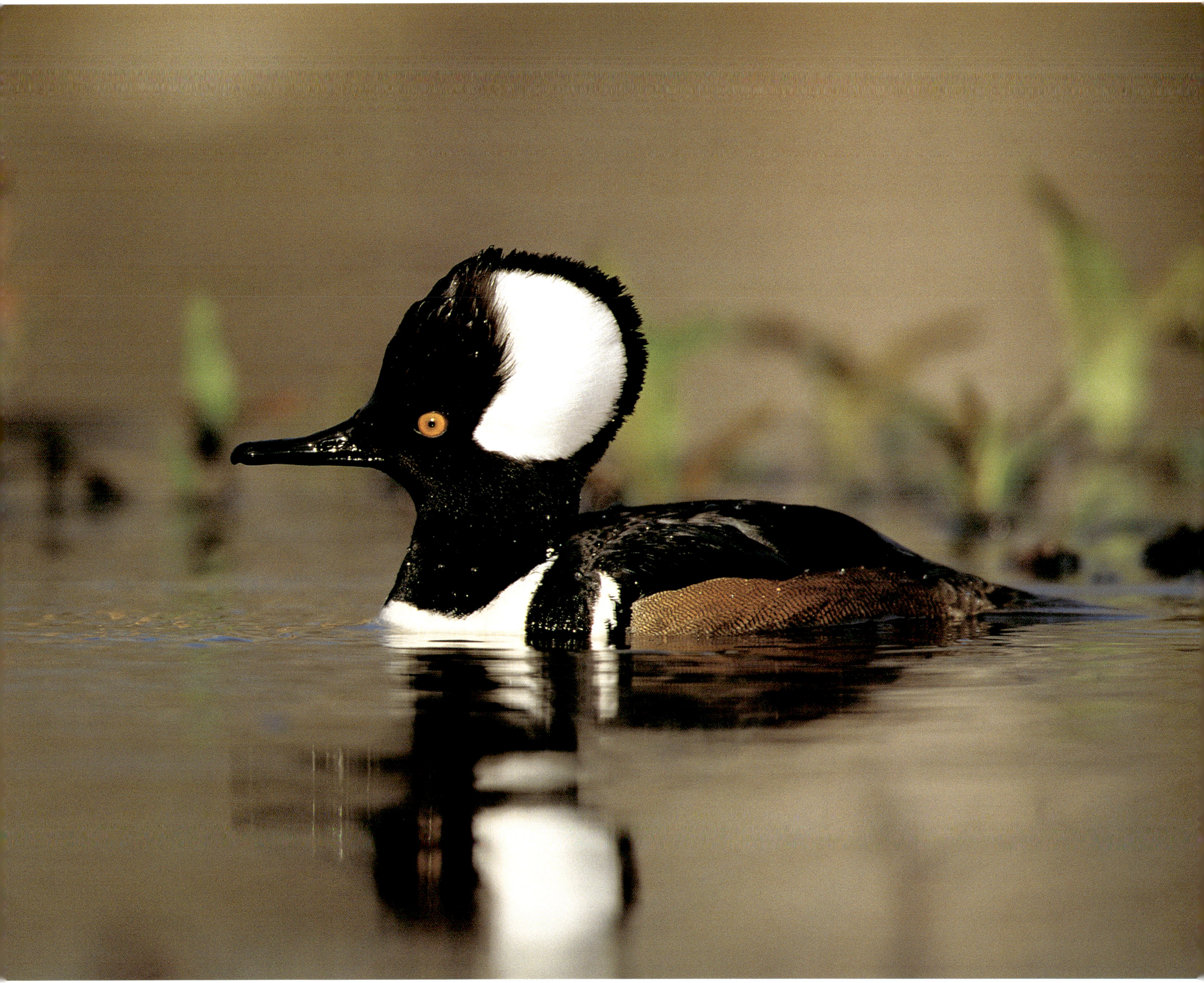

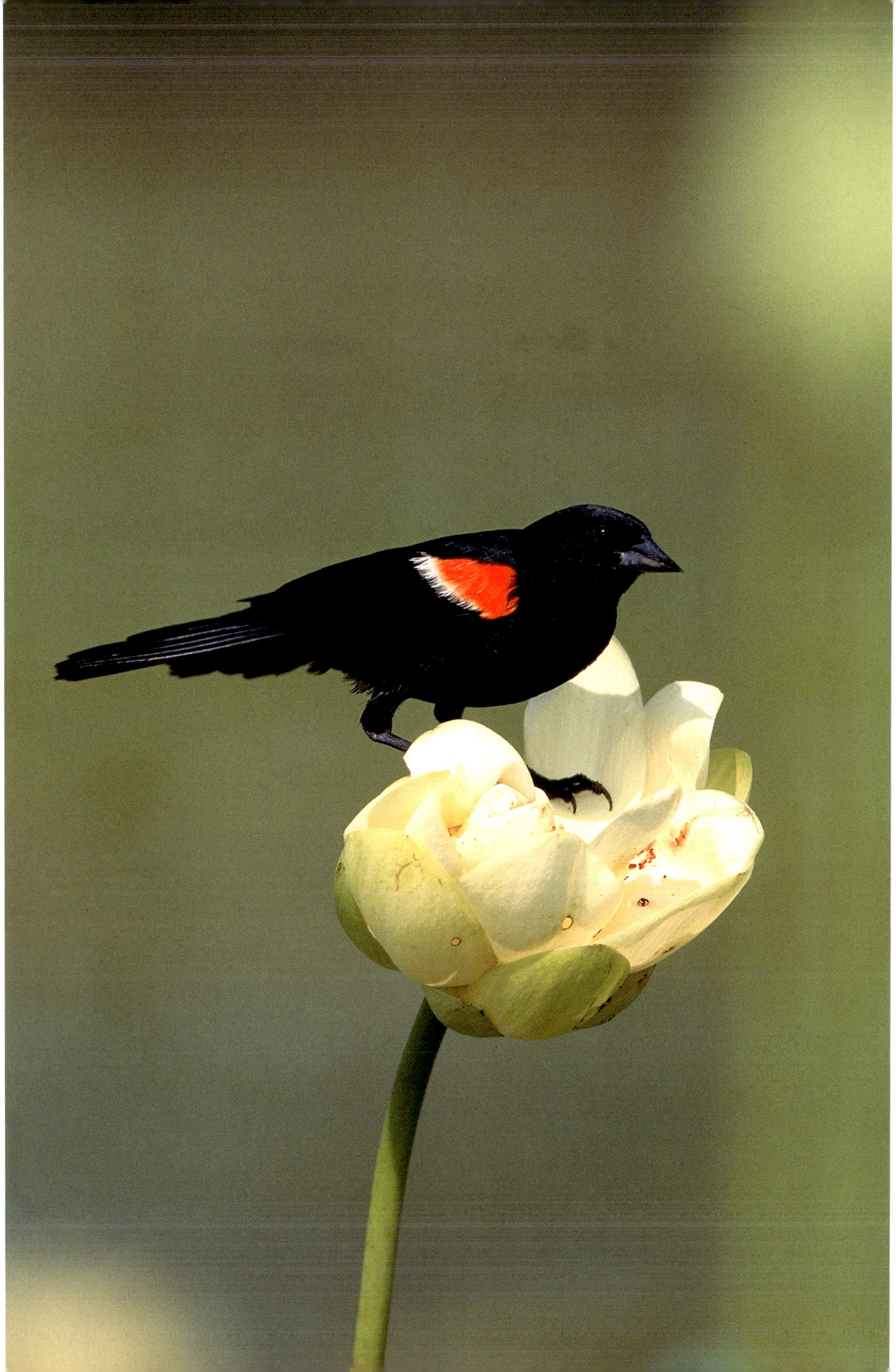

Red-winged blackbird on lotus

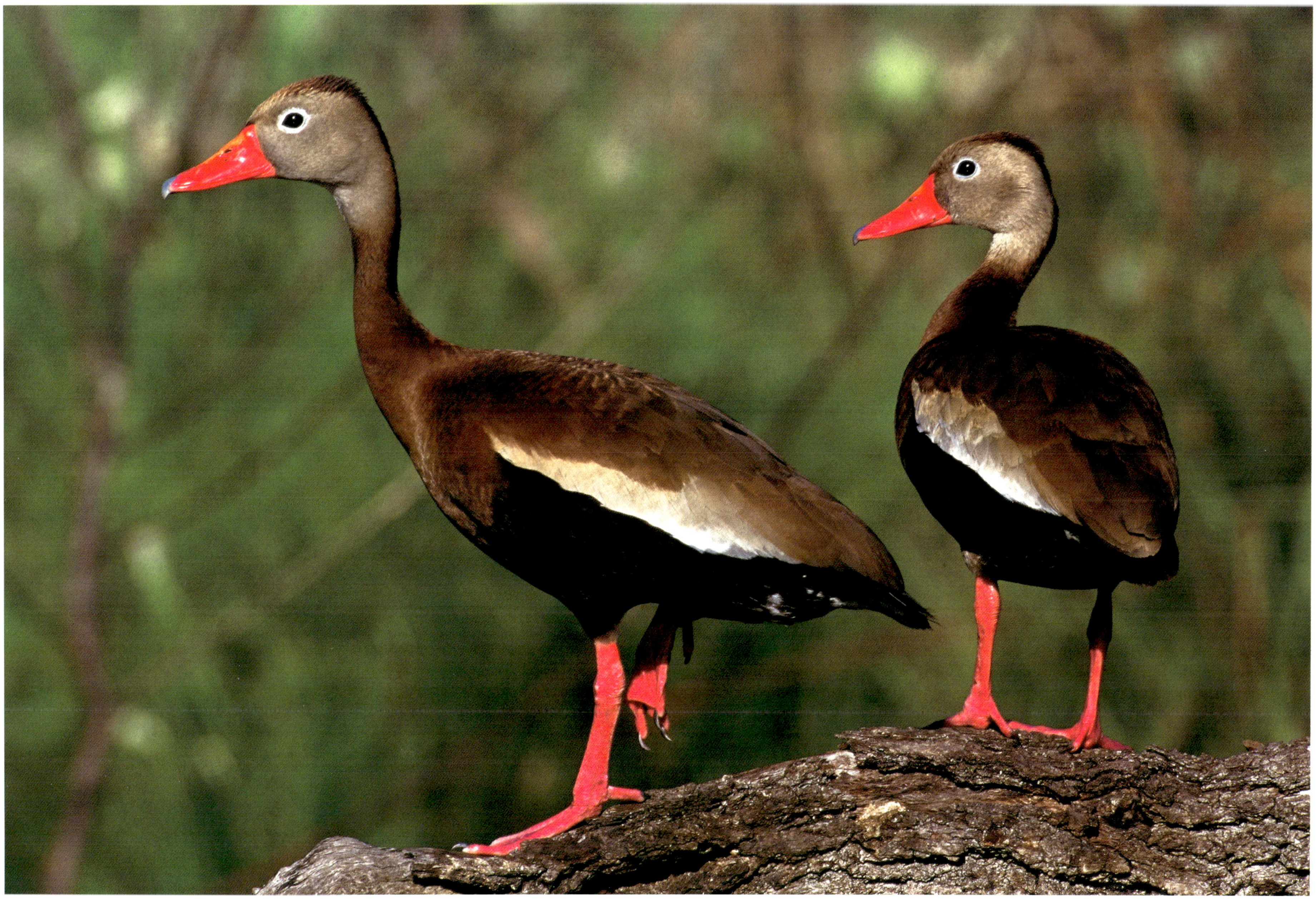

Black-bellied whistling ducks

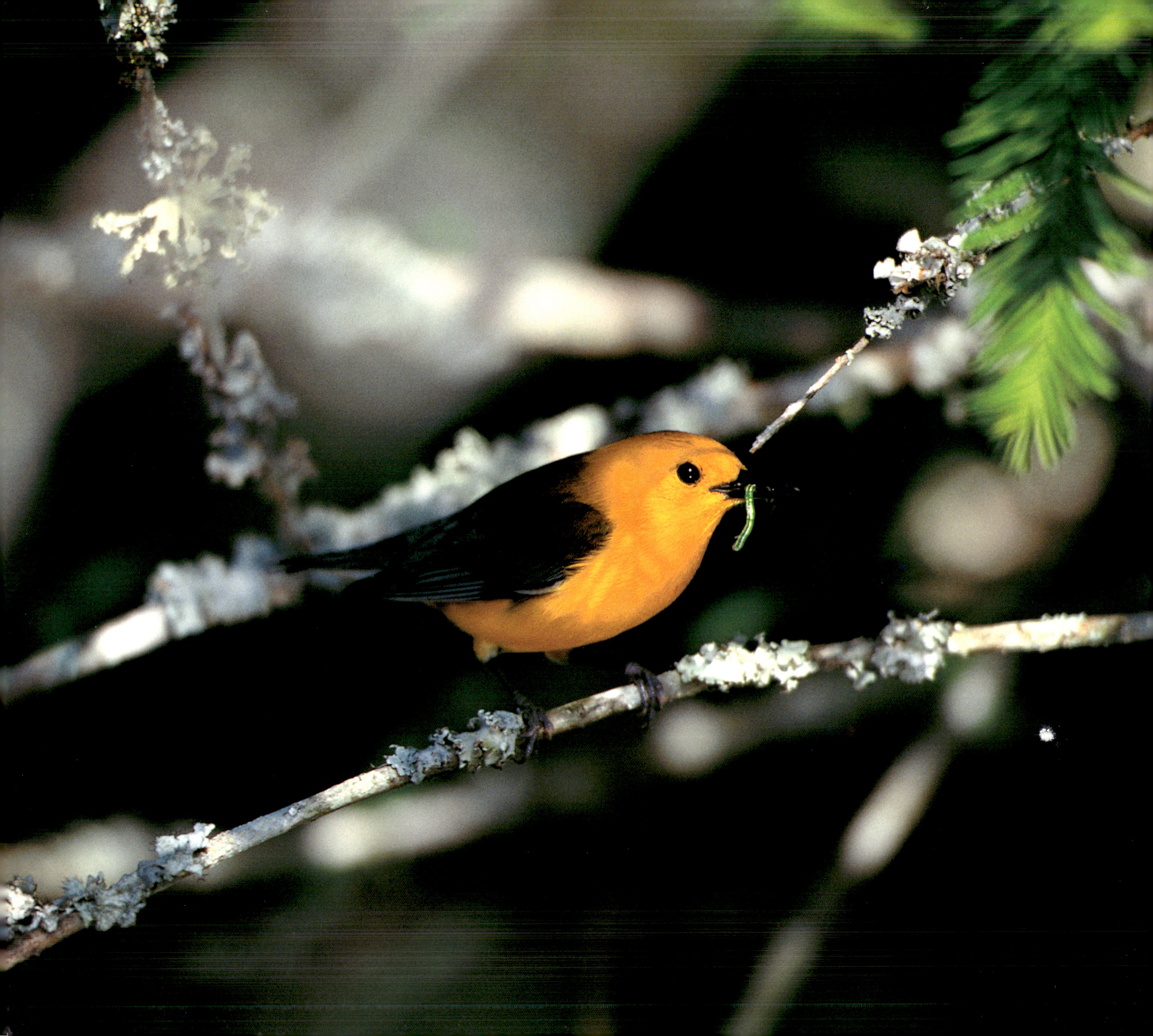

Prothonatary warbler

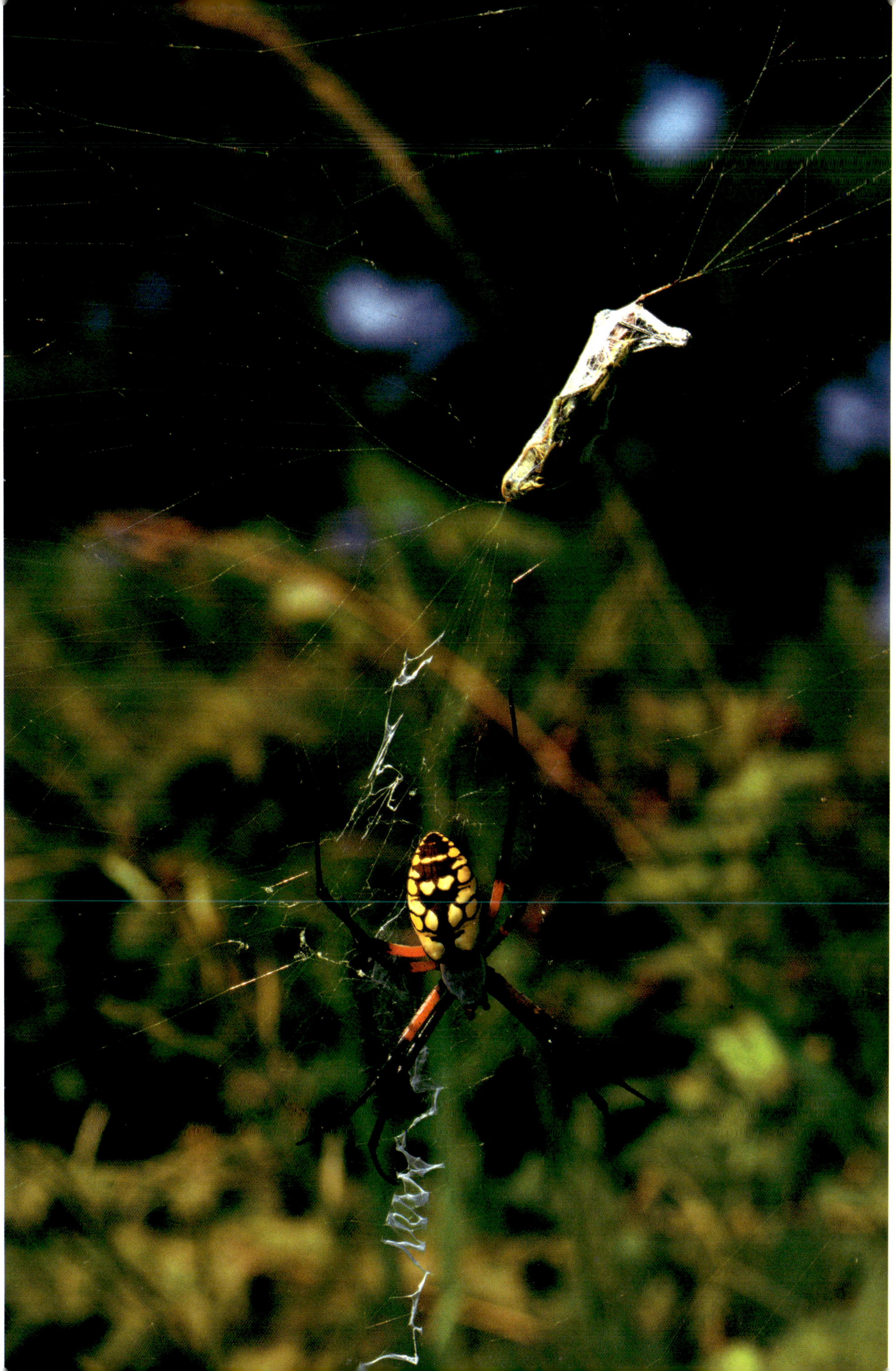

Garden spider with prey

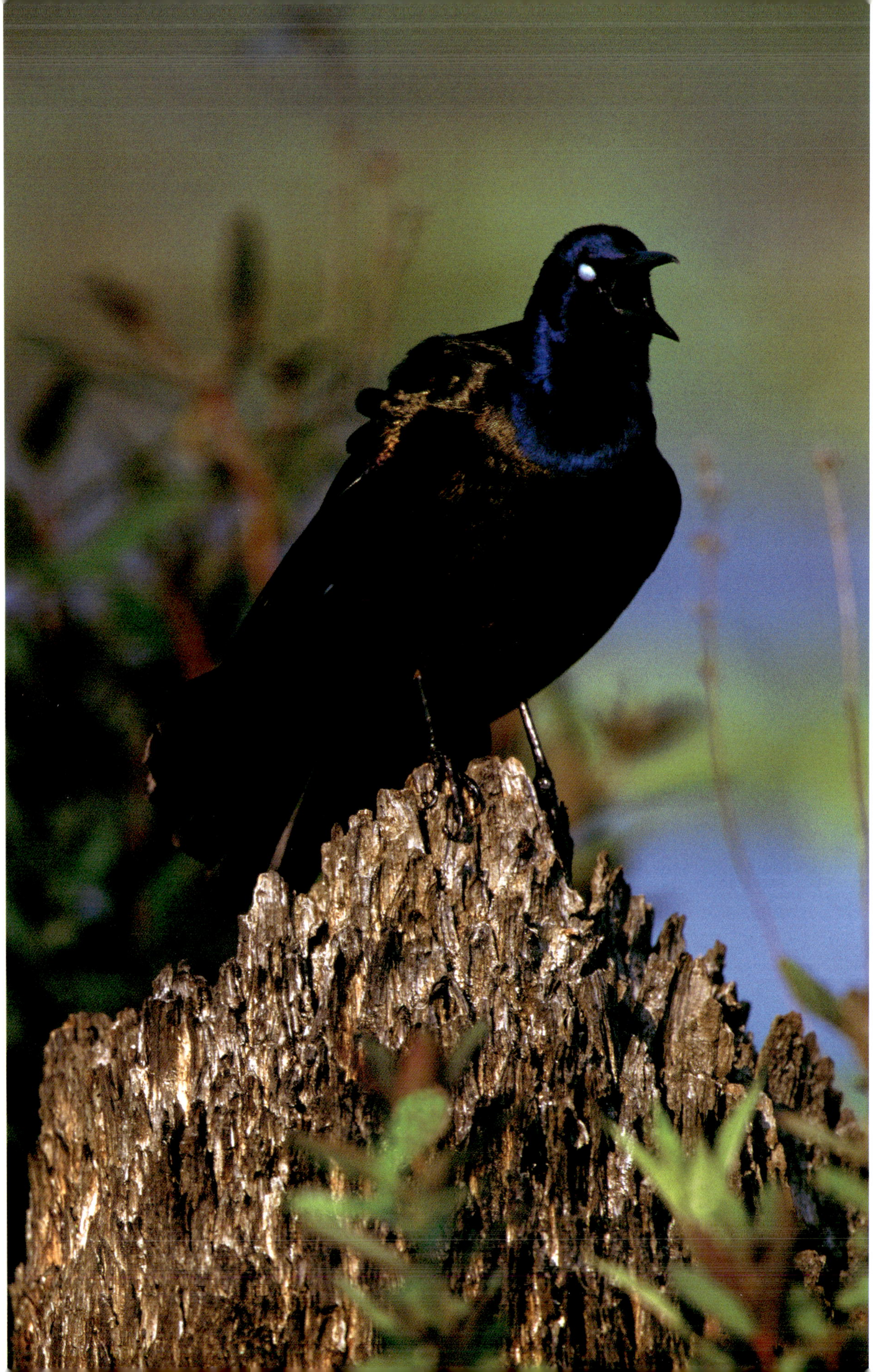

Common grackle

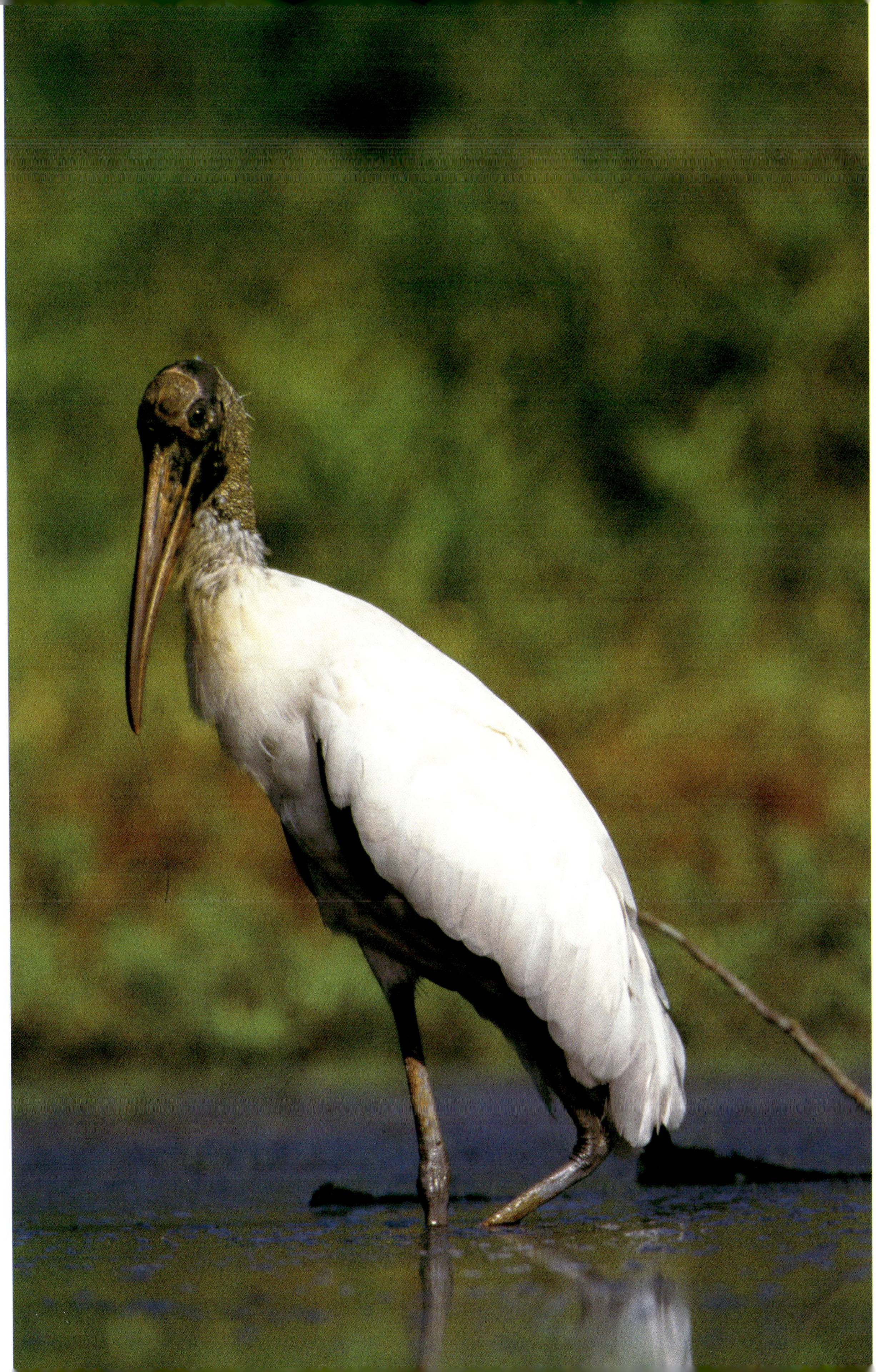

Wood stork

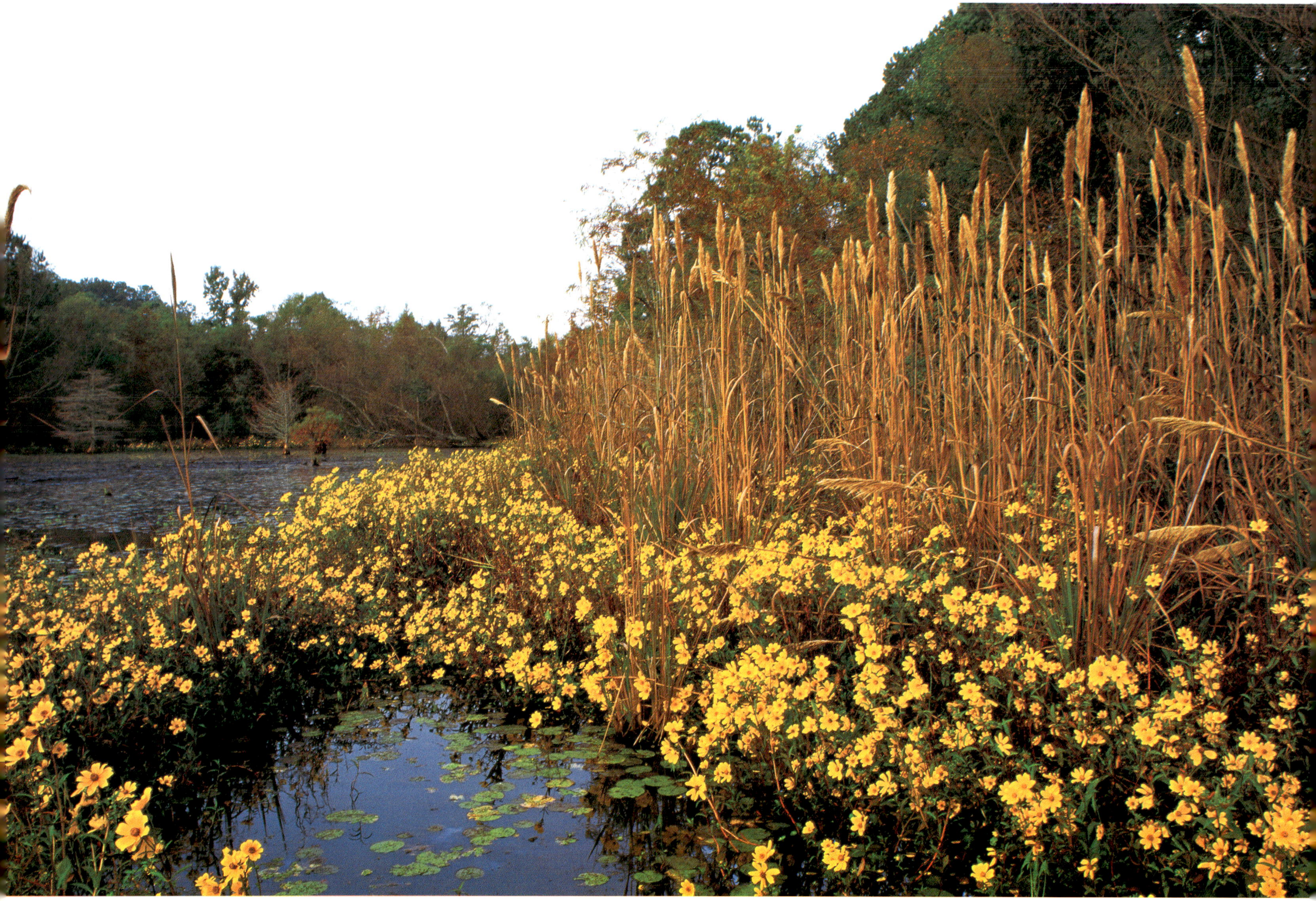

Sugarcane plumegrass and wildflowers

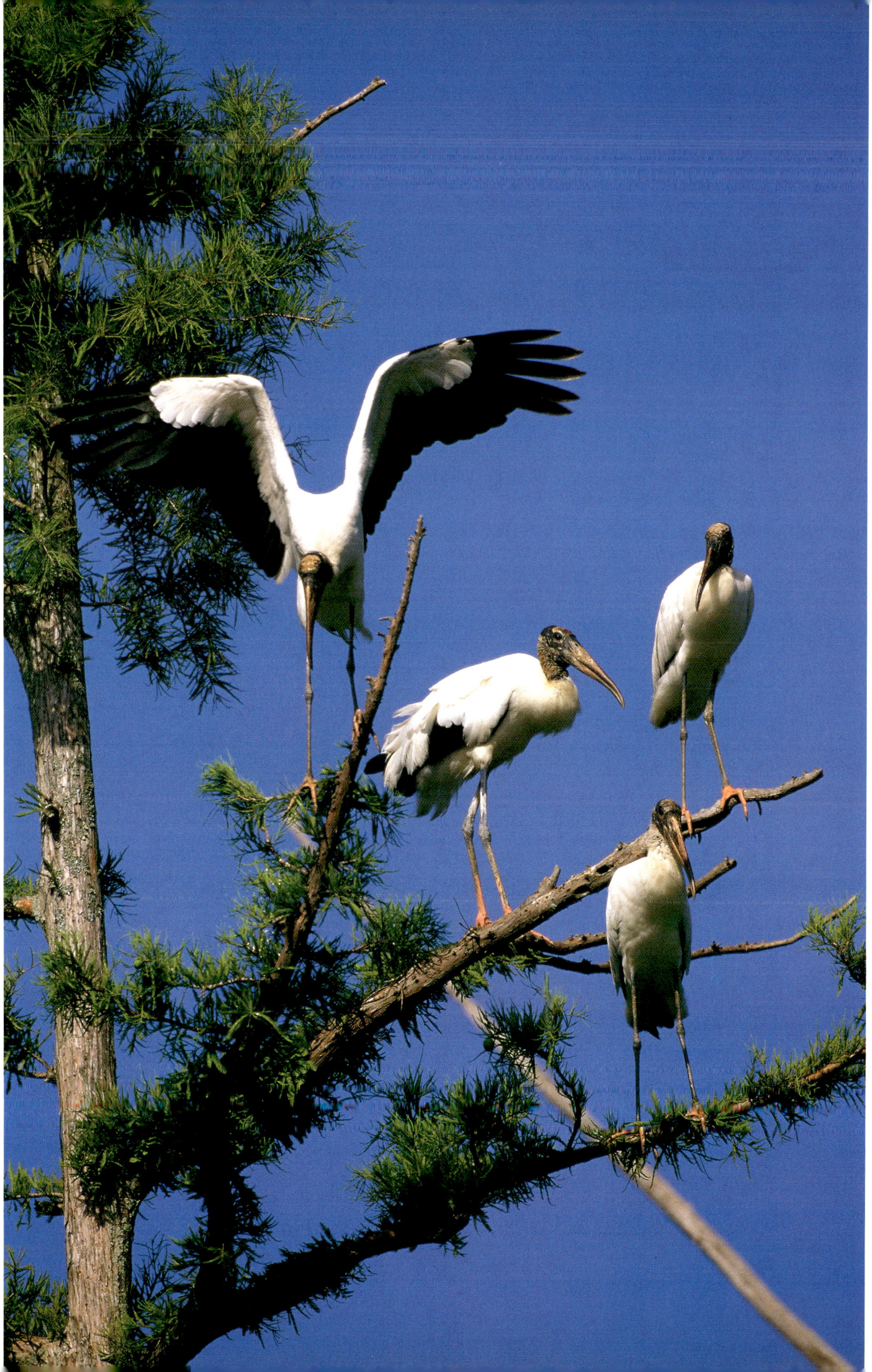

Wood storks

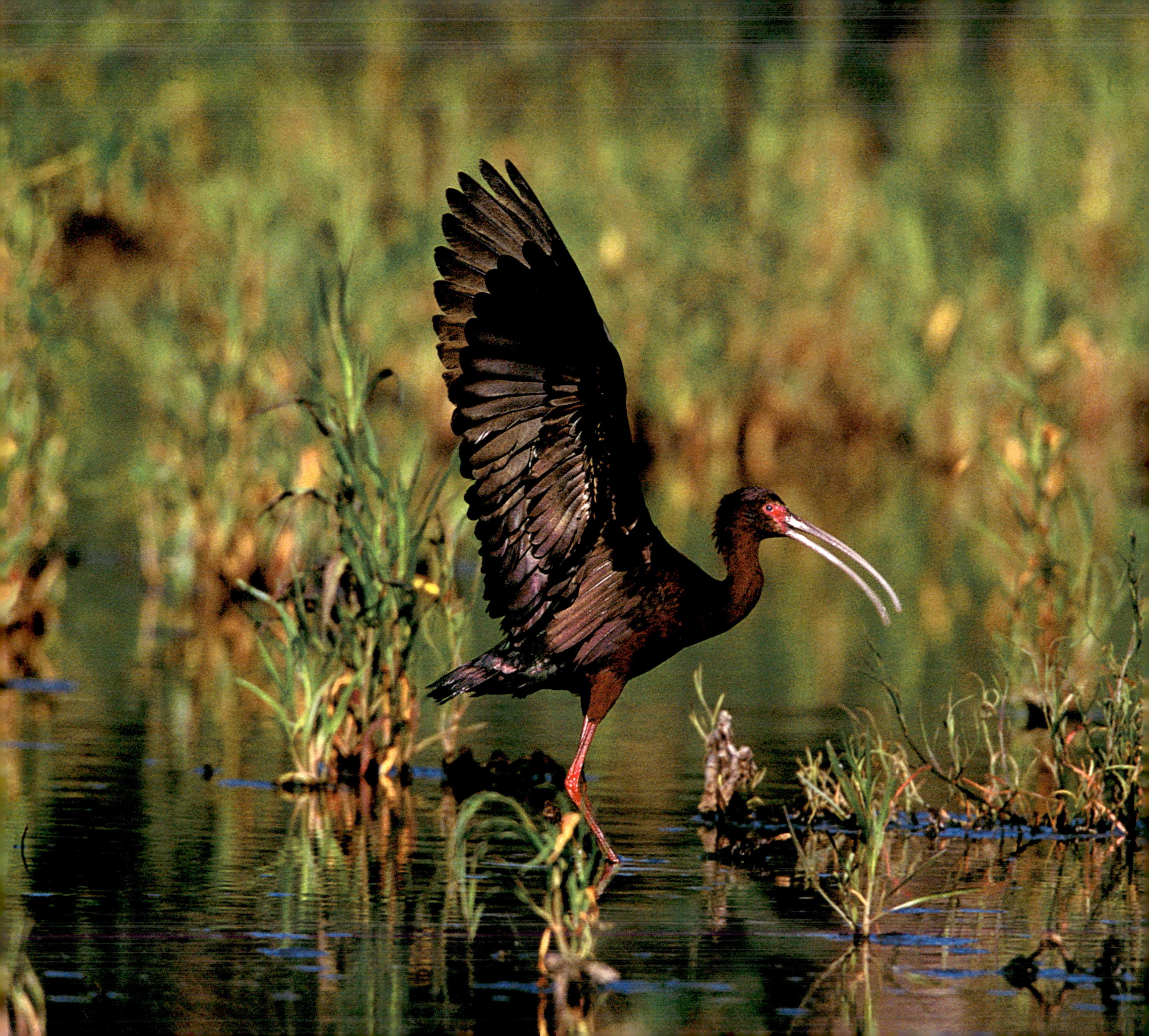

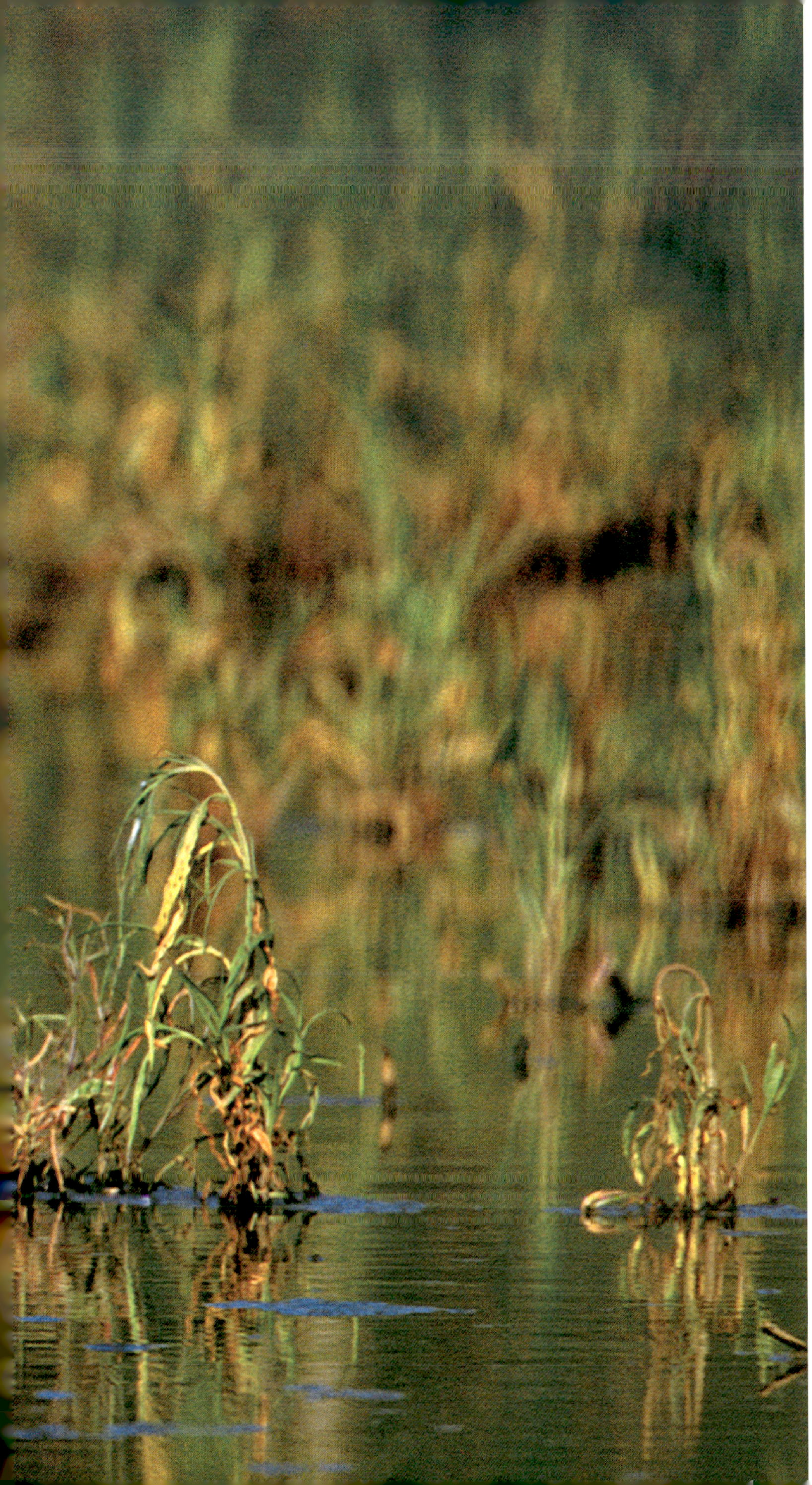

Dark ibis

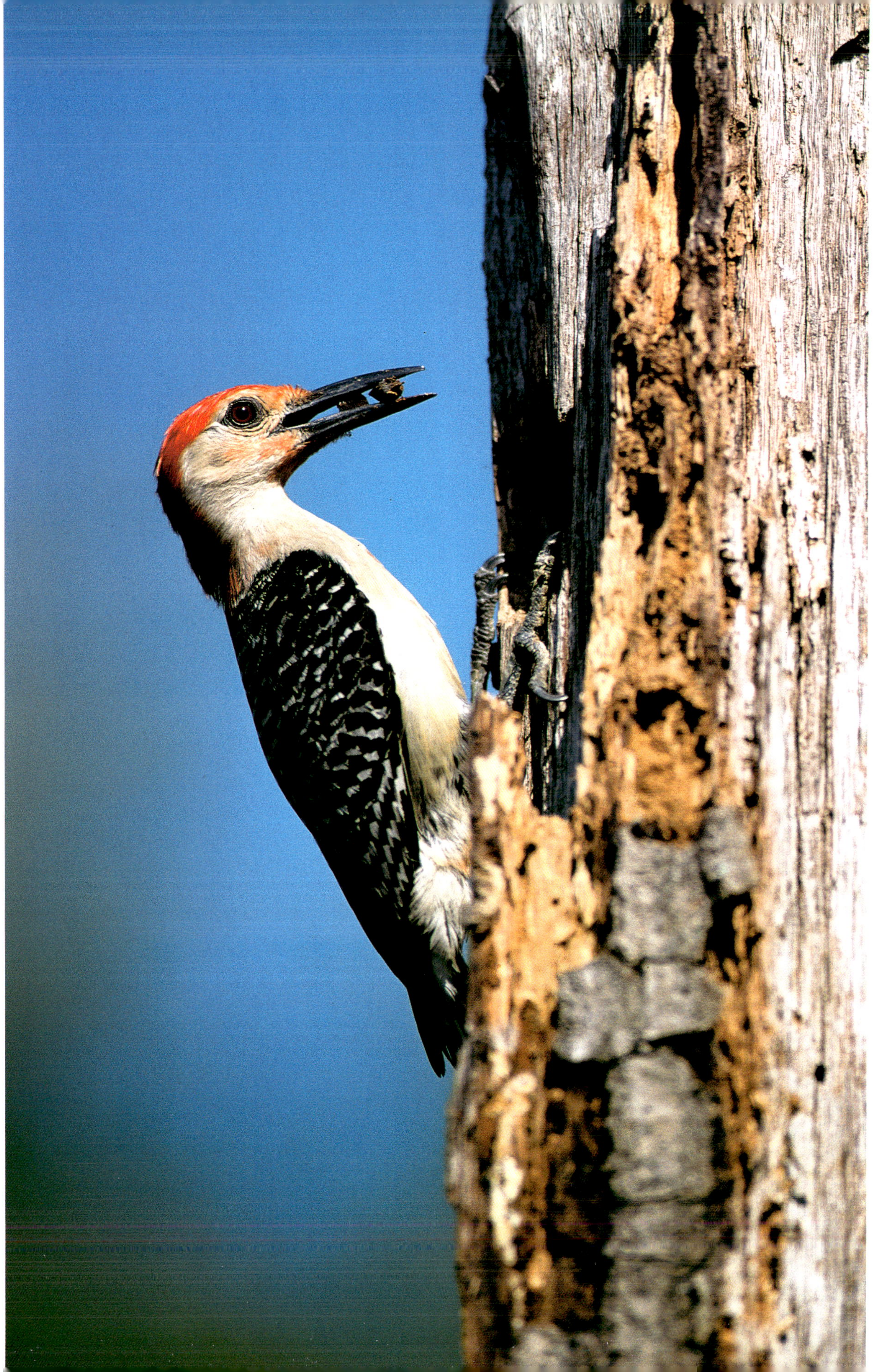

Red-bellied woodpecker

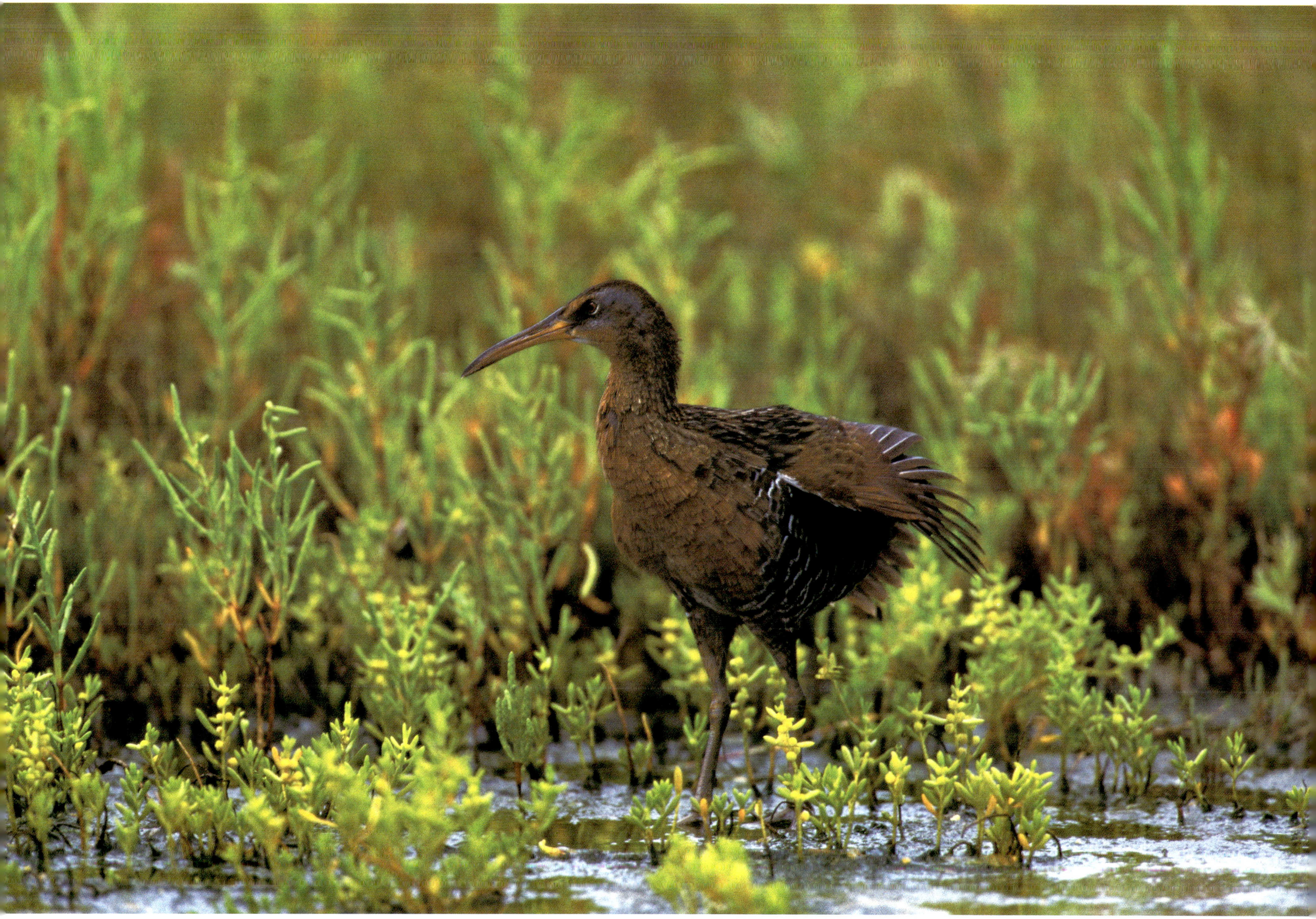

King rail

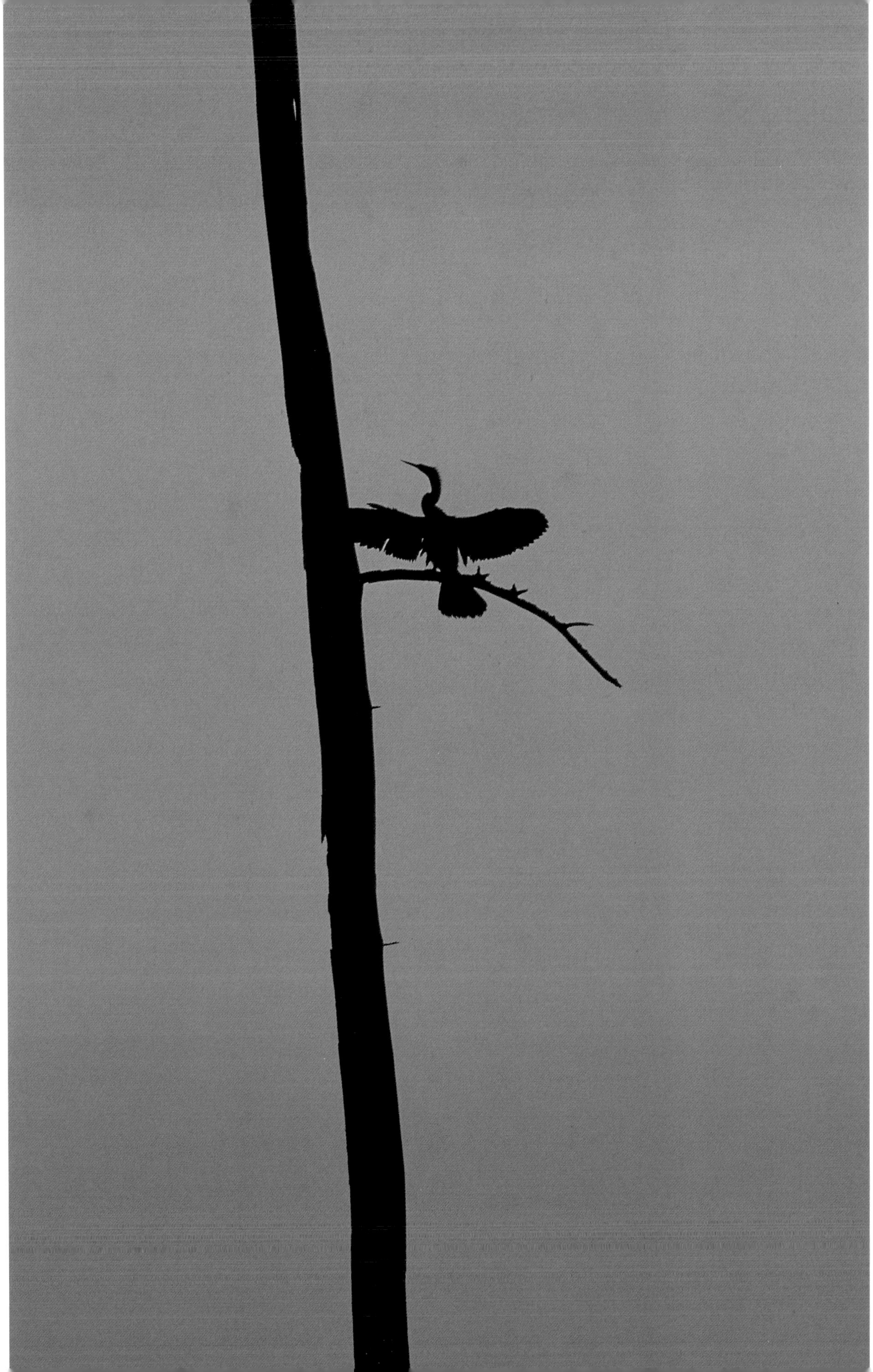

Anhinga

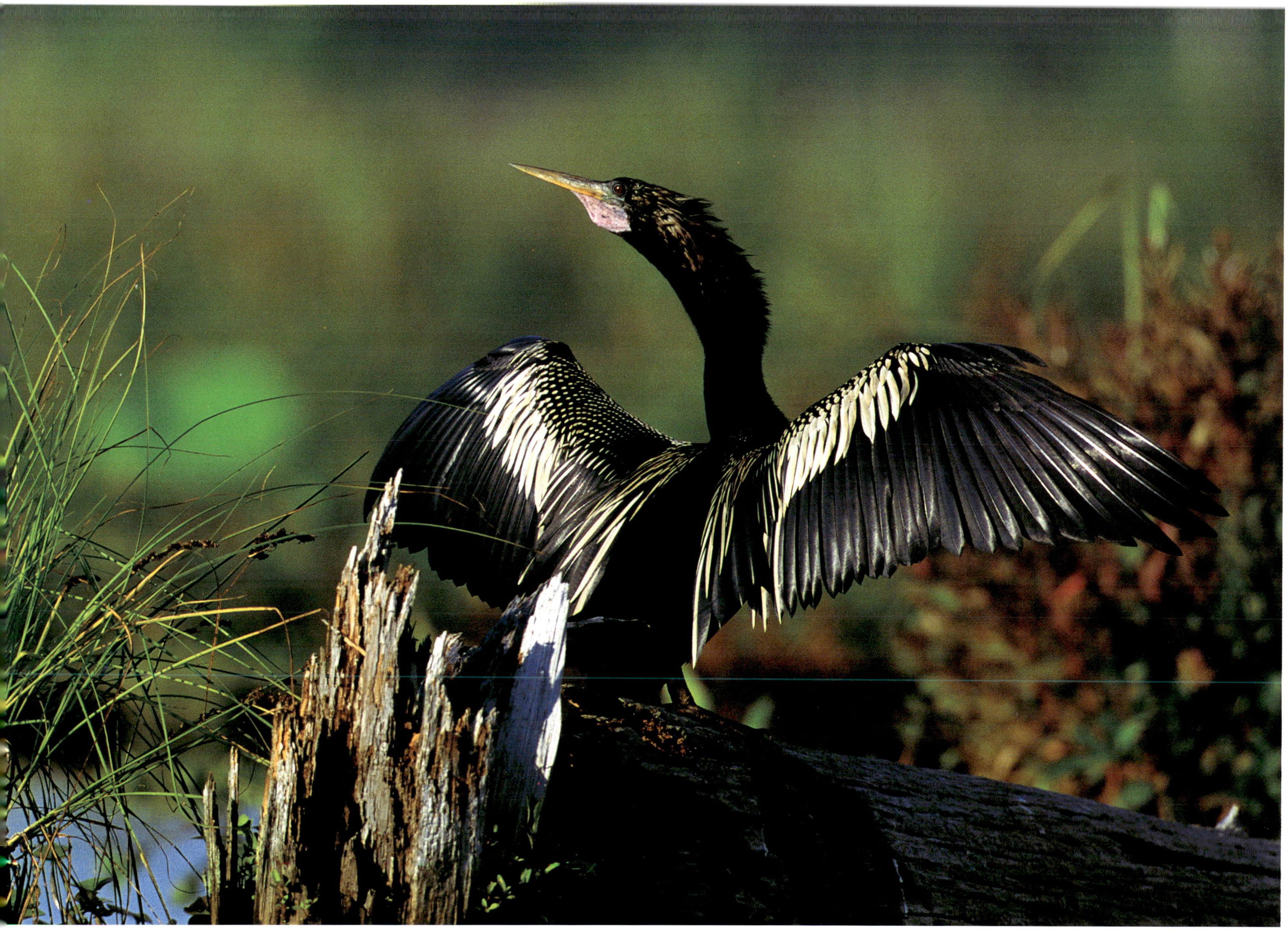

Anhinga

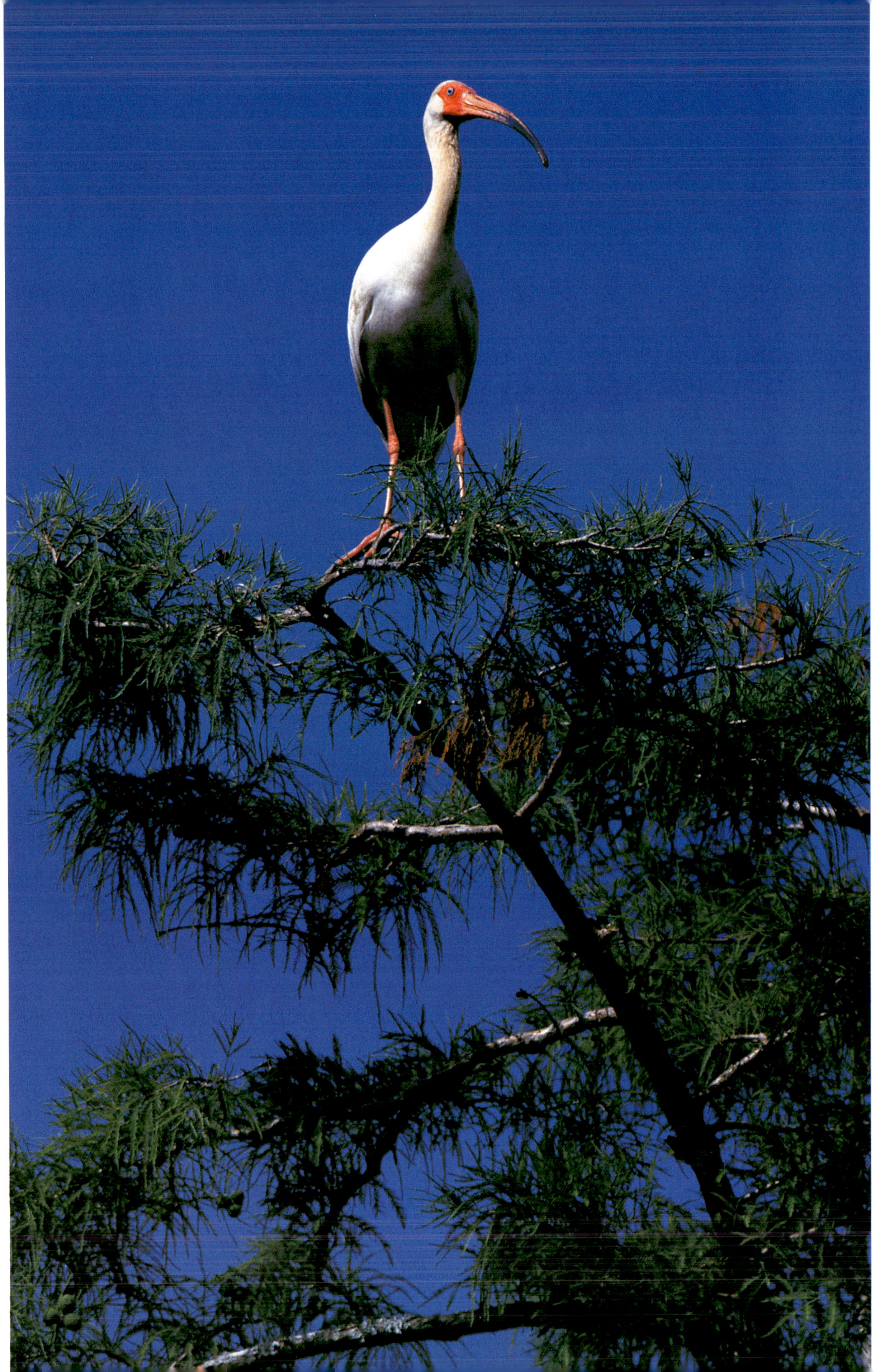

White ibis

Spicebush swallowtail on fragrant water lily

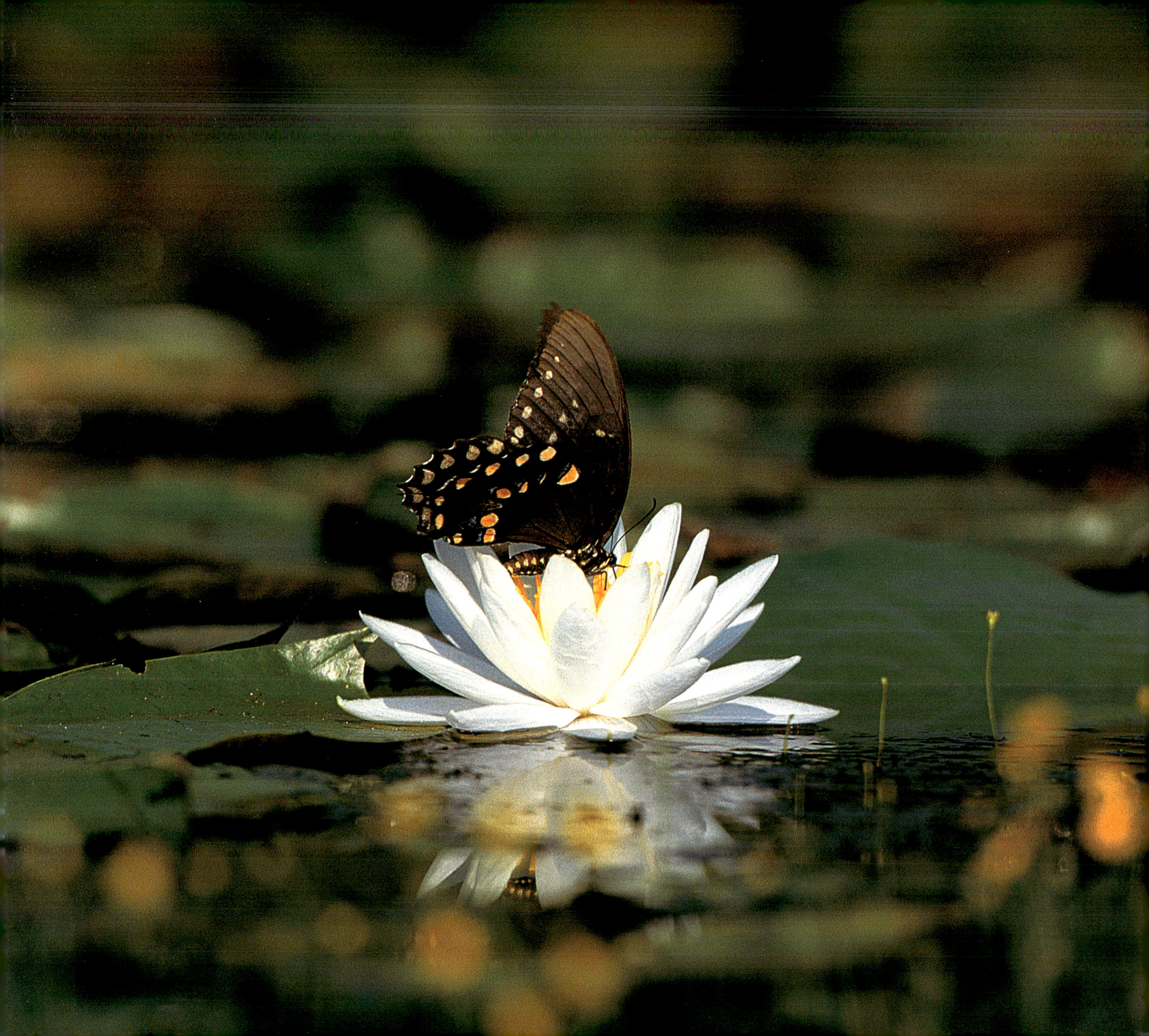

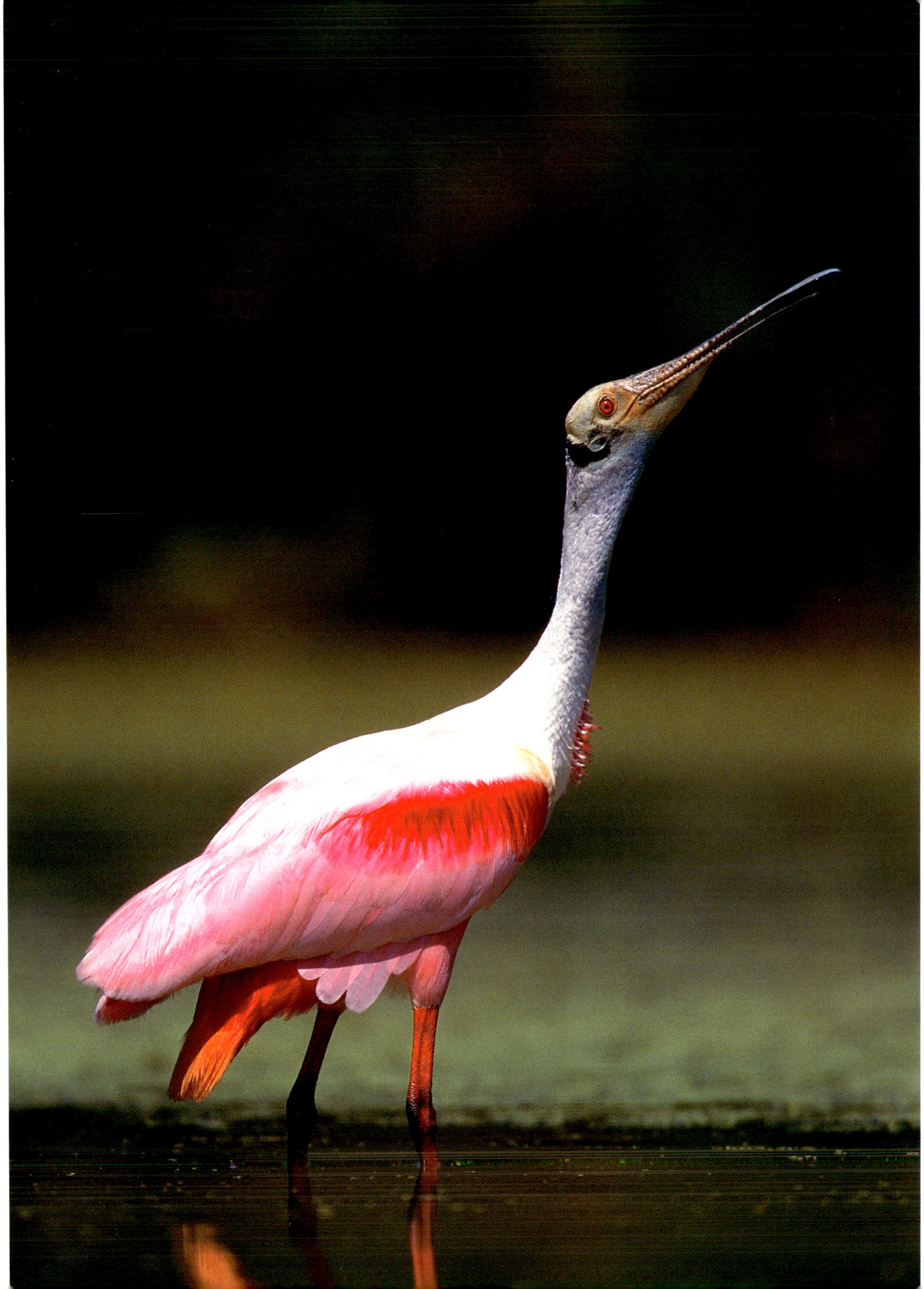

Roseate spoonbill

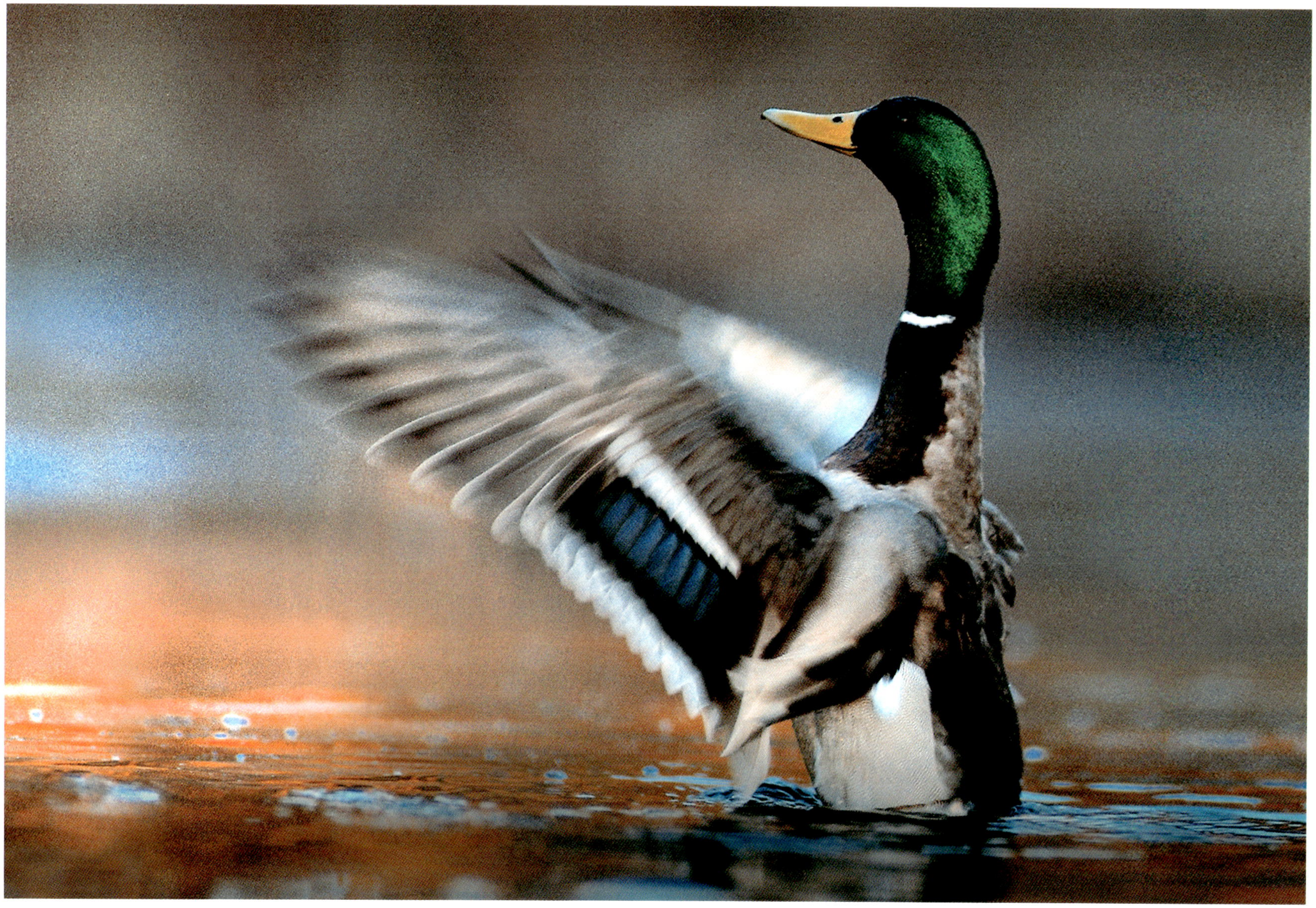

Mallard

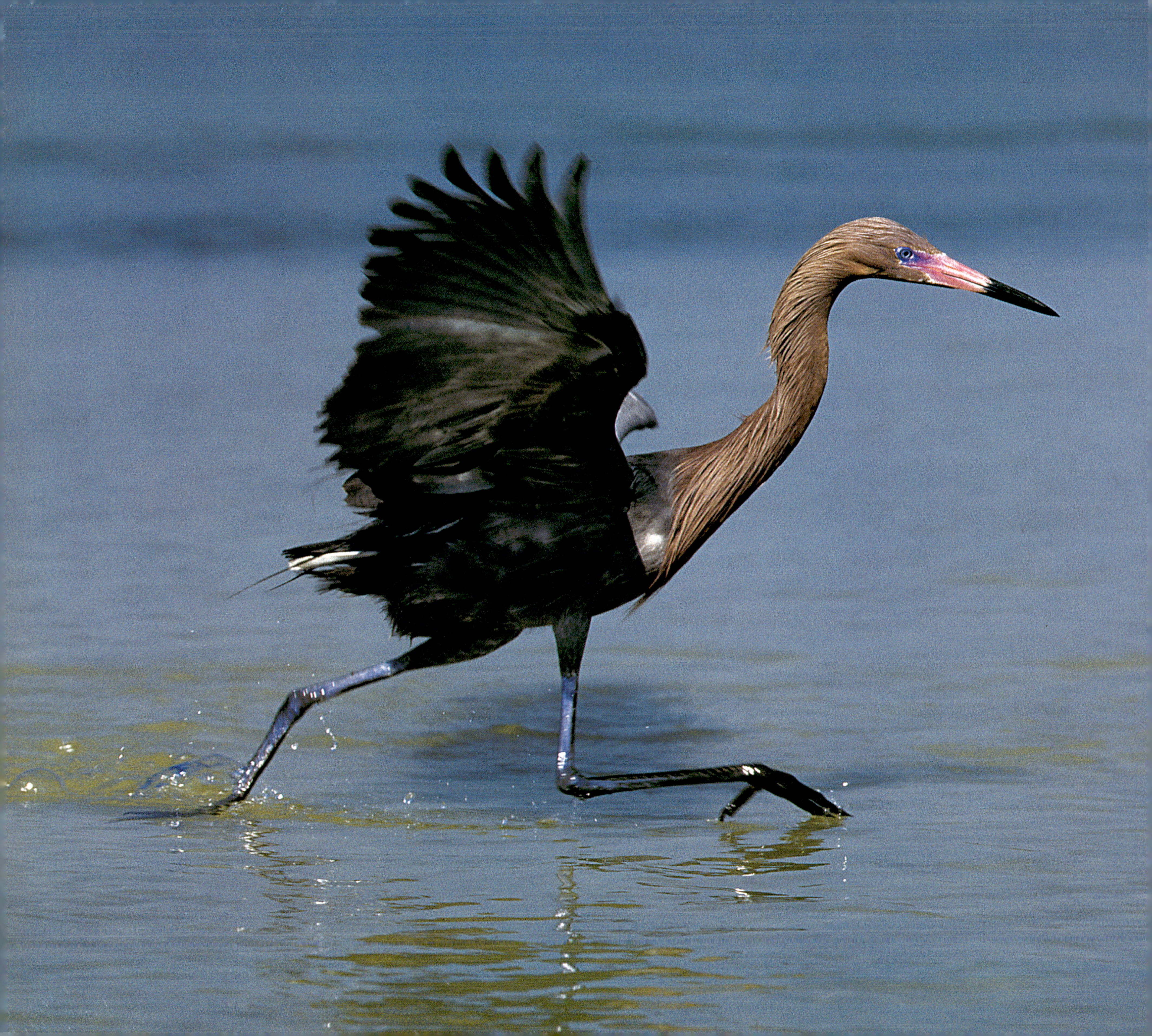

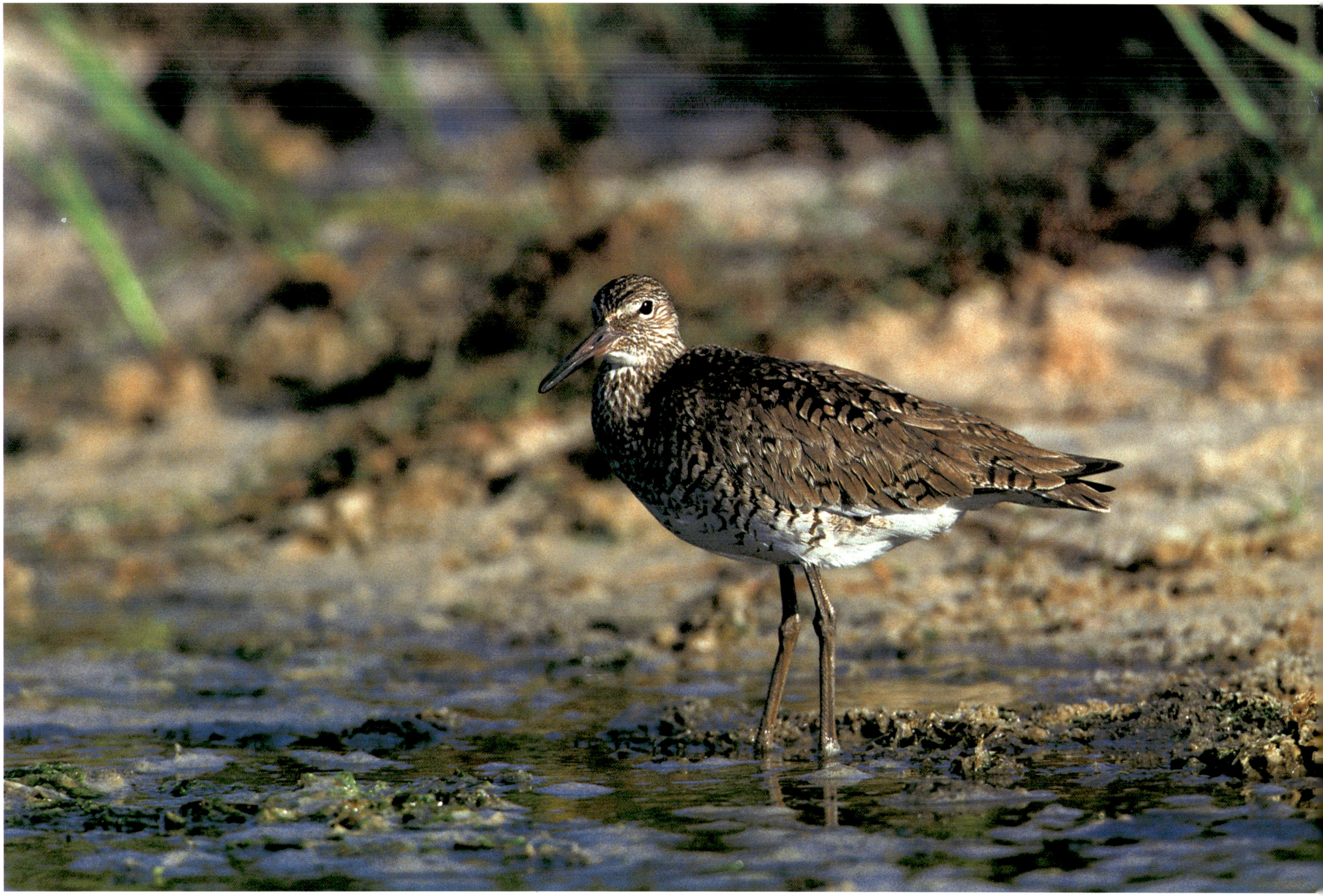

Willet

Reddish egret

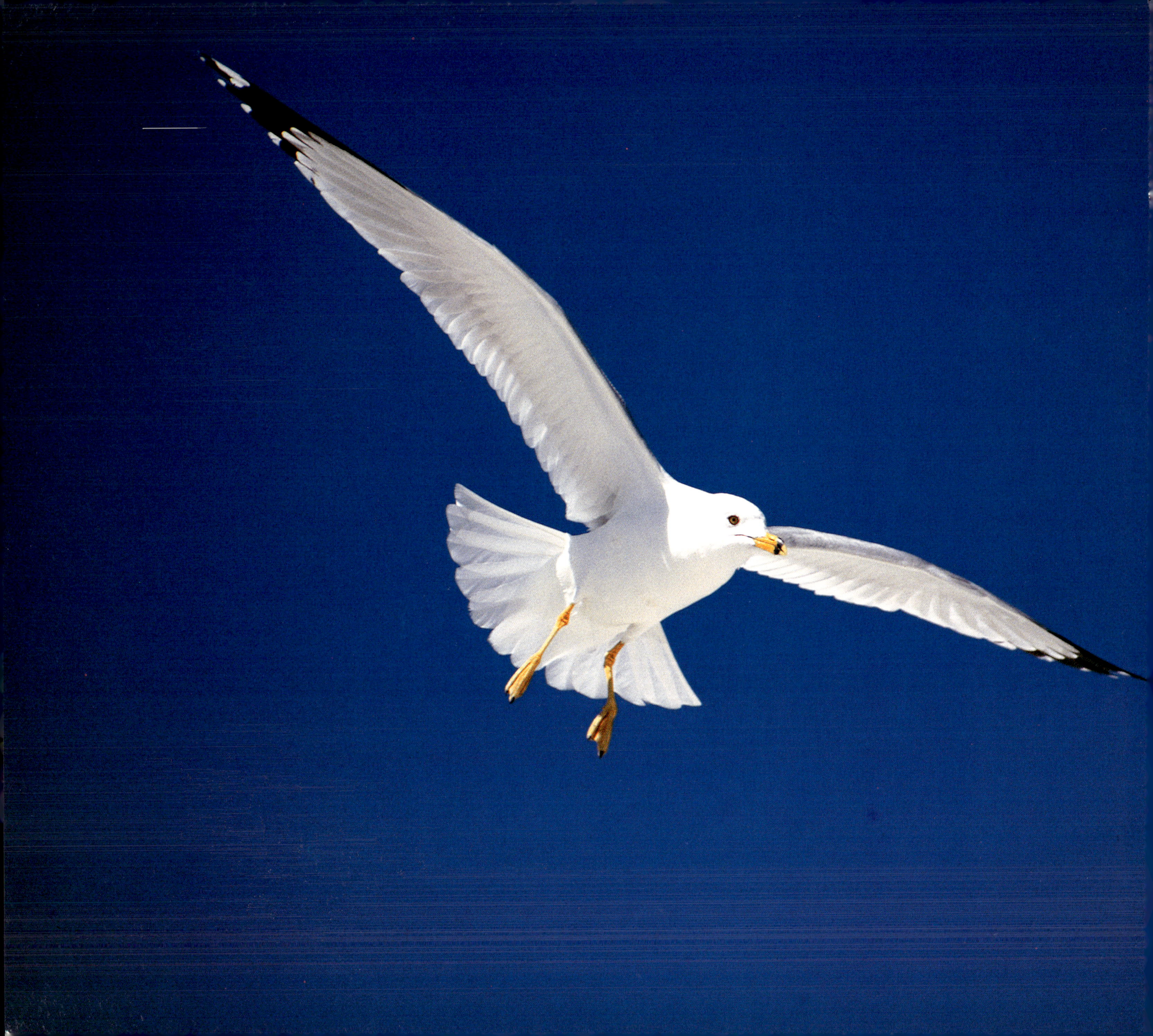

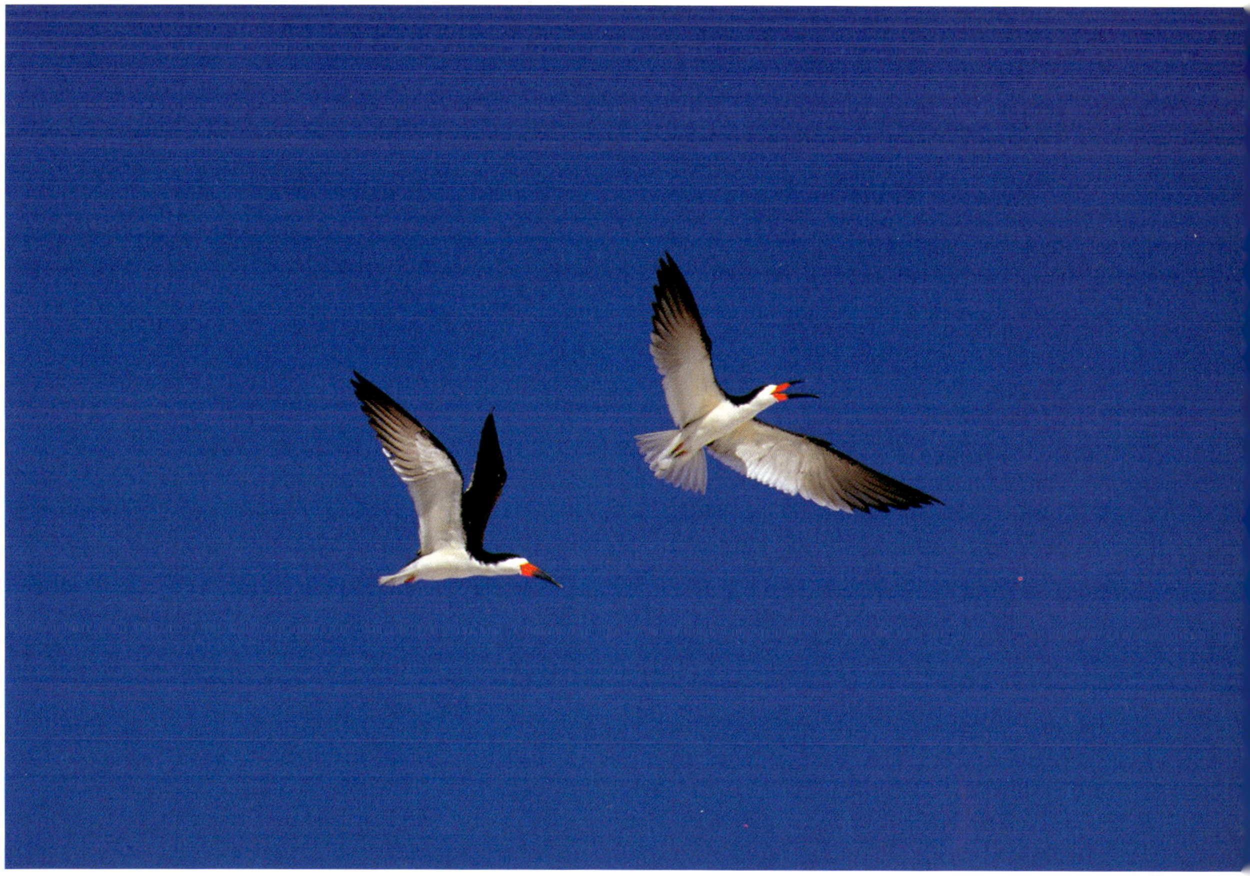

Black Skimmers

Ringed-bill gull

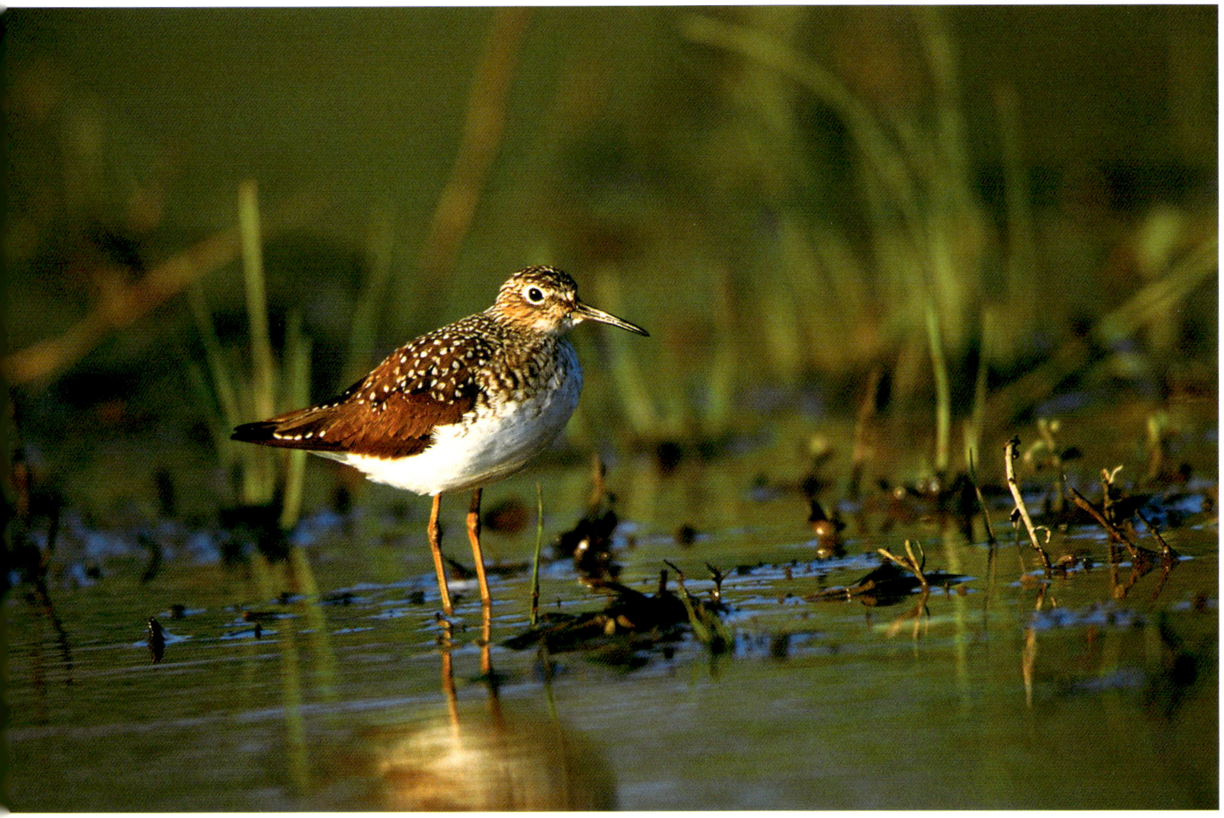

Solitary sandpiper

White pelicans

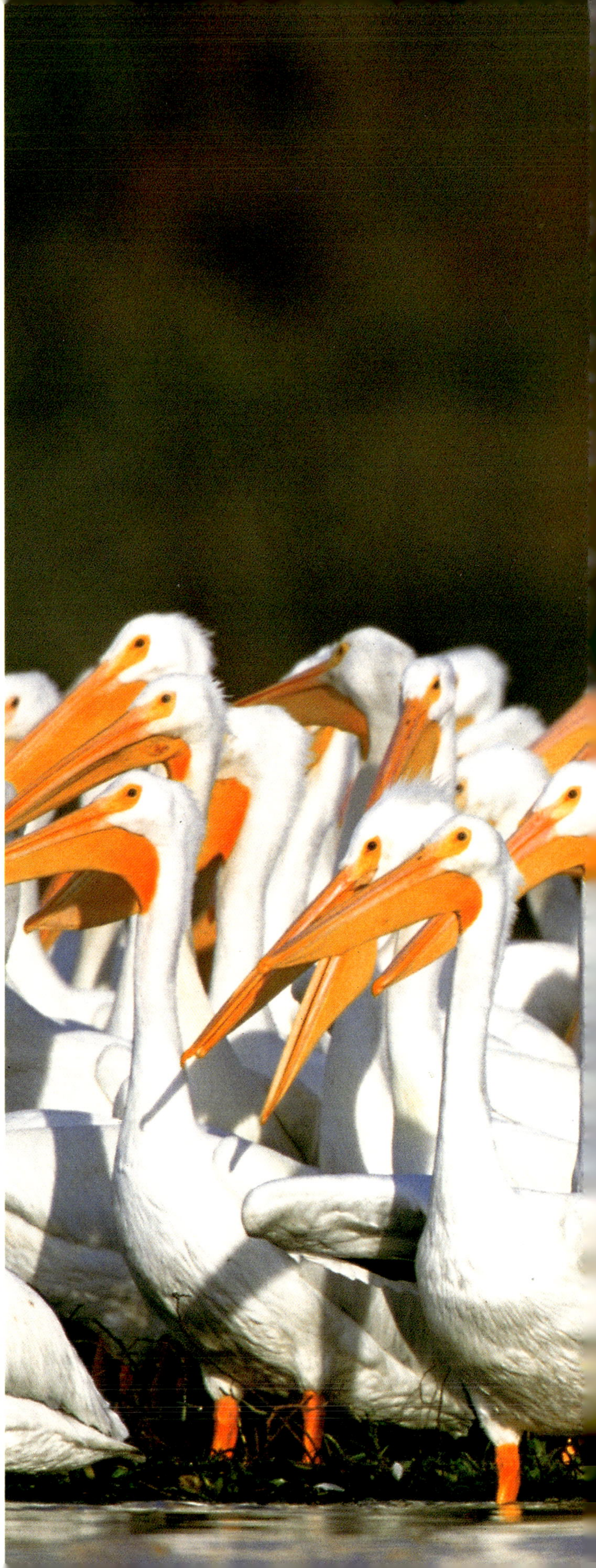

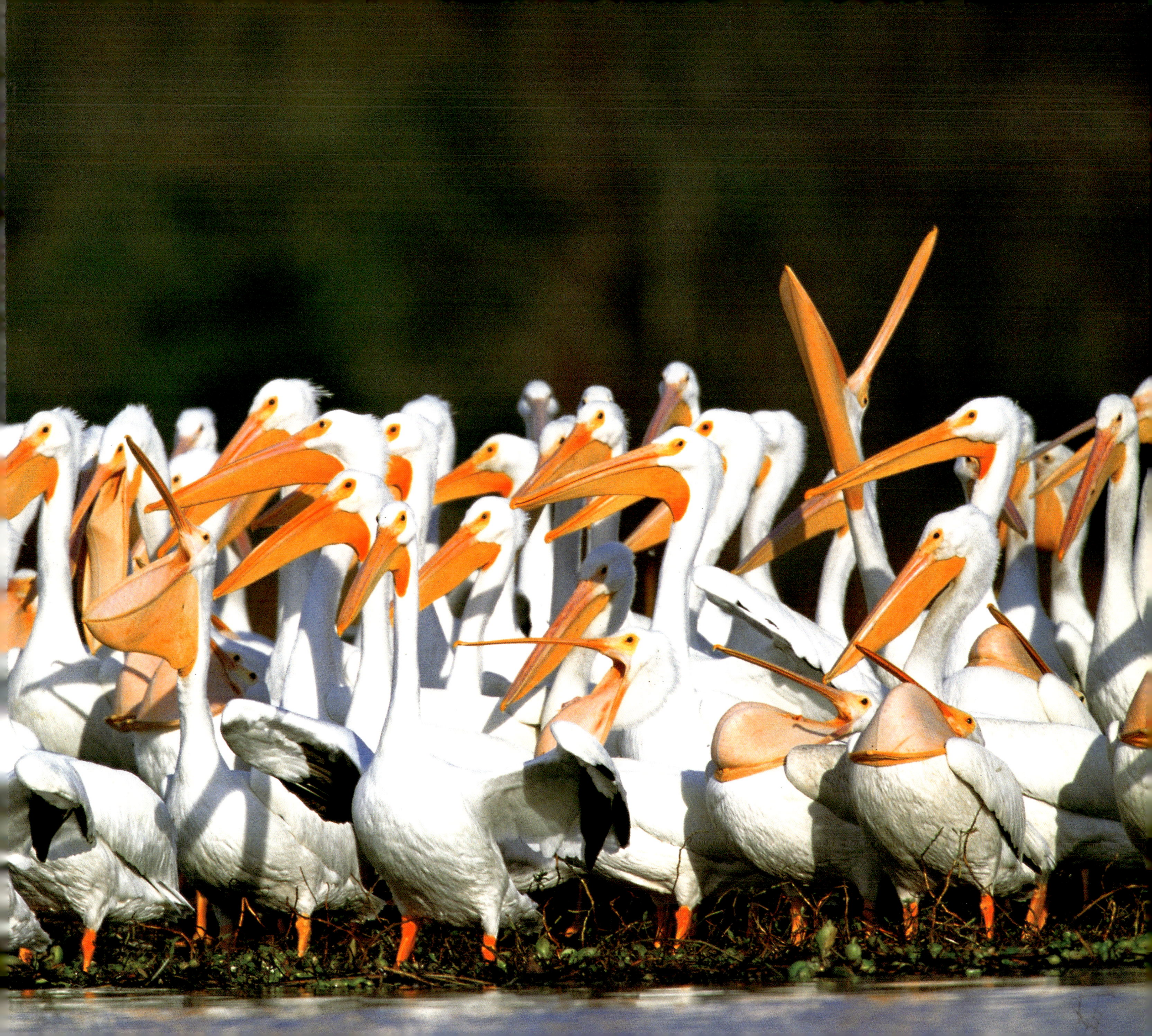

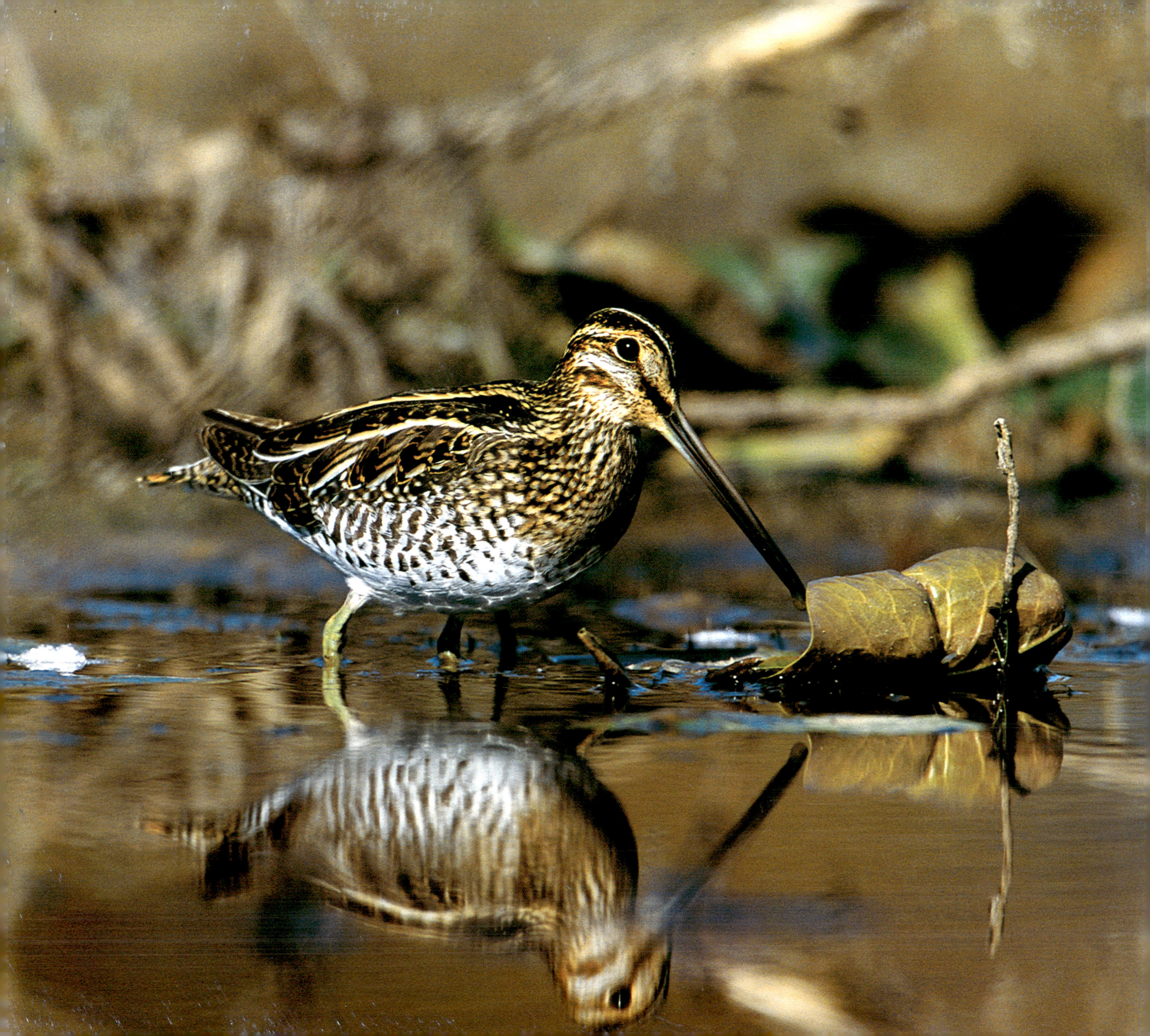

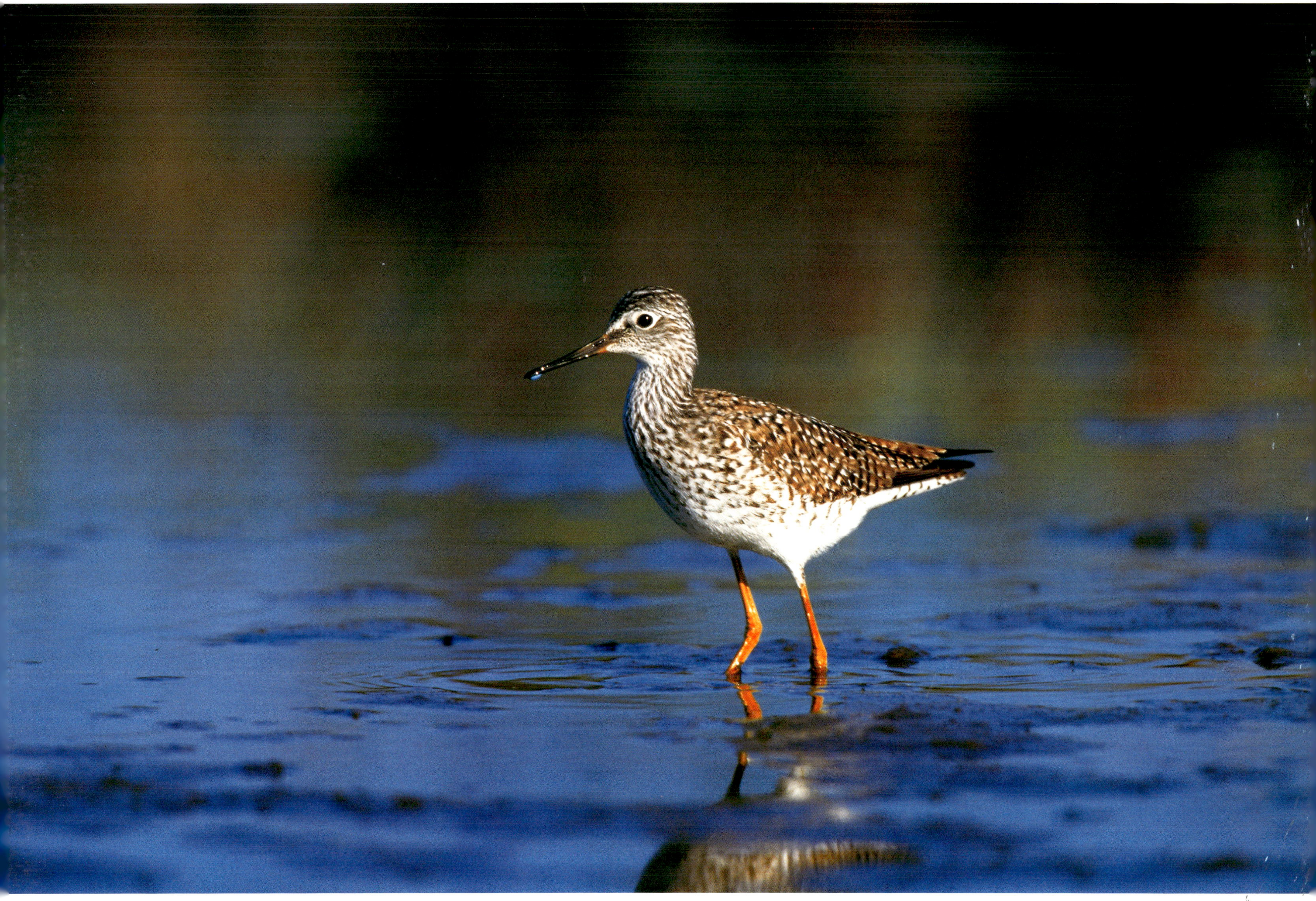

Lesser yellowlegs

Common snipe

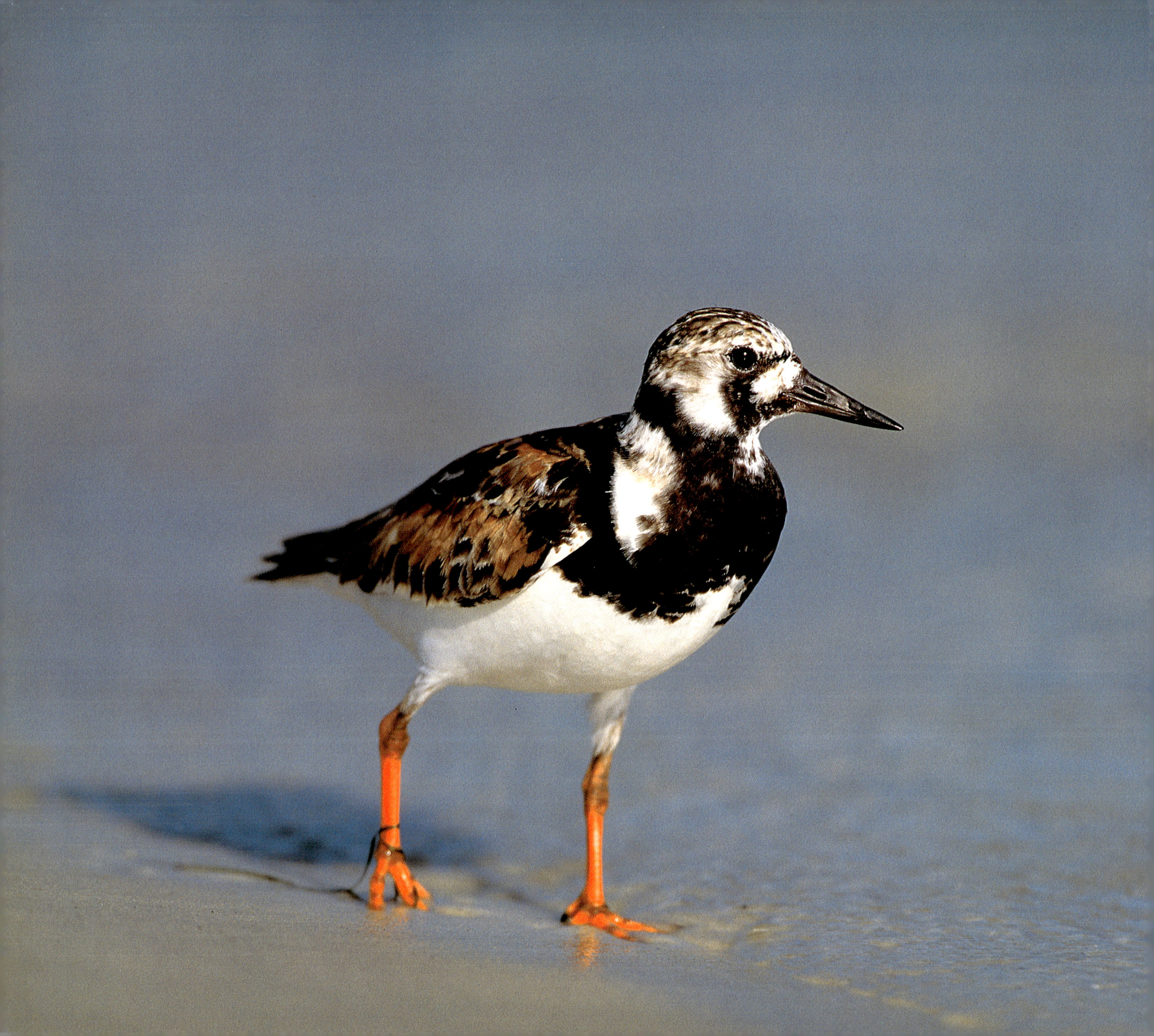

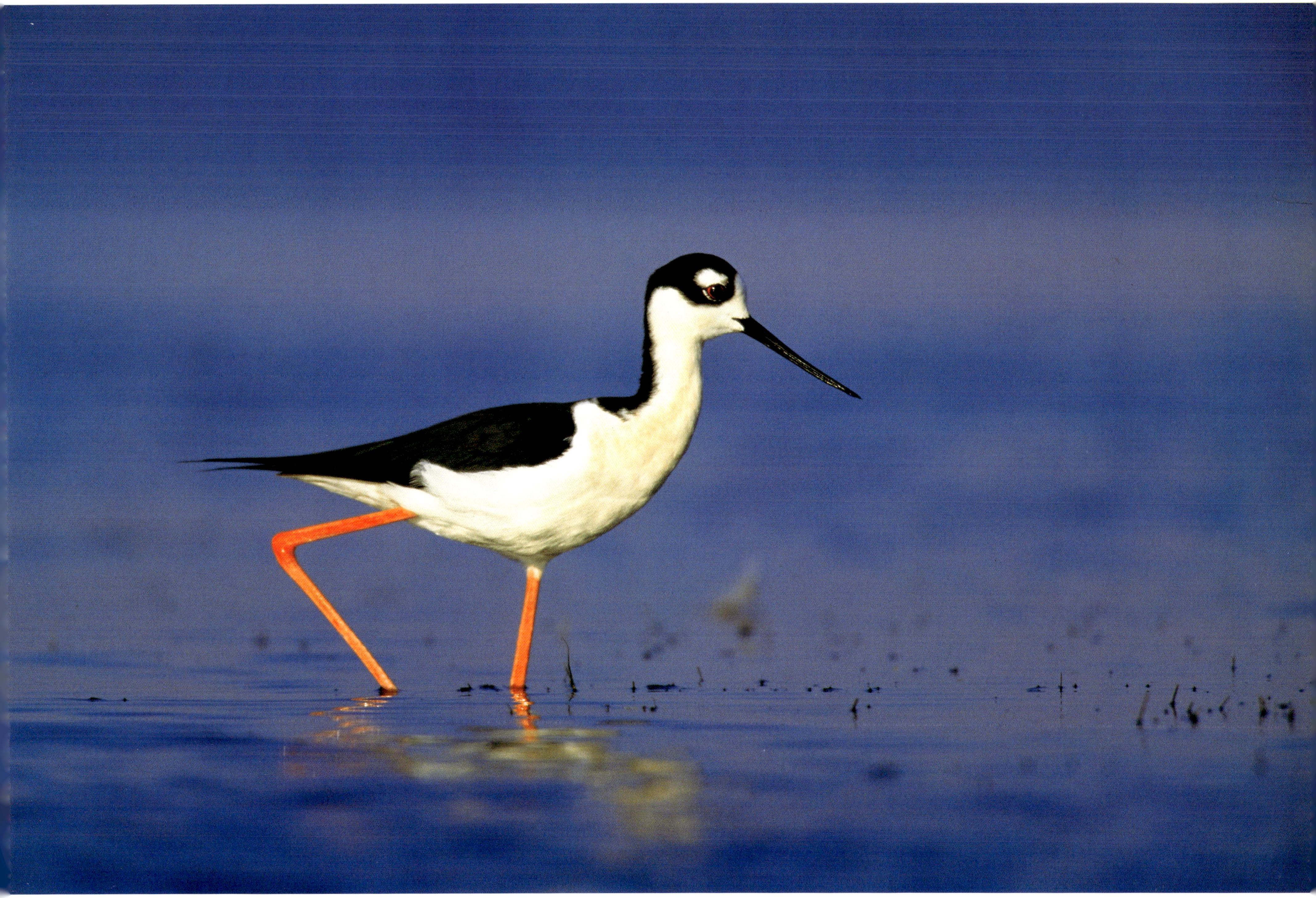

Black-necked stilt

Ruddy turnstone

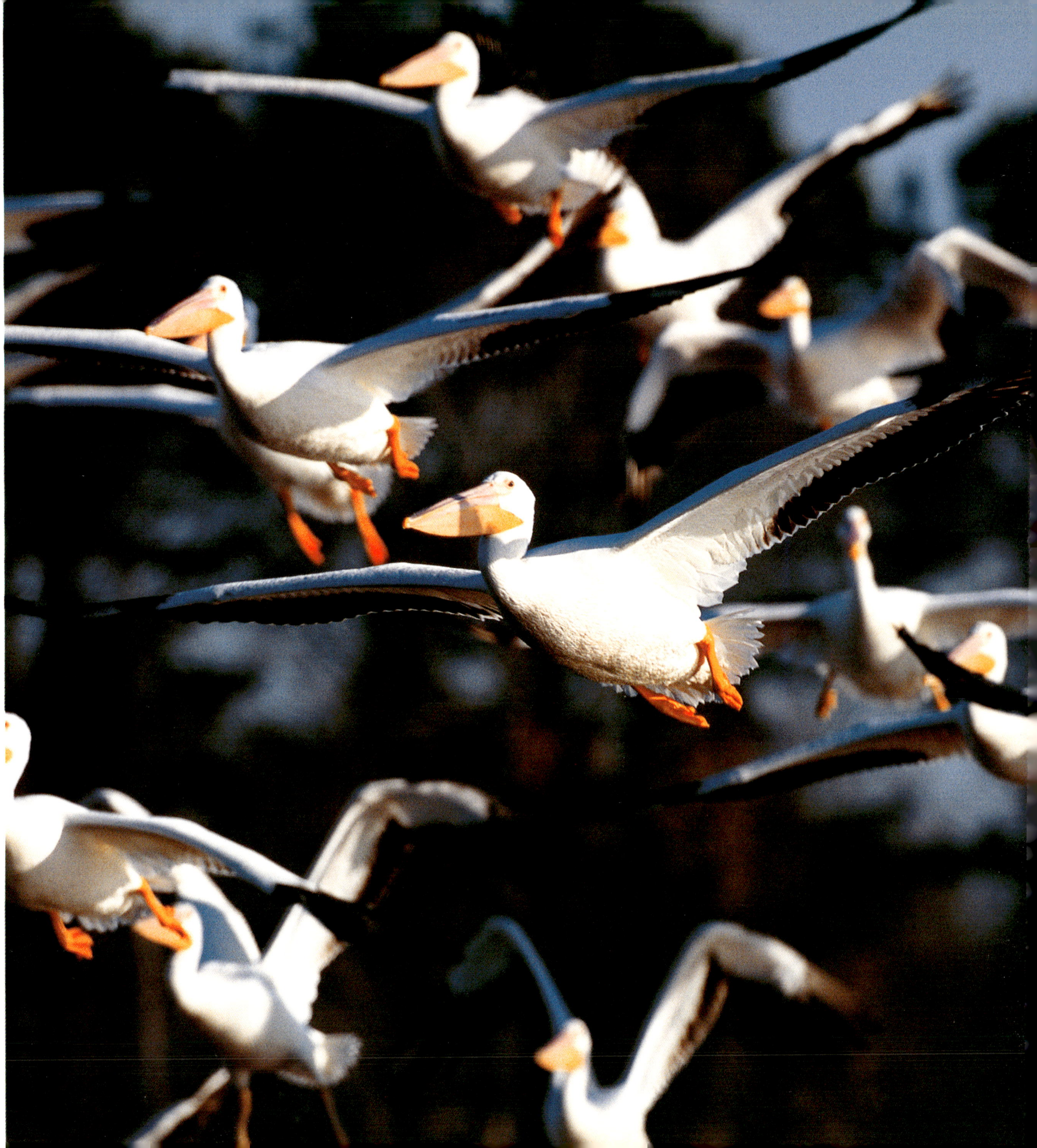

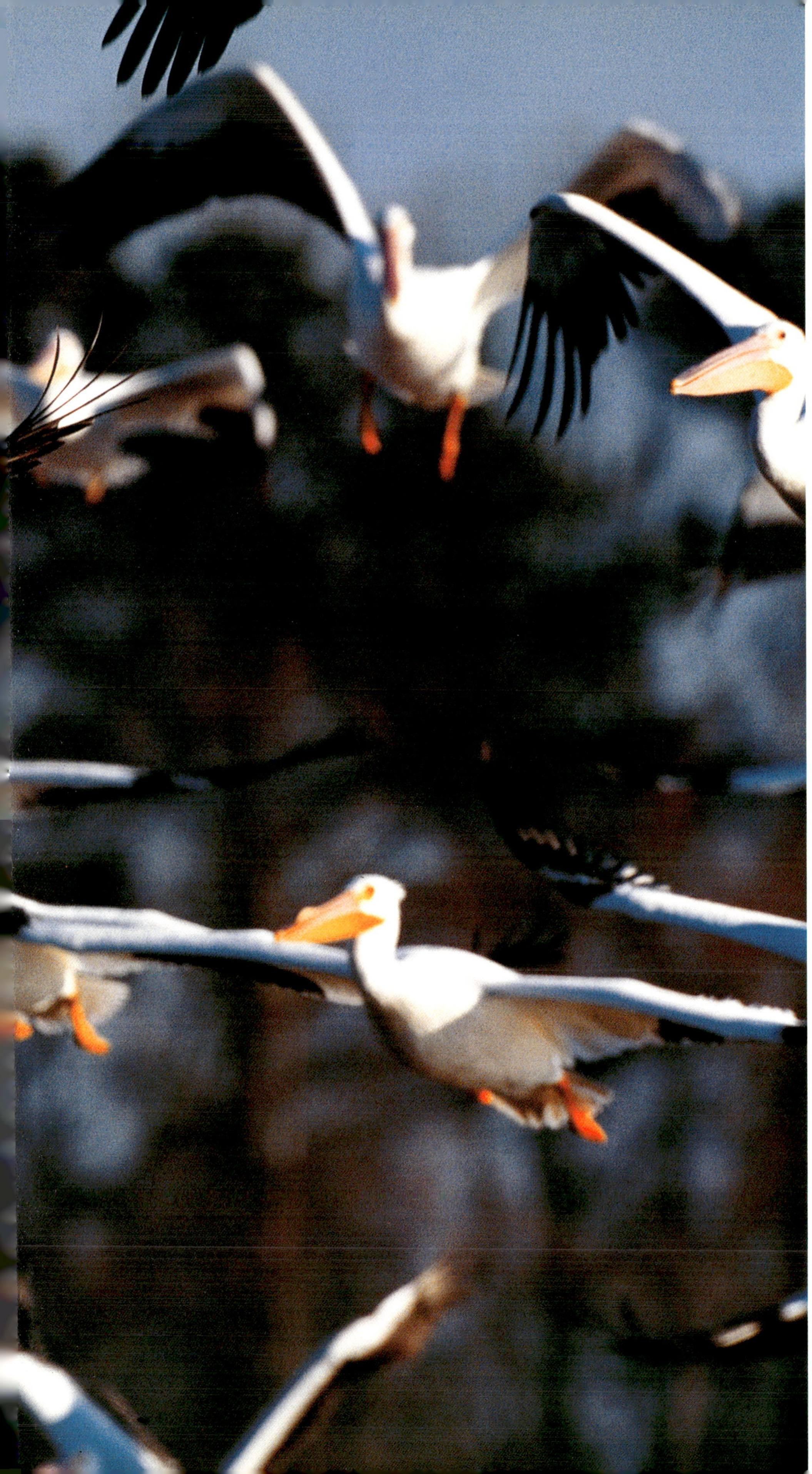

White pelicans

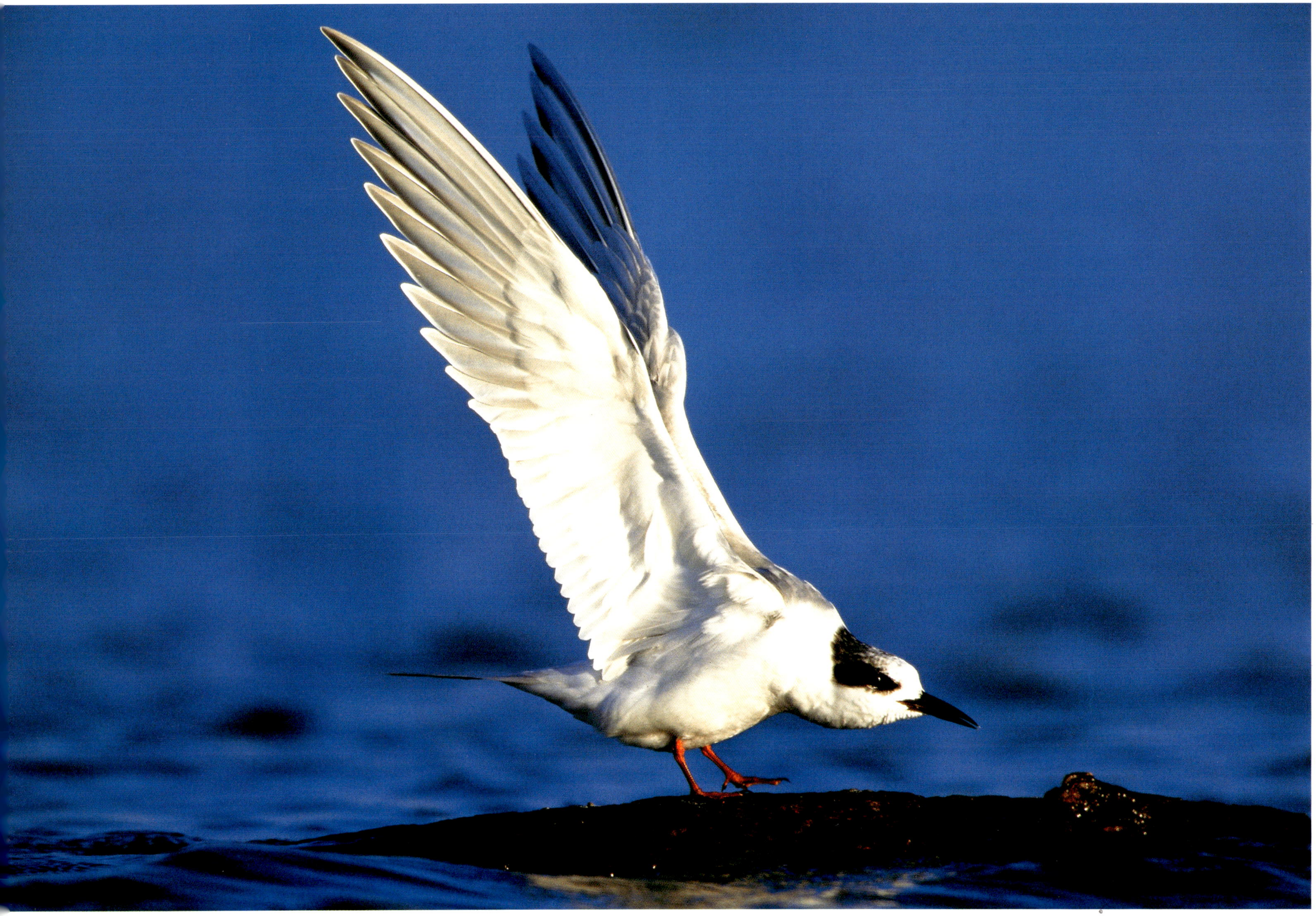

Foster's tern

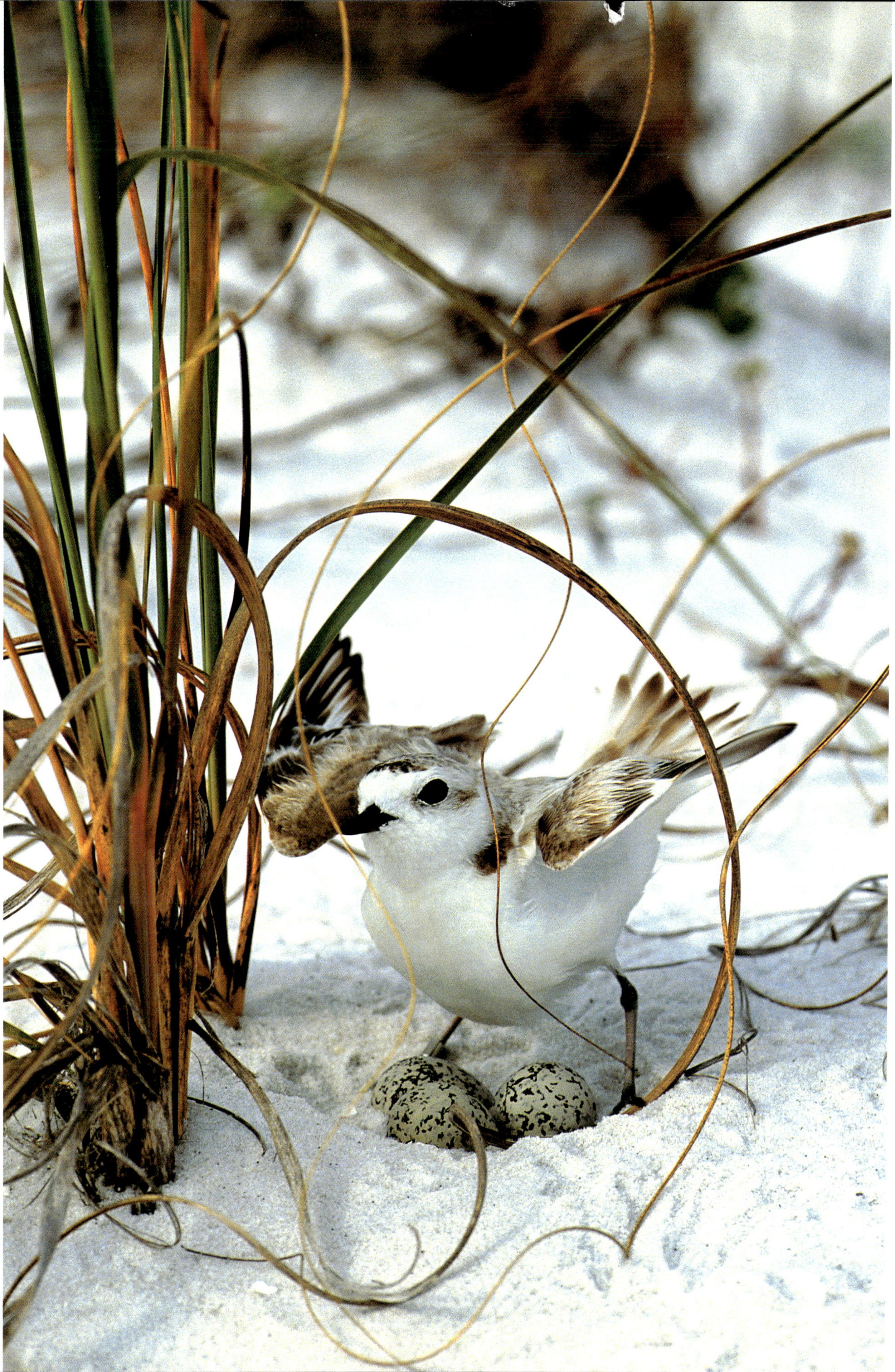

Snowy plover

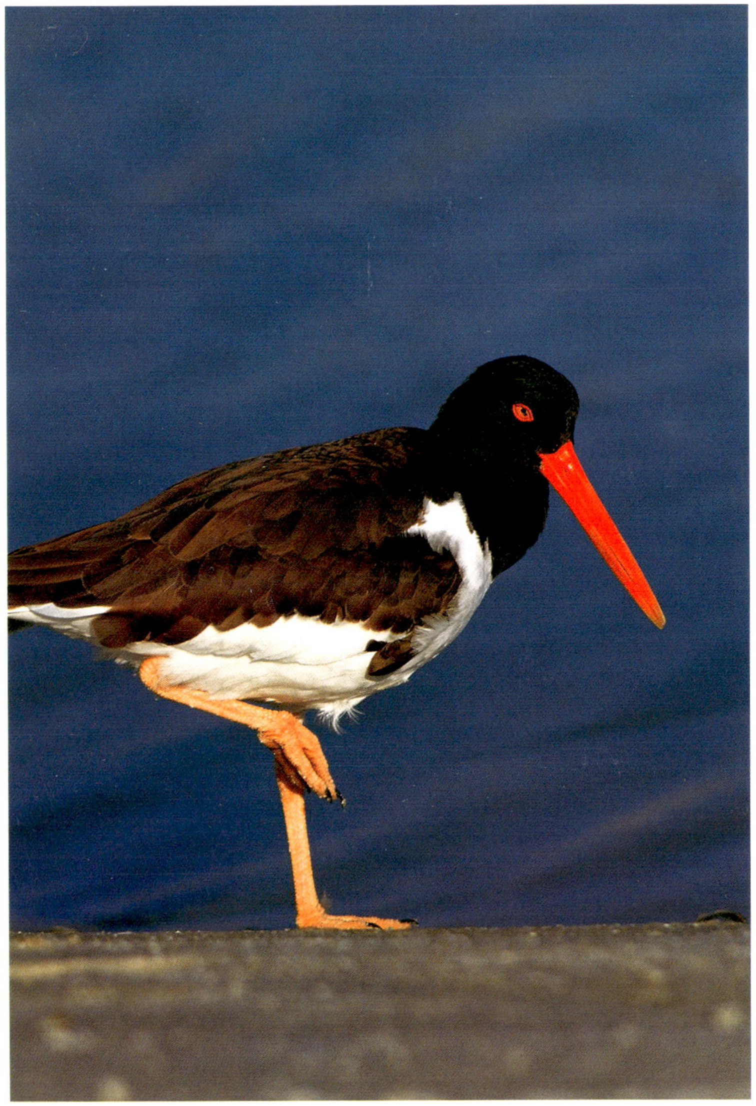

American oystercatcher

Red-winged blackbird flock at sunset

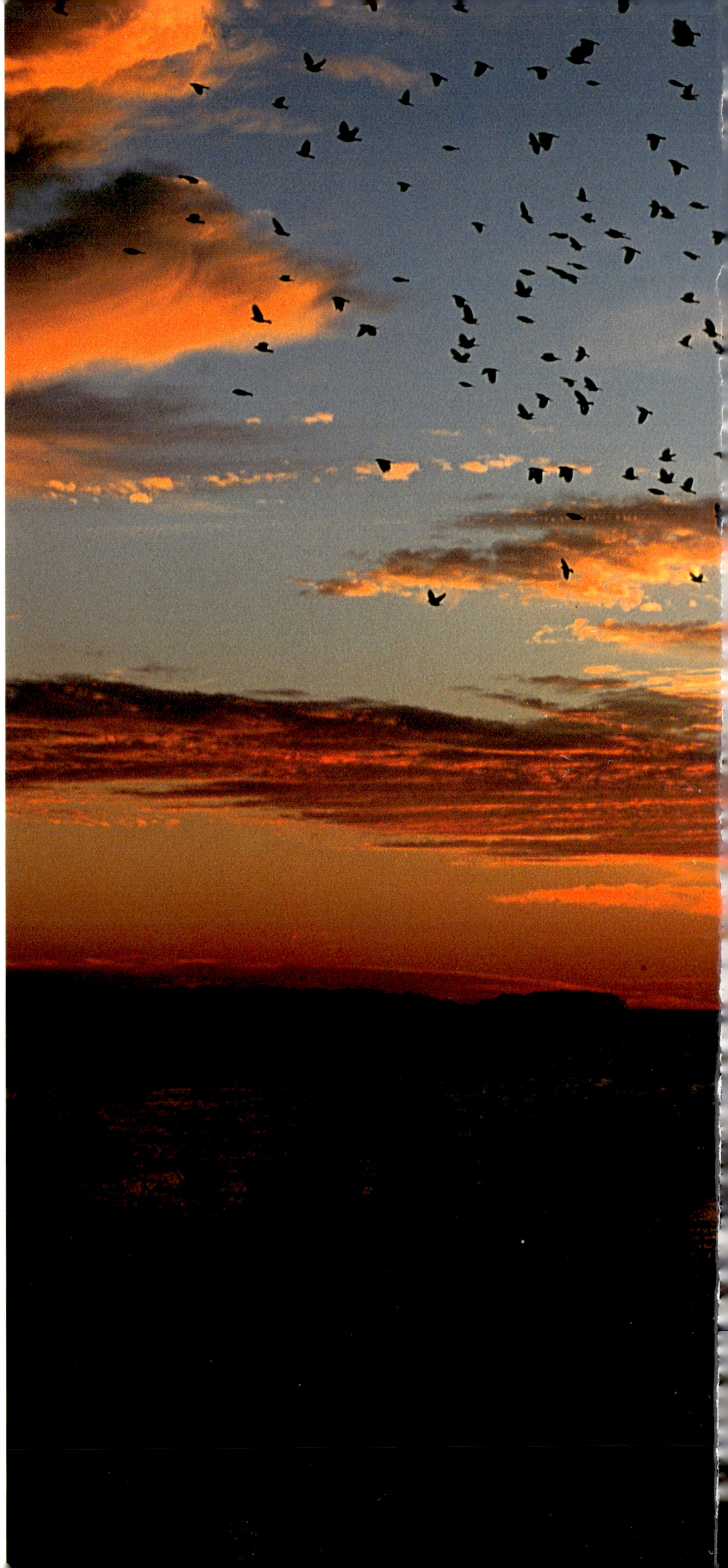